Chinese Link

中 文 天 地
Zhōng　Wén　Tiān　Dì

Beginning Chinese

Second Edition

Simplified Character Version

| Level 1 | Part 2 |

吴素美　　　于月明　　　张燕辉　　　田维忠

Sue-mei Wu　**Yueming Yu**　**Yanhui Zhang**　**Weizhong Tian**

Prentice Hall

Boston　Columbus　Indianapolis　New York　San Francisco　Upper Saddle River
Amsterdam　Cape Town　Dubai　London　Madrid　Milan　Munich　Paris　Montréal　Toronto
Delhi　Mexico City　São Paulo　Sydney　Hong Kong　Seoul　Singapore　Taipei　Tokyo

Senior Acquisitions Editor: Rachel McCoy
Editorial Assistant: Noha Amer
Publishing Coordinator: Kathryn Corasaniti
Executive Marketing Manager: Kris Ellis-Levy
Senior Marketing Manager: Denise Miller
Marketing Coordinator: William J. Bliss
Senior Media Editor: Samantha Alducin
Development Editor for Assessment: Melissa Marolla Brown
Media Editor: Meriel Martinez
Senior Managing Editor: Mary Rottino
Associate Managing Editor: Janice Stangel
Senior Production Project Manager: Manuel Echevarria
Senior Manufacturing and Operations Manager, Arts and Sciences: Nick Sklitsis
Operations Specialist: Cathleen Petersen
Senior Art Director: Pat Smythe
Art Director: Miguel Ortiz
Text and Cover Designer: Wanda España, Wee Design Group
Manager, Visual Research: Beth Brenzel
Manager, Rights and Permissions: Zina Arabia
Image Permission Coordinator: Frances Toepfer
Manager, Cover Visual Research & Permissions: Karen Sanatar
Cover Image: Jochen Helle
Full-Service Project Management: Margaret Chan, Graphicraft Limited
Printer/Binder: Courier/Kendallville
Cover Printer: Lehigh-Phoenix Color/Hagerstown
Publisher: Phil Miller

Credits and acknowledgments borrowed from other sources and reproduced, with permission, in this textbook appear on page 313.

This book was set in 12/15 Sabon by Graphicraft Ltd., Hong Kong, and was printed and bound by Courier – Westford. The cover was printed by Phoenix Color Corp.

Library of Congress Cataloging-in-Publication Data

Chinese link : Zhong wén tian dì : beginning Chinese, level 1. Simplified character version / Sue-mei Wu … [et al.].—2nd ed.
    p. cm.
  Spine title: Zhongwen tiandi
  ISBN 978-0-205-69196-8 (alk. paper : pt. 2)
  1. Chinese language—Textbooks for foreign speakers—English. I. Wu, Sue-mei, 1968– II. Title: Zhong wén tian dì. III. Title: Beginning Chinese, level 1. IV. Title: Zhongwen tiandi.
  PL1129.E5C4195 2011
  495.1'82421—dc22

2010000450

Printed in the United States of America
10 9 8 7 6 5 4 3 2 1

Prentice Hall
is an imprint of

PEARSON

www.pearsonhighered.com

ISBN 10: 0-205-69196-X
ISBN 13: 978-0-205-69196-8

目录　CONTENTS

范围和顺序
SCOPE AND SEQUENCE

Lessons & Topics	Objectives & Communications	Grammar	Culture Link
15 Location and Position 地点和位置 *p. 69*	■ Describe location with position words ■ Ask where something is located ■ Describe rooms in a house	1. Position Words 2. Expressing Location and Existence with 在, 有, and 是	**Culture Notes:** Feng Shui 风水 **Fun With Chinese:** Saying: 有缘千里来相会，无缘对面不相识。 **Let's Go:** Map of Scenic Spots in Beijing 北京景点地图
16 Hobbies and Sports 爱好和运动 *p. 89*	■ Describe how an action is performed ■ Talk about hobbies, sports, and exercise	1. Degree of Complement Sentences	**Culture Notes:** Chinese Martial Arts (Kung Fu) 中国功夫 **Fun With Chinese:** Saying: 高人一等 **Let's Go:** Competition Results (Game Results) 比赛结果
17 Weather and Seasons 天气和四季 *p. 109*	■ Describe the weather ■ Talk about the four seasons ■ Say that something will happen in the near future	1. 就要/快要……了 2. 最 3. Adjective + 极了	**Culture Notes:** The Main Chinese Festivals 中国的主要节庆 **Fun With Chinese:** Saying: 雨过天晴 **Let's Go:** Weather Forecast 天气预报
18 Travel and Transportation 旅行和交通 *p. 127*	■ Describe means of transportation ■ Talk about travel plans	1. 离 2. 先……再……然后 3. 坐, 骑, and 开	**Culture Notes:** Traveling by Train or Boat in China 在中国：坐火车或者坐船旅行 **Fun With Chinese:** Saying: 读万卷书，行万里路。 **Let's Go:** Train Station 火车站

Lessons & Topics	Objectives & Communications	Grammar	Culture Link
19 **Health and Medicine** 健康和医药 *p. 153*	■ Describe the symptoms of an illness ■ Describe something that has happened ■ Describe a changing situation	1. Expressing Completed Action with 了 2. Expressing a Change of State/New Situation with 了 3. 的, 得, and 地	**Culture Notes:** Traditional Chinese Medicine 中医中药 **Fun With Chinese:** Saying: 良药苦口，忠言逆耳。 **Let's Go:** Traditional Chinese Supplements 传统中医补品
20 **Renting an Apartment** 看房和租房 *p. 173*	■ Talk about renting an apartment ■ Indicate the direction of a movement ■ Specify the effects or results of an action on an object	1. Simple Directional Complements (Simple DC) 2. Compound Directional Complements (Compound DC) 3. 把 Sentences 4. 把 Sentences and the Directional Complement 5. When to Use Sentences with 把	**Culture Notes:** Houses in China 中国的住房 **Fun With Chinese:** Saying: 秀才不出门，能知天下事。 **Let's Go:** Apartment Rental Ad 租屋广告
21 **Future Plans** 未来计画 *p. 197*	■ Talk about future plans ■ Express blessings and wishes	1. 一面……一面…… 2. Summary of Verbal Aspects	**Culture Notes:** Summer Study in China 暑假在中国 **Fun With Chinese:** Saying: 活到老，学到老。 **Let's Go:** Overseas Student Application Form 入学申请表

Lessons & Topics	Objectives & Communications	Grammar	Culture Link
22 **Arts and Culture** 艺术和文化 *p. 217*	■ Give examples ■ Describe cause and effect ■ Describe your current situation	1. 比如 2. 因为……所以……	**Culture Notes:** Peking Opera and Chinese Calligraphy 京剧和书法 **Fun With Chinese:** Idiom: 心想事成 **Let's Go:** Calligraphy and Painting Exhibition 书画展

Appendices

Recognizing that the world is becoming increasingly interlinked and globalized, the goal of the **CHINESE LINK: Zhongwen Tiandi** 中文天地 (Beginning Chinese) project has been to integrate the "5Cs" principles of the National Standards for Foreign Language Education—Communication, Cultures, Comparisons, Connections, and Communities—throughout the program in order to provide a new approach for the teaching and learning of Chinese language in the 21st century. The program aims to help beginners develop their communicative competence in the four basic skills of listening, speaking, reading, and writing, while gaining an understanding of Chinese culture, exercising their ability to compare aspects of different cultures, making connections to their daily life, and building links among communities.

A language curriculum should be attractive to both students and instructors; therefore the authors provide a practical, learner-centered, and enjoyable language and culture learning experience for beginners in Chinese, as well as an efficient and comprehensive teaching resource for instructors.

Proficiency in a language involves knowing both the structural forms of the language and their appropriate use in different cultural contexts. Care has been taken to introduce and explain grammar points clearly and systematically without overwhelming beginners. In keeping with the communicative focus of the text, grammar points are related to communicative, task-oriented content.

Each version of the text (Traditional and Simplified) presents both traditional and simplified versions of Chinese characters since it is likely that students will encounter both forms. Similarly, care has been taken to present both Taiwan and Mainland China usage where they differ, and to incorporate new vocabulary items, such as *Internet* and *cell phone*. Culture Notes at the end of each lesson are thematically linked to the chapter. They are designed to capture the student's interest and to explain important features of Chinese culture. Attractive photographs and illustrations are provided to support this information by providing visual cues to aid students in learning and participation in communicative activities.

Features of CHINESE LINK: Zhongwen Tiandi 中文天地 (Beginning Chinese)

- The **5Cs** (**National Standards**) are integrated consistently into the content and exercises in the program.
- From the beginning, the text helps students build from words and phrases to sentences and cohesive passages, and then to application in **communicative tasks**.
- The textbook contains many **illustrations** and **photographs** and utilizes a clear, attractive layout.
- Both **traditional and simplified** character forms are listed for each **vocabulary** item. Seeing the two forms side-by-side helps students make the connection between the two.

- Differences in usage between **Mainland China and Taiwan** are consistently identified.
- Interesting **Cultural Notes** are included in each lesson and supplemented with photographs from Mainland China, Taiwan, and Hong Kong.

What's New to this Edition

Thanks to the many instructors and students who provided valuable feedback on the first edition, the second edition incorporates several new features that will make the materials more effective and easier to use. These new features are highlighted below:

1. In General

- Lessons have been revised to provide greater balance, add more review and recycling of materials, enhance consistency, and emphasize student outcomes. More engaging and communicative exercises for learners have been added and several of the Culture Notes have been updated.

2. Full-Color Design

- The use of a full-color design now provides clear delineation between various items and makes the text more appealing to today's learner.

3. Chapter Opening

- Opening photos have been updated and highlight the lesson theme.
- A "Connections and Communities Preview" section has been added to help learners make connections to their daily life and build links among their communities. Questions focus on the lesson and Culture Link themes.

4. Sentence Patterns

- Key grammar points in the Sentence Pattern section are highlighted to show the grammar in context.

5. Language Notes

- Notes have been placed next to the Language in Use texts for ease of reference.

6. Grammar

- Pinyin has been added to the examples to provide a more effective illustration of the key grammar notes.
- Grammar explanations have been simplified and clarified.
- A new "Try it!" section has been added to provide guided communicative practice and reinforcement immediately following grammar points.

7. Supplementary Practice

- Questions have been added for reading comprehension practice of the supplementary texts.

8. Activities

- Activities have been updated and additional communicative activities have been added.

9. Culture Notes

- Culture Notes, thematically linked to the content of the lesson, have been updated with new information and new topics of interest for today's students.
- A "Do you know . . ." section of introductory questions has been added before the reading to increase student motivation, attention, and interest before reading the Culture Notes.
- Comparison questions after the reading help learners compare their culture to Chinese culture and discuss the differences or similarities. Questions also encourage discussion of issues related to the reading and lesson's theme.
- Photos have been updated to present scenes related to the reading. Captions encourage reflection of information learned in the reading.

10. Fun with Chinese

- Activity questions have been added to highlight familiar words in the sayings and to help students connect real-life situations with the sayings.

11. Let's Go!

- Information and activities have been updated and strongly relate to the lesson's theme.

12. Student Activities Manual

- The **Student Activities Manual** incorporates listening, character, grammar, and comprehensive exercises into each lesson homework.
- More challenging and authentic materials have been added to the listening exercises. Situational dialogues have been created for each lesson to incorporate themes, expressions, and pragmatic settings of the lesson. Dialogues also contain some vocabulary and expressions that the students have not yet studied. These situational dialogues will challenge students from the very beginning and help them develop the skill of picking out useful information, even if they don't fully understand everything they hear. This helps develop an important survival skill for students who will encounter real-life settings in Chinese society through study abroad, travel, or interaction with Chinese communities in their own countries.
- At the end of each *Student Activities Manual* chapter, a "Progress Checklist" has been added for students to monitor their progress and their accomplishment of lesson goals and language competencies in each lesson.

13. Character Book

- The character exercises have been put into a separate volume for more efficiency and convenience. Both traditional and simplified characters are included, thus making the learning of both forms easy for the students.

14. MyChineseLab™

- MyChineseLab™, part of Pearson's MyLanguageLabs™, is a new, nationally hosted online learning system created for students and instructors of language courses. It brings together—in one convenient, easily navigable site—a wide array of language-learning tools and resources, including an interactive version of the *Chinese Link* student text,

Student Activities Manual, downloadable PDFs of the *Character Book*, a file of the artwork in the text, and all materials from the audio programs. Readiness checks, chapter tests, and tutorials personalize instruction to meet the unique needs of individual students. Instructors can use the system to devise assignments, set grading parameters, listen to student-created audio recordings, and provide feedback on student work. Student access codes to MyChineseLab™ are available for purchase. Take a tour! Visit www.MyLanguageLab.com

Organization of the Textbook

The textbook is divided into three main parts: **Foundation, Core Lessons,** and **Appendices.** The flexible design of the text allows instructors to use it in varying ways. Sample syllabi are available in the Instructor's Resource Manual.

Foundation (See *Chinese Link, 2e Level 1/Part 1*)

The **Foundation** module provides fundamental knowledge about Chinese and learning Chinese that is useful for beginners. It contains linguistic as well as cultural background material. Following are the major sections of the **Foundation** unit:

- Introduction to Chinese: This section briefly introduces some characteristics of Chinese language such as tones, the importance of word order, pictographic characters, and the history and development of Chinese.

- Pinyin Foundation and Exercises: Pinyin is the most widely used phonetic transliteration system for representing the sounds of Chinese. This section introduces the Pinyin system as well as the structural components of Chinese syllables: initials, finals, and tones. There are many Pinyin exercises. Tongue twisters are introduced to show different aspects of rhythm and rhyme and the sounds of Chinese.

- The Chinese Writing System: This section discusses the formation of Chinese characters. It introduces the common components, radicals, and structure of Chinese characters. Exercises are included.

- Classroom Expressions and Practice: This section introduces the most useful and common phrases encountered in the Chinese classroom. Introducing these phrases early helps the instructors to limit use of English in the classroom. It also allows students to learn some phrases that they can make use of right away.

- Abbreviations of Parts of Speech: This section lists the abbreviations used later in the grammar notes and vocabulary sections.

Core Lessons

The content of the 22 lessons (Part 1 contains Lessons 1–11; Part 2 contains Lessons 12–22) is selected to meet the practical needs and interests of students. The focus of the content begins with individual, family, and school activities, then gradually expands to include wider social occasions and societal contact. Great care has been taken to clearly and systematically present and practice the Core Vocabulary and grammatical expressions of elementary Chinese.

The major sections of each **Core Lesson** are described below:

- Core Vocabulary: Core vocabulary that appears in the **Language Link** section is introduced here. For each vocabulary item, traditional and simplified character forms are presented along with Pinyin pronunciation, grammatical function, and English meaning. This section also highlights the differences between Mainland China and Taiwan usage.

- Language Link: This section contains **Sentence Patterns** that incorporate the lesson's core vocabulary and grammar points. It is accompanied by illustrations that add context and make the lesson more interesting. **Language Link** serves as a model of the correct usage of the vocabulary and grammar points introduced in the lesson. Notes are provided to further explain the text. For most of the lessons, **Language Link** includes dialogues; for some lessons it includes essays, diaries, emails, and letters. The length of **Language Link** is carefully controlled and gradually increases to provide pedagogical sufficiency and challenge.

- Grammar: Core grammar points from **Language Link** are explained in this section. We adopt the pedagogical grammar approach to better fit with the communicative approach to language learning. Grammar explanations are supplemented with examples that use vocabulary items previously covered in the textbook. We have tried to avoid linguistic jargon, with the exception of such commonly used terms as *syntax*, *sentence*, *clause*, *subject*, *predicate*, *object*, and *modifier*. For review and consolidation, the communicative exercises of each lesson elicit the use of grammatical structures introduced in the lesson.

- Supplementary Practice: Each lesson contains a **Supplementary Practice** section with themes, vocabulary, and grammar similar to those found in **Language Link**. This allows students to practice immediately what they have learned from their study of the main text. A different format from that found in **Language Link** is used. For example, if **Language Link** contains a dialogue, **Supplementary Practice** includes a prose format, and vice versa. The pedagogical purpose is to help students learn to use vocabulary and grammar structures in varying forms of communication.

- Activities: This section is designed primarily for classroom use. Listening, character, grammar, and communicative exercises are included throughout the text. Care has been taken to provide balance between structural drills and real-life communicative tasks. The exercises integrate with the grammar points to provide a systematic extension of usage skills from vocabulary-item level to sentence level and on to discourse-level narration and description. Since these exercises are for class time, they are designed to be dynamic and interactive. Most involve interaction between instructor and students, student and student, or group and group. Communicative activities are based on situations that will elicit the grammar points and vocabulary students have learned in the lesson and in prior lessons. Illustrations set the context for the communicative activities. The classroom exercises are provided to save the instructor time, which makes the text convenient and efficient.

- Culture Link: This part contains three sections:

  - **Culture Notes:** The topics of the **Culture Notes** are carefully chosen to relate to those of the core lessons. **Culture Notes** will help students better understand the Chinese society, as well as how language reflects culture. Photos create a vivid and interesting learning experience. The discussion questions encourage students to discuss and compare cultural differences by helping them to be aware of the features of their own culture while gaining understanding of other cultures.

- **Fun with Chinese:** This section introduces a common saying that either utilizes new vocabulary presented in the lesson or is closely related to the theme of the lesson. Illustrations help make this section more fun and eye-catching. Discussion questions offer another way to relate the common Chinese sayings to the theme of the lesson.
- **Let's Go!:** This section provides students an opportunity to interact with Chinese in an authentic context. It helps them connect to Chinese society and communities, increases their motivation, and develops their survival skills for life in Chinese society.

Appendices

The **Appendices** serve as a learning resource for both students and instructors. They can also be used for review exercises in class or for self-study. The Appendices include the following:

- Grammar Summary
- Traditional/Simplified Character Table
- Chinese Transcriptions of **Language in Use**
- English Translations of **Language in Use**. These can be used for translation or interpretation practice, for self-study, or for in-class review.
- Glossaries (Pinyin and English)
- Characters in the *Character Book*

Supplements

Instructor Resources

Instructor's Resource Manual

The **Instructor's Resource Manual** provides sample syllabi, daily schedules, and the answer keys for in-class and homework exercises. This manual is available in print or electronically for download at the Instructor Resource Center (IRC) to qualified adopters. Upon adoption or to preview the online resources, please go to PearsonSchool.com/Access_Request and select "Online Teacher Supplements." You will be required to complete a one-time registration subject to verification. Upon verification of educator status, access information and instructions will be sent via email.

Testing Program

This provides sample test questions for each lesson and is available in a printed format, as well as on MyChineseLab™.

Student Resources

Student Activities Manual

The **Student Activities Manual** contains homework assignments for each lesson in the main textbook. Homework activities are selected from listening, character recognition and writing, grammar exercises, and communicative tasks.

Character Book

The **Character Book** provides the Chinese characters for the Core Vocabulary in every lesson. It shows the following for each character:

1. Character with its stroke order indicated by numbers.
2. Traditional form of the character.
3. Simplified form of the character.
4. Pinyin pronunciation, grammatical usage, and sample sentences or phrases.
5. Stroke order illustrated by writing the character progressively.
6. Radical of the character with its Pinyin pronunciation and meaning.
7. Dotted graph lines to aid students' practice.

Blank boxes are also included for students to practice writing the character. As a handy reference, four types of glossaries are provided in the *Character Book*: (1) By Number of Strokes; (2) By Lesson Number; (3) Alphabetic by Pinyin; (4) Common Radicals.

Audio Materials

The audio recordings for each lesson's texts, vocabulary, listening exercises, tongue twisters, and poems, as well as the listening exercises in the *Student Activities Manual* are provided in the audio program.

Online Resources

Companion Web Site <www.pearsonhighered.com/chineselink>

This open-access site offers the complete audio program, as well as Web resource links for completing Internet-based activities in the textbook.

MyChineseLab™

MyChineseLab™ is a new, nationally hosted online learning system created for students and instructors of language courses. It brings together—in one convenient, easily navigable site—a wide array of language-learning tools and resources, including an interactive version of the *Chinese Link* student text, *Student Activities Manual*, downloadable PDFs of the *Character Book*, a file of the artwork in the text, and all materials from the audio programs. Readiness checks, chapter tests, and tutorials personalize instruction to meet the unique needs of individual students. Instructors can use the system to devise assignments, set grading parameters, listen to student-created audio recordings, and provide feedback on student work. Student access codes to MyChineseLab™ are available for purchase. Take a tour! Visit www.MyLanguageLab.com

致谢 ACKNOWLEDGMENTS

We would like to give our sincerest thanks to the Pearson Education's World Languages team for bringing their talent and professional publishing experience to this project. Many thanks to Rachel McCoy, Senior Acquisitions Editor, for her enthusiasm, sincere dedication, and professional guidance. We appreciate Phil Miller for his faith, commitment and warm encouragement to this project. Thanks to Bethany Gilmour Williamson and Noha Amer, Editorial Assistants, for helping with every aspect of preparing for the revision and ensuring the manuscript was ready for production. Mary Rottino, Senior Managing Editor; Janice Stangel, Associate Managing Editor; and Manuel Echevarria, Senior Production Editor, have been wonderful conduits for channeling the vision of editorial for the second edition, into the development of this revision, on to the final phase of production, all of which were handled with outstanding knowledge of how to turn raw manuscript into a beautiful final product. Meriel Martínez, Media Editor, has continued to carefully oversee the production of the Audio program and Companion Web Site. Melissa Marolla Brown, Development Editor for Assessment, was terrific in providing guidance in preparing various manuscripts, ensuring their readiness for the online environment of MyChineseLab™. Samantha Alducin, Senior Media Editor receives a big thanks for her ability to work with many Pearson team members in order to create MyChineseLab™. Christina Schafermeyer and Dana Bourgerie provided tremendous developmental guidance that enabled this second edition to be more outstanding than the first.

Margaret Chan, Project Manager, and her Graphicraft team members have been wonderful to work with since the first edition. Their prompt communication and hard work helped the production stage go smoothly and efficiently. Thanks to Mark Haney for his assistance with English proofreading of the manuscript during the many different stages of its preparation. With Mark's devotion and patience, the *Chinese Link* project moved along smoothly and well.

We would like to conclude by thanking our families, without whose love and support this project would not have been possible. Many thanks to our husbands, Mark, Dejun, and Jinghong, for enduring our long hours. Special thanks to our children, Carrie, Marion, Lauren, Sara, and Ryan, for giving up a lot of time with their moms so that this project could be completed.

We extend our sincere thanks and appreciation to the colleagues who reviewed the manuscript and provided valuable input. Their detailed comments and insightful suggestions helped us to further refine our manuscript.

Sara Bosa, New Trier High School, IL

Dana Scott Bourgerie, Brigham Young University, UT

Liana Chen, The Pennsylvania State University, PA

Mingjung Chen, De Anza College, CA

Wenze Hu, United States Naval Academy, MD

Weijia Huang, Boston University, MA
Dela Jiao, New York University, NY
George Kang, New Trier High School, IL
Julia Hongwei Kessel, New Trier High School, IL
Xue Guang Lian, City College of San Francisco, CA
Weihsun Mao, Ohlone College, CA
Gary Quinlivan, Saint Vincent College, PA
Chao-mei Shen, Rice University, TX
Xiaohong Wen, University of Houston, TX
Jean Yuanpeng Wu, University of Oregon, OR
Jun Yang, University of Chicago, IL
Jean Yu, The Hotchkiss School, CT
John Yu, Baruch College, NY
Zheng-sheng Zhang, San Diego State University, CA

Sue-mei Wu 吴素美, Ph.D.
Lead author of *Chinese Link*
Carnegie Mellon University

中国地图 MAP OF CHINA

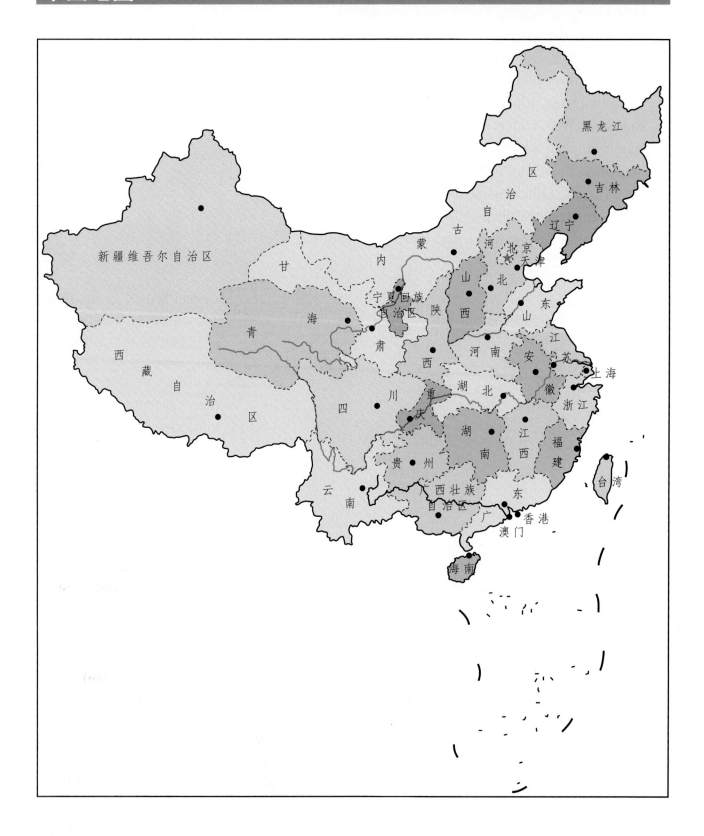

中文简介　INTRODUCTION TO CHINESE

Chinese is a language spoken by about a quarter of the world's population. It is also one of the six working languages of the United Nations. It is called 汉语 [Hànyǔ] (Hanyu) in Chinese because it is spoken by the Han people, the largest ethnic group in China.

A member of the Sino-Tibetan language family, Chinese differs from other languages in many respects. Following are a few of its distinctive characteristics:

- It has no inflection of words to indicate person, gender, number, tense, or mood. The meaning of a sentence relies heavily on the context and word order.

- It is a tonal language. There are many Chinese words whose meanings are differentiated solely by which of the four tones is assigned to them.

- It consists of a large number of dialects, which share the same written form but can be mutually unintelligible when spoken. The Chinese dialects are generally categorized into eight groups: Mandarin (Northern), Northern Min (Northern Fujian), Southern Min (Southern Fujian, Taiwan), Xiang (Hunan), Gan (Jiangxi), Wu (Jiangsu and Zhejiang), Hakka (Guangdong, Guangxi), and Yue (Guangdong).

- The written form of the language consists of roughly square-shaped characters, each of which is formed by a number of strokes. The number of Chinese characters keeps growing. Scholars believe that 3,000 years ago there were around 4,500 characters in use. More recently the Kangxi Dictionary, first compiled in 1710, lists about 48,000 characters. A dictionary published in 1994 lists around 86,000 characters! But don't let the sheer number of characters scare you away from studying Chinese. According to a list of commonly used Chinese characters published by China's Education Commission, only 3,500 characters are commonly used in daily life. It is generally acknowledged that a well-educated Chinese person has mastered 6,000 to 7,000 characters.

- Radicals often provide clues to the meaning of the character. The radical is also important for ordering and grouping characters. For example, dictionaries often have characters grouped by radical and then by the number of strokes required to write the character. According to Chinese linguists, there are approximately 1,500 radicals in total, but most modern Chinese dictionaries only include 214.

About 400 years ago, a unified system of pronunciation for Chinese, which would be intelligible to everybody in the country, began to be established. These efforts continued up until the beginning of the 20th century. As a result, *Guoyu* (the National Language) developed and became the language for all official communication. *Guoyu* takes the Beijing Dialect as the standard for pronunciation and is based on dialects used in the northern part of the country. It also incorporates some language features of other dialects.

After the People's Republic of China was founded in 1949, some changes in the pronunciation of *Guoyu* were made and its name was changed to *Putonghua*, which means "common language." *Putonghua* has been the official language in Mainland China ever since, while *Guoyu* is still being used in Taiwan. In Singapore, Chinese is referred to locally as *Huawen*. In the West, "Mandarin Chinese" is the common term.

Phonetic Transliteration Systems

In the last few centuries there have been efforts to develop a method of representing the Chinese language using the Latin alphabet. The most widely used system is called *Pinyin*. It was developed in Mainland China in the 1950s and officially adopted in 1979. *Pinyin*, which literally means "spell the sounds," is used to help people learn the pronunciation of characters or to look up words in dictionaries. The **Pinyin Foundation** section of this textbook gives a more detailed introduction to this phonetic system.

Characters

Legend says that Chinese characters were created by Cang Jie, an official recorder of the Yellow Emperor, over 5,000 years ago. But the earliest use of a fully developed form of Chinese characters can be traced back to around 3,300 years ago in the Shang Dynasty. These writings, called the "Oracle Bone Scripts," consist of characters carved on ox bones or tortoise shells. Scholars believe that Chinese characters originally were pictographs that represented objects in the real world. Recent archeological discoveries also show that character-like pictographs existed as far back as 7,000 years ago. Xu Shen (58–147 A.D.), a well-known linguist of the Eastern Han Dynasty (25–220 A.D.), analyzed the existing characters, examined their shapes, pronunciations, and meanings, traced their roots, and finally compiled the first ever Chinese dictionary in history—*Shuo Wen Jie Zi*《说文解字》—in which he collected over 9,000 characters categorized under 540 radicals. He concluded that Chinese characters were basically formed in six ways, called *Liu Shu* (the six writings):

1. *Xiang xing* (Pictograph: the character represents a picture of an object), e.g., 木、日、月
2. *Zhi shi* (Ideogram: the character is an indicative sign or indirect symbol), e.g., 上、下、本
3. *Hui yi* ("Meeting of ideas": characters combine to form a new meaning), e.g., 明、休、好
4. *Xing sheng* ("Picture and sound": one part shows the pronunciation, other parts show the meaning), e.g., 想、清、爸
5. *Zhuanzhu* ("Transferable meaning": transformed characters or characters influenced by other words), e.g., 考、老
6. *Jiajie* (Borrowed or loaned characters: meanings come from phonetic association), e.g., 莫、其

Shuo Wen Jie Zi is not only the first dictionary in Chinese history, it is also a scholarly masterpiece with great theoretical and practical value. Xu Shen's analysis of "Liu Shu" has been followed by scholars in China and other East Asian countries as well.

The section **The Chinese Writing System** (on F-22) provides a more detailed introduction to writing Chinese characters.

Simplification of Characters

Because of a belief that the complexity of Chinese characters was both an obstacle to raising the nation's literacy level and also to learning of the language by non-Chinese, efforts to simplify the characters began in the 19th century. In the 1950s, a simplified system of characters was promulgated in Mainland China. This system eliminated 1,053 variant characters and reduced the number of strokes for many other characters. The "Complete List of Simplified Characters" published in May 1964 listed 2,236 simplified characters. This system of simplified characters has become the major writing system used in Mainland China and Singapore. The traditional forms are still the standard way of writing in Taiwan and many overseas Chinese communities.

China has a history of several thousand years. In spite of periods of unity and disunity, China has remained intact as a country and is one of the only ancient civilizations that still exists today. It is believed that the Chinese writing system has played a crucial role by serving as an important binding factor in the cohesiveness of the country.

请求
Making Requests

As the automobile industry in China continues to grow, an increasing number of Chinese people are learning to drive.

教学目标 OBJECTIVES

- Make requests and give permission
- Express wishes, obligations, capabilities, and possibilities
- Talk about driving a car

CONNECTIONS AND COMMUNITIES PREVIEW

Discuss the following questions with a partner or your class. What similarities and differences do you think there might be between Chinese culture and your own culture?

1. How do you make requests or ask for permission in your culture? Are there certain words or phrases people use? Are any gestures used?

2. What words are used in your language to express different feelings such as hopes, wants, and obligations, or to give advice?

生词 VOCABULARY

核心词 Core Vocabulary

	SIMPLIFIED	TRADITIONAL	PINYIN		
1.	可以	可以	kěyǐ	Aux.	can, may
2.	借	借	jiè	V.	to borrow
3.	明天	明天	míngtiān	N.	tomorrow
4.	用	用	yòng	V.	to use
5.	得	得	děi	Aux.	must, have to
6.	机场	機場	jīchǎng	N.	airport
7.	接	接	jiē	V.	to pick up
8.	妹妹	妹妹	mèimei	N.	younger sister
9.	玩	玩	wán	V.	to play, to have fun
10.	飞机	飛機	fēijī	N.	airplane
11.	到	到	dào	V.	to arrive
12.	手排挡	手排擋	shǒupáidǎng	N.	manual transmission (手排 in Taiwan)
	手	手	shǒu	N.	hand
13.	开	開	kāi	V.	to drive, to turn on, to open
14.	应该	應該	yīnggāi	Aux.	should
15.	问题	問題	wèntí	N.	problem, question
16.	白	白	bái	Adj.	white
17.	色	色	sè	N.	color
18.	停	停	tíng	V.	to park
19.	停车场	停車場	tíngchēchǎng	N.	parking lot

	SIMPLIFIED	TRADITIONAL	PINYIN		
20.	这次	這次	zhècì	Pron.	this time
21.	练习	練習	liànxí	V.	to practice
22.	这样	這樣	zhèyàng	Pron.	thus, in this way, like this
23.	就	就	jiù	Adv.	then (connects two clauses, the first being the premise of the second)
24.	能	能	néng	Aux.	can, may, be able to
25.	进步	進步	jìnbù	V.	to improve

专名 Proper Nouns

	SIMPLIFIED	TRADITIONAL	PINYIN		
1.	于影	于影	Yú Yǐng	N.	(name) Ying Yu
2.	王本乐	王本樂	Wáng Běnlè	N.	(name) Benle Wang
3.	上海	上海	Shànghǎi	N.	Shanghai
4.	洛杉矶	洛杉磯	Luòshānjī	N.	Los Angeles

补充词 Supplementary Vocabulary

	SIMPLIFIED	TRADITIONAL	PINYIN		
1.	自动排挡	自動排擋	zìdòngpáidǎng	Adj.	automatic transmission (自排 in Taiwan)

语文知识 LANGUAGE LINK

Read and listen to the following sentence patterns. These patterns use vocabulary, expressions, and grammar that you will study in more detail in this lesson. After reading the sentence patterns, read and listen to the Language in Use section that follows.

句型 Sentence Patterns

A: 我可以借你的车吗?
   Wǒ kěyǐ jiè nǐde chē ma?

B: 可以。
   Kěyǐ.

A: 你要去接谁?
   Nǐ yào qù jiē shéi?

B: 我要去接我妹妹。
   Wǒ yào qù jiē wǒ mèimei.

A: 你会不会开车?
   Nǐ huìbuhuì kāi chē?

B: 我不会开车。
   Wǒ bú huì kāi chē.

🔊 **课文 Language in Use: 我可以借你的车吗？**

于影： 本乐，明天下午你用不用车？
Běnlè, míngtiān xiàwǔ nǐ yòngbuyòng chē?

王本乐： 我不用。你有什么事儿吗？
Wǒ búyòng. Nǐ yǒu shénme shèr ma?

于影： 我得去机场接人，可以借你的车吗？
Wǒ děi qù jīchǎng jiē rén, kěyǐ jiè nǐde chē ma?

王本乐： 可以。你要去接谁？
Kěyǐ. Nǐ yào qù jiē shéi?

于影： 我妹妹和她男朋友。他们
Wǒ mèimei hé tā nánpéngyou. Tāmen

从上海坐飞机去洛杉矶
cóng Shànghǎi zuò fēijī qù Luòshānjī

玩儿，明天会到我这儿来。
wár, míngtiān huì dào wǒ zhèr lái.

坐 [zuò]

坐 means "sit." When its object is a means of transportation, 坐 means "to take" or "to ride."

For example, 坐飞机 literally means "to take an airplane," i.e., "to fly."

王本乐： 我的车是手排挡的，
Wǒde chē shì shǒupáidǎng de,

你会不会开？
nǐ huìbuhuì kāi?

手排挡 [shǒupáidǎng]

手排挡 literally means "hand handle gear." It refers to a manual transmission. In Taiwan, 手排 is commonly used.

于影： 应该没问题。我爸爸的车也是
Yīnggāi méi wèntí. Wǒ bàbade chē yěshì

手排挡的，我常开他的车。
shǒupáidǎng de, wǒ cháng kāi tāde chē.

王本乐： 我的车是白色的，车号是
Wǒde chē shì báisè de, chēhào shì

BD5730，停在五号停车场。
BD wǔ qī sān líng, tíng zài wǔ hào tíngchēchǎng.

于影: 知道了。谢谢!

Zhīdào le. Xièxie!

王本乐: 不谢。你妹妹他们会说英文吗?

Búxiè. Nǐ mèimei tāmen huì shuō Yīngwén ma?

于影: 会一点儿,这次他们想多学习一点儿英文。

Huì yìdiǎr, zhècì tāmen xiǎng duō xuéxí yìdiǎr Yīngwén.

王本乐: 太好了,我得跟他们多练习一点儿中文。

Tàihǎo le, wǒ děi gēn tāmen duō liànxí yìdiǎr Zhōngwén.

这样,我的中文就能

Zhèyàng, wǒde Zhōngwén jiù néng

就 [jiù]
就 here is used as a conjunction meaning "then."

进步了。

jìnbù le.

语法 GRAMMAR

I. Optative Verbs: 要, 想, 应该, 得, 能, 可以, and 会

Optative verbs (verbs that express wishes or hopes) are placed before the main verb to express wishes, desires, obligations, capabilities, possibilities, or to give permission. The most commonly used optative verbs are as follows.

Optative verb	Meaning	Example	Negation
要 [yào]	1. want, will, to be going to	我要去机场。 Wǒ yào qù jīchǎng. (I'm going to go to the airport.)	不想 (irregular negation)
	2. have to, should	你要多练习中文。 Nǐ yào duō liànxí Zhōngwén. (You should practice Chinese more.)	不用 (irregular negation)

想 [xiǎng]	want, intend, would like to	我想吃饺子。 Wǒ xiǎng chī jiǎozi. (I would like to eat dumplings.)	不想
应该 [yīnggāi]	should, ought to, to be supposed to	你应该在宿舍学习。 Nǐ yīnggāi zài sùshè xuéxí. (You should study at the dorm.)	不应该
得 [děi]	have to, to be required to	我得去机场接人。 Wǒ děi qù jīchǎng jiē rén. (I have to pick someone up from the airport.)	不用 (irregular negation)
能 [néng]	1. have the ability to, can	我能开手排挡的车。 Wǒ néng kāi shǒupáidǎng de chē. (I'm able to drive a car with manual transmission.)	不会 (irregular negation)
	2. can (depending on circumstances)	他明天能来上课。 Tā míngtiān néng lái shàngkè. (He can come to class tomorrow.)	不能
	3. permission — may	我能借他的车。 Wǒ néng jiè tāde chē. (We may borrow his car.)	不能
可以 [kěyǐ]	1. permission — may	我可以借他的车。 Wǒ kěyǐ jiè tāde chē. (I may borrow his car.)	不可以 不能 (irregular negation)
	2. can (depending on circumstances)	他明天可以来。 Tā míngtiān kěyǐ lái. (He can come tomorrow.)	不能 (irregular negation)
会 [huì]	1. know how to, have the ability to	我会开车。 Wǒ huì kāichē. (I know how to drive.)	不会
	2. be likely to, will	他明天会来。 Tā míngtiān huì lái. (He will come tomorrow.)	不会

>>Try it!   With a partner, ask and answer the following questions with optative verbs.

1. A: 你想喝什么?
      Nǐ xiǎng hē shénme?

   B: 我 ＿＿＿ 喝 ＿＿＿。
      Wǒ ＿＿＿ hē ＿＿＿.

2. A: 你爸爸常说你应该做什么?
      Nǐ bàba cháng shuō nǐ yīnggāi zuò shénme?

   B: 爸爸常说我 ＿＿＿＿＿＿＿＿＿。
      Bàba cháng shuō wǒ ＿＿＿＿＿＿＿＿＿ .

3. A: 你 ＿＿ 不 ＿＿ 开车?
      Nǐ ＿＿ bù ＿＿ kāichē?

   B: ＿＿＿＿＿＿＿＿＿＿＿＿＿＿。

4. A: 你得去接人吗?
      Nǐ děi qù jiērén ma?

   B: 今天不 ＿＿＿ 接人。明天 ＿＿＿ 去。
      Jīntiān bù ＿＿＿ jiērén. Míngtiān ＿＿＿＿ qù.

5. A: ＿＿ 不 ＿＿ 喝红茶?
      ＿＿ bù ＿＿ hē hóngchá?

   B: 我不 ＿＿＿ 喝茶，＿＿＿ 喝可乐。
      Wǒ bù ＿＿＿ hē chá, ＿＿＿ hē kělè.

6. A: 我 ＿＿＿ 不 ＿＿＿ 跟你一起去玩儿?
      Wǒ ＿＿＿ bù ＿＿＿ gēn nǐ yìqǐ qù wár?

   B: 可以! 你 ＿＿＿ 去哪儿?
      Kěyǐ! Nǐ ＿＿＿ qù nǎr?

II. 从......去/到......

从......去/到...... [cóng . . . qù/dào . . .] (from . . . to . . .) is a common pattern that is used to describe the movement of something from one place to another. Note that when describing an event, Chinese word order begins with the starting point, then proceeds to the means, to the arriving point, and then to the action. This reflects the temporal sequence of the event.

Subj.		Place 1	Means		Place 2	V.
他们	从	上海	坐飞机	去	洛杉矶	玩。
Tāmen	cóng	Shànghǎi	zuò fēijī	qù	Luòshānjī	wán.

(Literally: They, from Shanghai, took a flight, arrived in Los Angeles, and had fun.)

When talking about time, only 从……到…… is used.

这个学期是从一月到五月。

Zhège xuéqī shì cóng yīyuè dào wǔyuè.

(This semester runs from January to May.)

>> Try it! | **With a partner, ask and answer the following questions with 从……去/到……**

1. A: _____ 纽约坐飞机 _____ 洛杉矶要几个小时[1]?

   _____ Niǔyuē zuò fēijī _____ Luòshānjī yào jǐge xiǎoshí?

   B: _____ 纽约坐飞机 _____ 洛杉矶要五个小时。

   _____ Niǔyuē zuò fēijī _____ Luòshānjī yào wǔge xiǎoshí.

2. A: 你想 _____ 洛杉矶 _____ 哪儿玩?

   Nǐ xiǎng _____ Luòshānjī _____ nǎr wán?

   B: 我想 _____ 洛杉矶 _____ 玩。

   Wǒ xiǎng _____ Luòshānjī _____ wán.

3. A: _____ 你小的时候[2] _____ 现在[3],你喜欢吃什么?

   _____ nǐ xiǎode shíhou _____ xiànzài, nǐ xǐhuān chī shénme?

   B: _____ 小的时候 _____ 现在,我喜欢吃 _____。

   _____ xiǎode shíhou _____ xiànzài, wǒ xǐhuān chī _____ .

4. A: 这个学期是 _____ 几月 _____ 几月?

   Zhège xuéqī shì _____ jǐyuè _____ jǐyuè?

   B: _____ 。

5. A: 我们 _____ 这里怎么 _____ 那里?

   Wǒmen _____ zhèlǐ zěnme _____ nàlǐ?

   B: 我们 _____ 这里 _____ 。

   Wǒmen _____ zhèlǐ _____ .

Notes:
1. 小时(小時) [xiǎoshí]: hour
2. 小的时候(小的時候) [xiǎode shíhou]: when young, during childhood
3. 现在(現在) [xiànzài]: now

III. 多/少 + V./V.P.

多/少 [duō/shǎo] can be placed before a verb or verb phrase to indicate doing more or less of the action. 多/少 + V.P. is often preceded by an optative verb (modal verb) to give advice or to express wishes.

你要多学习。
Nǐ yào duō xuéxí.

You need to study more.

他应该少喝咖啡。
Tā yīnggāi shǎo hē kāfēi.

He should drink less coffee.

你应该多练习汉字。
Nǐ yīnggāi duō liànxí Hànzì.

You should practice characters more.

请多吃一点儿。
Qǐng duō chī yìdiǎr.

Please eat a little bit more.

我要多睡一点儿。
Wǒ yào duō shuì yìdiǎr.

I want to sleep a little more.

>>Try it! | With a partner, take turns completing the following sentences with 多/少.

1. 你要 ＿＿ 喝水。
   Nǐ yào ＿＿ hēshuǐ.

2. 我们应该 ＿＿ 看电视吧。
   Wǒmen yīnggāi ＿＿ kàn diànshì ba.

3. 姐姐得 ＿＿ 练习一点儿。
   Jiějie děi ＿＿ liànxí yìdiǎr.

4. 要学中文，要 ＿＿ 跟中国人说中文。
   Yào xué Zhōngwén, yào ＿＿ gēn Zhōngguórén shuō Zhōngwén.

补充课文 SUPPLEMENTARY PRACTICE

Read the following passage. Then listen and repeat.

　　我妹妹和她男朋友要来美国度假¹，他们要先从上海坐飞机去洛杉矶玩儿，然后再到我这儿来。我得去机场接他们，可是我没有车，我就跟我朋友本乐借车。本乐的车是手排挡的，他问我会不会开。我告诉²他我比较³喜欢开自排的车⁴，可是我也会开手排的车，所以⁵应该没问题。

　　妹妹他们这次来，除了⁶要玩儿以外，他们也想多了解⁷美国文化⁸，多学一点儿英文。本乐说他也想多练习一点儿中文。他问我可不可以跟他们一起去玩儿。我说当然⁹可以！

Notes:

1. 度假 [dùjià]: to spend one's vacation
2. 告诉(告訴) [gàosu]: to tell (pronounced as [gàosù] in Taiwan)
3. 比较(比較) [bǐjiào]: relatively, comparatively
4. 自排 [zìpái]: automatic transmission
5. 所以 [suǒyǐ]: therefore, so
6. 除了……以外 [chúle . . . yǐwài]: besides
7. 了解(瞭解) [liǎojiě]: to understand
8. 文化 [wénhuà]: culture
9. 当然(當然) [dāngrán]: of course

Pinyin version:

Wǒ mèimei hé tā nánpéngyou yào lái Měiguó dùjià, tāmen yào xiān cóng Shànghǎi zuò fēijī qù Luòshānjī wár, ránhòu zài dào wǒ zhèr lái. Wǒ děi qù jīchǎng jiē tāmen, kěshì wǒ méiyǒu chē, wǒ jiù gēn wǒ péngyou Běnlè jièchē. Běnlè de chē shì shǒupáidǎng de, tā wèn wǒ huìbuhuì kāi. Wǒ gàosu tā wǒ bǐjiào xǐhuān kāi zìpái de chē, kěshì wǒ yě huìkāi shǒupái de chē, suǒyǐ yīnggāi méiwèntí.

Mèimei tāmen zhècì lái, chúle yào wár yǐwài, tāmen yě xiǎng duō liǎojiě Měiguó wénhuà, duō xué yìdiǎr Yīngwén. Běnlè shuō tā yě xiǎng duō liànxí yìdiǎr Zhōngwén. Tā wèn wǒ kě bù kěyǐ gēn tāmen yìqǐ qù wár. Wǒ shuō dāngrán kěyǐ!

Read the following statements and choose whether they are true or false.

1. 本乐's sister is coming to visit.	True	False
2. 本乐's sister is coming here to work.	True	False
3. The speaker prefers a car with automatic transmission.	True	False
4. 本乐's sister is interested in studying English more.	True	False
5. The speaker tells 本乐 he can go out with them.	True	False

练习 ACTIVITIES

I. Listening Exercises

12-1 Listen and write the Pinyin for the words you hear. Then check your answers with a partner or the class.

1. _____   2. _____   3. _____

4. _____   5. _____   6. _____

7. _____   8. _____   9. _____

10. _____   11. _____   12. _____

12-2 Listen and complete each phrase with the correct Pinyin. Then check your answers with a partner or the class.

1. _____ liànxí _____ _____ jìnbù   2. wǒ _____ qù _____ rén

3. _____ Niǔyuē dào _____ _____   4. hái bú _____ _____ chē

5. xiǎng _____ _____ sè de chē   6. wǒ _____ shàng _____ chē

12-3 Work in small groups. Take turns reading the lines of the following poem, paying special attention to the tones and rhythm.

Lè Yóuyuán (Lǐ Shāngyǐn)	乐游原 (李商隐)	Wandering about the Pleasant Plateau (Li, Shangyin)
Xiàng wǎn yì bú shì,	向晚意不适，	Feeling slightly sad near dusk,
Qū chē dēng gǔyuán.	驱车登古原 。	I drive up to the ancient plateau.
Xīyáng wúxiàn hǎo,	夕阳无限好，	The sunset is endlessly beautiful,
Zhǐshì jìn huánghūn.	只是近黄昏 。	But dusk is drawing near.

II. Character Exercises

12-4   Match each Chinese word with its English meaning. Then check your answers with a partner.

___ 1. 开车
      kāichē

    a. to improve

___ 2. 停车
      tíngchē

    b. to drive a car

___ 3. 接
      jiē

    c. airplane

___ 4. 借
      jiè

    d. to pick up

___ 5. 练习
      liànxí

    e. to borrow

___ 6. 进步
      jìnbù

    f. problem

___ 7. 问题
      wèntí

    g. to park a car

___ 8. 飞机
      fēijī

    h. to practice

12-5   Match each character with its radical. Check your answers with a partner and discuss how each radical contributes to the meaning of the character. Try to think of another character with each of the radicals.

___ 1. 问   a. 土 (earth)

___ 2. 接   b. 女 (female)

___ 3. 场   c. 日 (sun, day)

___ 4. 妹   d. 手 (扌) (hand)

___ 5. 进   e. 走 (辶) (walk)

___ 6. 明   f. 口 (mouth)

III. Grammar Exercises

12-6   Look at the following example. With a partner, take turns extending the following words into phrases and then sentences. See how long you can keep extending the sentences.

Example: A: 到   dào

B: 到机场   dào jīchǎng

A: 从学校到机场   cóng xuéxiào dào jīchǎng

B: 从学校到机场接人   cóng xuéxiào dào jīchǎng jiē rén

A: 能从学校到机场接人
néng cóng xuéxiào dào jīchǎng jiē rén

B: 你能从学校到机场去接人吗？
Nǐ néng cóng xuéxiào dào jīchǎng qù jiē rén ma?

1. 借   2. 用   3. 玩   4. 色   5. 停   6. 会   7. 排   8. 进
jiè   yòng   wán   sè   tíng   huì   pái   jìn

12-7   With a partner, take turns using words from the boxes to complete and practice the dialogues. Look carefully at the sentences to see which words fit most appropriately.

Example: A: 你会不会<u>开车</u>？   Nǐ huìbuhuì <u>kāichē</u>?

B: 我会<u>开车</u>。   Wǒ huì <u>kāichē</u>.

1. A: 你会不会 _____？
Nǐ huìbuhuì _____ ?

用电脑	写电子邮件	开车
yòng diànnǎo	xiě diànzǐ yóujiàn	kāichē
说法文	开飞机	
shuō Fǎwén	kāi fēijī	

B: 我(不)会 _____ 。
Wǒ (bú) huì _____ .

2. A: 你现在能 _____ 吗？
Nǐ xiànzài néng _____ ma?

上网	看中国文学书
shàngwǎn	kàn Zhōngguó wénxué shū
看电视	跟我一起喝茶
kàn diànshì	gēn wǒ yìqǐ hēchá

B: 我现在 _____ 。
Wǒ xiànzài _____ .

3. A: 王老师要从 _____
   Wáng lǎoshī yào cóng _____

   到 _____ 做什么?
   dào _____ zuò shénme?

   B: 王老师要从 _____
   Wáng lǎoshī yào cóng _____

   到 _____ _____ 。
   dào _____ _____ .

公寓 gōngyù	图书馆 túshūguǎn	看书 kànshū
英国 Yīngguó	日本 Rìběn	学习 xuéxí
家 jiā	学校 xuéxiào	打球 dǎqiú
六点 liùdiǎn	八点 bādiǎn	跟朋友吃饭 gēn péngyou chīfàn

12-8 With a partner, match each Chinese sentence with its English meaning, paying special attention to the optative verbs.

___ 1. 我今天得开车去学校。
    Wǒ jīntiān děi kāichē qù xuéxiào.

a. I should drive to school today.

___ 2. 我今天要开车去学校。
    Wǒ jīntiān yào kāichē qù xuéxiào.

b. I will drive to school today.

___ 3. 我今天应该开车去学校。
    Wǒ jīntiān yīnggāi kāichē qù xuéxiào.

c. I am likely to drive to school today.

___ 4. 我今天能开车去学校。
    Wǒ jīntiān néng kāichē qù xuéxiào.

d. I have to drive to school today.

___ 5. 我今天会开车去学校。
    Wǒ jīntiān huì kāichē qù xuéxiào.

e. I am able to drive to school today.

12-9 With a partner, match each Chinese sentence with its English meaning, paying special attention to the negative optative verbs.

___ 1. 他不可以打手机。
    Tā bù kěyǐ dǎ shǒujī.

a. He doesn't want to use the cell phone.

___ 2. 他不会打手机。
    Tā búhuì dǎ shǒujī.

b. He shouldn't use the cell phone.

___ 3. 他不用打手机。
    Tā búyòng dǎ shǒujī.

c. He is not allowed to use the cell phone.

___ 4. 他不想打手机。
    Tā bù xiǎng dǎ shǒujī.

d. He doesn't know how to use the cell phone.

___ 5. 他不应该打手机。
    Tā bù yīnggāi dǎ shǒujī.

e. He doesn't need to use the cell phone.

IV. Communicative Activities

12-10 With a partner, role-play the following situation.

Situation: You and a friend are going on an overseas trip together next month. You discuss your plans. Your friend asks how long the flight will take and where both of you should go. You ask your friend what food both of you should try on the trip. You both talk about places you wish to see or things you shouldn't miss. You and your friend also talk about how to stay healthy while traveling (for example, what you should do more or less of).

Words and expressions to use:

很好玩儿/很美[1]
hěn hǎowár/hěnměi

从......坐......到/去......
cóng . . . zuò . . . dào/qù . . .

多/少 + V.P.
duō/shǎo

要/得/应该/可以
yào/děi/yīnggāi/kěyǐ

喜欢......
xǐhuān . . .

Note:
1. 美 [měi]: beautiful

12-11 Work in small groups to role-play the following situation.

Situation: You are on an advice radio talk show. One person gives advice. The others are callers with different problems. The advisor uses optative verbs, 多/少 + V.P., and the words and expressions below. Begin with the sample problems and then think of some new problems.

Sample problems:

要学中文，可是不认识中国朋友
yào xué Zhōngwén, kěshì bú rènshi Zhōngguó péngyou

每天都很累
měitiān dōu hěnlèi

不懂[1]功课
bù dǒng gōngkè

要去机场接人可是没有车
yào qù jīchǎng jiērén kěshì méiyǒu chē

Note:
1. 懂 [dǒng]: to understand

Words and expressions to use:

我有一个问题......   怎么办? (What should I do?)
wǒ yǒu yíge wèntí . . .   zěnmebàn?

要/得/应该   多/少 + V.P.
yào/děi/yīnggāi   duō/shǎo

谢谢
xièxie

文化知识 Culture Link

文化点滴 CULTURE NOTES

汽车在中国 Cars in China

The car industry in China has developed relatively recently. Though cars were imported earlier, the first cars produced by a Chinese manufacturer were built in 1953. One was a truck called the Liberation and the other was a limousine called the Red Flag. However, it wasn't until the mid-1990s that private car ownership began to be permitted. Since then, the number of families owning a car in China has grown.

When private car ownership was first allowed, only the very wealthy could afford a car. They often purchased imported vehicles from foreign embassies. The license plate fees and various other fees made it difficult for most people to buy and use a car in everyday life. With the growing affluence in China's cities along with changes in tax and bank loan policies, more people today are able to buy a car for their families than ever before. For many families it helps to increase their status, sometimes bringing about increased business opportunities.

As the car industry has grown, so have some interesting trends. The appeal of luxury cars has caught on with some people

Do you know...

- what the name of the first car produced by Chinese manufacturers was?
- what some recent car trends are?
- what some concerns about increased car ownership in China are?

Read and find out!

buying expensive cars as a status symbol. In fact, the more affluent Hong Kong is often known as the Rolls Royce capital of the world. Cars are increasingly used for recreation: drive-in movie theaters have sprung up and car clubs promote group road trips in self-driving tours to different places in China. Another trend started when McDonald's introduced the first drive-through restaurant in China in 2006.

Increased car ownership and roads that cannot handle a huge increase in traffic, have caused the government to introduce many fees for maintaining and registering a car (as well as road tolls and parking fees) to help limit the number of cars on the roads. However, car ownership in China is expected to continue growing and the market is expected to exceed many other international markets. With this growth comes increasing concern for the environment and worry about the impact of the increasing traffic problems China will have. To help ameliorate these problems, many car manufacturers are introducing ecologically friendly electric cars and hybrid cars to China's growing market.

A new hydrogen-cell–powered car displayed near the Great Wall. Why are some car manufacturers hoping to market such cars in China?

McDonald's has recently opened drive-through restaurants in China. What other car trends have developed in China?

Discuss the following with a group or your class.

1. What changes do you think increases in car ownership will bring to China's society? Do you think the new trends will affect Chinese society?

2. Some people say that, with a population of 1.3 billion, it is not appropriate for China to encourage its people to purchase their own cars. Do you agree with them? Why or why not?

趣味中文 FUN WITH CHINESE

有借有还，再借不难。

If you return what you borrow, it will be easy to borrow again.

yǒu	jiè	yǒu	huán	zài	jiè	bù	nán
有	借	有	还	再	借	不	难
have	borrow	have	return	again	borrow	not	difficult

Work in small groups or with your class.

1. Practice reading the saying aloud, paying attention to the pronunciation and rhythm.
2. Take a closer look at these two characters: 再 在
   What are the similarities and differences between them in pronunciation and meaning?
3. Do you agree with the saying? Do you know of any similar sayings in other languages or cultures?

🔊 行动吧！ LET'S GO!

租车表 Car Rental Form

Work with a partner or small groups. Read the following car rental form that 于影 has filled out.

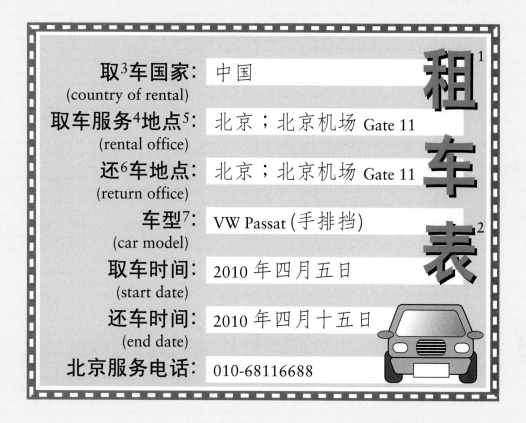

取³车国家： (country of rental)	中国
取车服务⁴地点⁵： (rental office)	北京；北京机场 Gate 11
还⁶车地点： (return office)	北京；北京机场 Gate 11
车型⁷： (car model)	VW Passat (手排挡)
取车时间： (start date)	2010 年四月五日
还车时间： (end date)	2010 年四月十五日
北京服务电话：	010-68116688

Notes:
1. 租 [zū]: to rent
2. 表 [biǎo]: form
3. 取 [qǔ]: to obtain, to take
4. 服务(服務) [fúwù]: service
5. 地点(地點) [dìdiǎn]: place
6. 还(還) [huán]: to return, to give back
7. 型 [xíng]: model, type

Answer the following questions with your partner or group.

1. 于影要从什么时候到什么时候用车？

   Yú Yǐng yào cóng shénme shíhou dào shénme shíhou yòng chē?

2. 她在哪儿取车？

   Tā zài nǎr qǔ chē?

3. 能不能在上海还车？

   Néngbunéng zài Shànghǎi huán chē?

4. 她应该会开什么样[1]的车？

   Tā yīnggāi huì kāi shénmeyàng de chē?

5. 有问题的时候，要给谁打电话？

   Yǒu wèntí de shíhou, yào gěi shéi dǎ diànhuà?

Note:

1. 什么样(什麼樣) [shénmeyàng]: what kind

第十三课
LESSON

13

衣服、逛街
Clothes and Shopping

A traveler shops for traditional Chinese clothing.

教学目标 OBJECTIVES

- Ask how much something costs
- Talk about clothing
- Express opinions

CONNECTIONS AND COMMUNITIES PREVIEW

Discuss the following questions with a partner or your class. What similarities and differences do you think there might be between Chinese culture and your own culture?

1. Are there any kinds of traditional clothing in your culture? Are there any occasions where people still wear traditional clothing?

2. Are there lucky colors in your culture? Do different colors have different meanings? Do you wear different colors for different occasions?

生词 VOCABULARY

核心词 Core Vocabulary

	SIMPLIFIED	TRADITIONAL	PINYIN		
1.	买	買	mǎi	V.	to buy
2.	件	件	jiàn	M.W.	(measure word for clothes)
3.	衬衫	襯衫	chènshān	N.	shirt
4.	店员	店員	diànyuán	N.	salesman, saleswoman
	店	店	diàn	N.	store
5.	条	條	tiáo	M.W.	(measure word for skirts/pants)
6.	裙子	裙子	qúnzi	N.	skirt
7.	或者	或者	huòzhě	Conj.	or, either . . . or . . .
8.	裤子	褲子	kùzi	N.	pants
9.	黄	黃	huáng	Adj.	yellow
10.	不错	不錯	búcuò	Adv.	not bad, pretty good
11.	比较	比較	bǐjiào	Adv.	relatively, comparatively
12.	穿	穿	chuān	V.	to wear (used with clothing in general)
13.	黑	黑	hēi	Adj.	black
14.	试试	試試	shìshi	V.	to try
15.	帮	幫	bāng	V.	to help
16.	好看	好看	hǎokàn	Adj.	good-looking
17.	让	讓	ràng	V.	to let, to allow
18.	觉得	覺得	juéde	V.	to think, to feel
19.	钱	錢	qián	N.	money
20.	块	塊	kuài	N.	dollar
21.	张	張	zhāng	M.W.	(measure word for piece of paper)

SIMPLIFIED	TRADITIONAL	PINYIN		
22. 电影	電影	diànyǐng	N.	movie
23. 票	票	piào	N.	ticket

专名 Proper Nouns

SIMPLIFIED	TRADITIONAL	PINYIN		
1. 毛爱红	毛愛紅	Máo Àihóng	N.	(name) Aihong Mao
2. 方子英	方子英	Fāng Zǐyīng	N.	(name) Ziying Fang

补充词 Supplementary Vocabulary

SIMPLIFIED	TRADITIONAL	PINYIN		
1. 贵	貴	guì	Adj.	expensive
2. 便宜	便宜	piányi	Adj.	inexpensive, cheap (pronounced as [piányí] in Taiwan)
3. 卖	賣	mài	V.	to sell
4. 几号	幾號	jǐ hào	Pron.	what size
号	號	hào	N.	size
5. 大	大	dà	Adj.	large
6. 中	中	zhōng	Adj.	medium
7. 小	小	xiǎo	Adj.	small
8. 衣服	衣服	yīfu	N.	clothes
9. 外套	外套	wàitào	N.	coat (used with M.W. 件)
10. 毛衣	毛衣	máoyī	N.	sweater (used with M.W. 件)
11. T-恤衫	T-恤衫	tīxùshān	N.	T-shirt (used with M.W. 件)
12. 短裤	短褲	duǎnkù	N.	shorts (used with M.W. 条)
13. 牛仔裤	牛仔褲	niúzǎikù	N.	jeans (used with M.W. 条)
14. 鞋子	鞋子	xiézi	N.	shoes (used with M.W. 双)
15. 袜子	襪子	wàzi	N.	socks (used with M.W. 双)

	SIMPLIFIED	TRADITIONAL	PINYIN		
16.	脱	脫	tuō	V.	to take off (used with clothing in general)
17.	戴	戴	dài	V.	to wear, to put on (used with accessories)
18.	摘	摘	zhāi	V.	to take off (used with accessories)
19.	手表	手錶	shǒubiǎo	N.	watch
20.	眼镜	眼鏡	yǎnjìng	N.	glasses (used with M.W. 副 [fù])
21.	耳环	耳環	ěrhuán	N.	earring (used with M.W. 对 for a pair of earrings)
22.	帽子	帽子	màozi	N.	hat (used with M.W. 顶 [dǐng])
23.	颜色	顏色	yánsè	N.	color
24.	橙色 (橘色)	橙色 (橘色)	chéngsè (júsè)	Adj.	orange
25.	蓝色	藍色	lánsè	Adj.	blue
26.	紫色	紫色	zǐsè	Adj.	purple
27.	棕色 (咖啡色)	棕色 (咖啡色)	zōngsè (kāfēisè)	Adj.	brown
28.	金黄色	金黃色	jīnhuángsè	Adj.	gold
29.	银灰色	銀灰色	yínhuīsè	Adj.	silver
30.	人民币	人民幣	Rénmínbì	N.	currency of the People's Republic of China
31.	新台币	新台幣	Xīntáibì	N.	currency of Taiwan (New Taiwan dollars). In the traditional character, it can be also written as 新臺幣 (臺 and 台 are both traditional forms, but 臺 is more formal than 台).
32.	港币	港幣	Gǎngbì	N.	currency of Hong Kong
33.	美金	美金	Měijīn	N.	U.S. dollar

语文知识 LANGUAGE LINK

Read and listen to the following sentence patterns. These patterns use vocabulary, expressions, and grammar that you will study in more detail in this lesson. After reading the sentence patterns, read and listen to the Language in Use section that follows.

句型 Sentence Patterns

A: 你想买什么？
   Nǐ xiǎng mǎi shénme?

B: 我想买一件衬衫。
   Wǒ xiǎng mǎi yíjiàn chènshān.

A: 你帮我看看，我穿裙子
   Nǐ bāng wǒ kànkan, wǒ chuān qúnzi

   好看还是穿裤子好看？
   hǎokàn háishì chuān kùzi hǎokàn?

B: 我觉得你穿裙子好看。
   Wǒ juéde nǐ chuān qúnzi hǎokàn.

A: 这条裙子多少钱？
   Zhètiáo qúnzi duōshǎo qián?

B: 十五块。
   Shíwǔ kuài.

🔊 **课文 Language in Use: 我想买一件衬衫**

店员:　两位小姐想买什么?
　　　　Liǎngwèi xiǎojiě xiǎng mǎi shénme?

毛爱红:　我想买一件衬衫。
　　　　Wǒ xiǎng mǎi yíjiàn chènshān.

方子英:　我想买一条裙子或者裤子。
　　　　Wǒ xiǎng mǎi yìtiáo qúnzi huòzhě kùzi.

店员:　这件黄衬衫怎么样?
　　　　Zhèjiàn huáng chènshān zěnmeyàng?

毛爱红:　还不错。可是我比较喜欢
　　　　Hái búcuò. Kěshì wǒ bǐjiào xǐhuān

　　　　穿黑色的,有没有黑色的?
　　　　chuān hēisède, yǒuméiyǒu hēisède?

店员:　有,在这儿,你试试!
　　　　Yǒu, zài zhèr, nǐ shìshi!

方子英:　爱红,来,你帮我看看,
　　　　Àihóng, lái, nǐ bāng wǒ kànkan,

　　　　我穿裙子好看还是穿
　　　　wǒ chuān qúnzi hǎokàn háishì chuān

　　　　裤子好看?
　　　　kùzi hǎokàn?

毛爱红:　你穿穿,让我看看。
　　　　Nǐ chuānchuan, ràng wǒ kànkan.

　　　　我觉得你穿这条裙子
　　　　Wǒ juéde nǐ chuān zhètiáo qúnzi

　　　　好看。
　　　　hǎokàn.

还不错 [Hái búcuò]

不错 literally means "not wrong." It means "good" in Chinese. 还不错 means "okay," "fine."

穿 [chuān] and 戴 [dài]

The verb 穿 [chuān] is used to refer to putting on or wearing clothing items in general, such as coats, pants/skirts, socks, and shoes.

穿一条裙子 [chuān yìtiáo qúnzi] means "wear a skirt."

The verb 戴 [dài] is used to refer to putting on or wearing accessories, such as glasses, hats, gloves, and jewelry.

戴一个手表 [dài yíge shǒubiǎo] means "wear a watch."

好看 [hǎokàn]

好看 means "good-looking." 好 is often used with a verb to form a new adjective to mean "good to V." or "easy to V." Other common examples include:

好吃 [hǎochī]: delicious (good to eat)

好喝 [hǎohē]: delicious to drink (good to drink)

好玩 [hǎowán]: funny, interesting (good to play)

好写 [hǎoxiě]: easy to write

Adding 不好 or 难 before a verb gives the opposite meaning "not good to V." or "not easy to V." For example, 不好吃 and 难吃 both mean something does not taste good.

觉得 [juéde]

When 觉 is used in 觉得, meaning "to feel" or "to think," it is pronounced as [jué]. When 觉 is used in 睡觉, meaning "to sleep," it is pronounced as [jiào].

When 得 is preceded by 觉 in 觉得, it is pronounced as [de]. When 得 is by itself, it has the meaning of "must" or "have to" and is pronounced as [děi].

方子英：　请问，这条裙子多少钱？
　　　　　Qǐngwèn, zhètiáo qúnzi duōshǎo qián?

> 多少钱 [duōshǎo qián]
> How much (money) is it?

店员：　　十五块。
　　　　　Shíwǔ kuài.

方子英：　好，我买了。
　　　　　Hǎo, wǒ mǎile.

毛爱红：　我要买这件黑衬衫。
　　　　　Wǒ yào mǎi zhèjiàn hēi chènshān.

店员：　　对了，小姐，这张电影票是你的吗？
　　　　　Duì le, xiǎojiě, zhèzhāng diànyǐngpiào shì nǐde ma?

方子英：　是的，这张电影票是我的。谢谢！我们等一下
　　　　　Shìde, zhèzhāng diànyǐngpiào shì wǒde. Xièxie! Wǒmen děngyíxià

　　　　　要去看电影。
　　　　　yào qù kàn diànyǐng.

语法 GRAMMAR

I.　The Conjunction 或者

或者 [huòzhě] is another conjunction meaning "or," similar to 还是 [háishì]. However, while 还是 [háishì] is used only in questions, 或者 [huòzhě] is used only in statements.

我想买一条裙子或者裤子。
Wǒ xiǎng mǎi yìtiáo qúnzi huòzhě kùzi.
(I would like to buy a skirt or a pair of pants.)

我喜欢红色或者白色的。
Wǒ xǐhuān hóngsè huòzhě báisède.
(I like red or white.)

>>**Try it!** With a partner, practice asking questions and answering with 或者.

1. A: 你想去哪儿?
   Nǐ xiǎng qù nǎr?

   B: 我想去中国 _____ 日本 。
   Wǒ xiǎng qù Zhōngguó _____ Rìběn.

2. A: 妈妈说妹妹应该学什么?
   Māma shuō mèimei yīnggāi xué shénme?

   B: 她说妹妹应该学法文 _____ 德文 。
   Tā shuō Mèimei yīnggāi xué Fǎwén _____ Déwén.

3. A: 今天你要吃什么?
   Jīntiān nǐ yào chī shénme?

   B: 今天我要吃 _____ 。
   Jīntiān wǒ yào chī _____ .

II. Measure Words (4): 件, 条, 双, and 张

In describing clothing, the measure words 件 [jiàn] and 条 [tiáo] are used. 件 [jiàn] is generally used for clothing worn on the upper body, but sometimes it can be used for clothing in general. 条 [tiáo] is a measure word used for long-shaped clothing, such as 裤子 [kùzi] and 裙子 [qúnzi].

Measure word	Usage	Example	
件 [jiàn]	For clothing in general	一件衬衫 [chènshān]	shirt
		一件大衣 [dàyī]	overcoat
		一件T-恤衫 [tīxùshān]	T-shirt
		一件外套 [wàitào]	coat
条 [tiáo]	For long-shaped items	一条裤子 [kùzi]	pants
		一条牛仔裤 [niúzǎikù]	jeans
		一条裙子 [qúnzi]	skirt

For clothing items that come in pairs, such as socks and shoes, 双 [shuāng], the measure word for pairs, is used.

两双鞋子 [liǎng shuāng xiézi]   two pairs of shoes

三双袜子 [sān shuāng wàzi]   three pairs of socks

Note that for pairs of accessories, other measure words are used, such as 副 [fù] for gloves and 对 [duì] for earrings.

Finally, 张 [zhāng] is used for flat objects and sheets of paper or tickets.

> **>>Try it!** With a partner, use the appropriate measure word to complete the dialogues.

1. A: 那 ___ 衬衫你喜欢不喜欢？
    Nà ___ chènshān nǐ xǐhuān bu xǐhuān?

    B: 我喜欢。我也喜欢那 ___ 鞋子。
    Wǒ xǐhuān. Wǒ yě xǐhuān nà ___ xiézi.

2. A: 你想买这 ___ 裤子还是那 ___ ？
    Nǐ xiǎng mǎi zhè ___ kùzi háishì nà ___ ?

    B: 我想买这 _____ 黑色的。
    Wǒ xiǎng mǎi zhè _____ hēisè de.

3. A: 你觉得穿什么颜色的鞋子好看？
    Nǐ juéde chuān shénme yánsè de xiézi hǎokàn?

    B: 我觉得那 _____ 白色的鞋子好看。
    Wǒ juéde nà _____ báisè de xiézi hǎokàn.

4. A: 我们今天要去看电影，那两 ___ 电影票在哪儿？
    Wǒmen jīntiān yàoqù kàn diànyǐng, nà liǎng ___ diànyǐngpiào zài nǎr?

    B: 噢[1]！在那 ___ 外套的口袋[2]！
    Òu! Zài nà ___ wàitào de kǒudài!

Notes:
1. 噢 [Òu]: Oh!
2. 口袋 [kǒudài]: pocket

III. Duplication of Verbs

Many verbs can be duplicated in spoken Chinese to indicate a quick action, doing a little bit of something, or doing something in a relaxed way. Only verbs that express active actions or behaviors can be duplicated. Verbs that indicate status or existence cannot be duplicated. Note that the duplicated syllable is always pronounced in the neutral tone.

试试 [shìshi]	to try	看看 [kànkan]	to have a look
穿穿 [chuānchuan]	to try on	写写 [xiěxie]	to write a little
说说 [shuōshuo]	to say a little	想想 [xiǎngxiang]	to think a little

If the verb has two syllables, the duplication is as follows:

介绍介绍 [jièshao jièshao]   to give a little introduction

学习学习 [xuéxi xuéxi]   to study a little

Verbs that can be duplicated may also be followed by 一下(儿) [yíxià(r)] instead of duplication. This usage has the same effect as duplication. Monosyllabic verbs can also be duplicated with the word 一 [yí] in between, such as 看一看 or 想一想.

| 看看 | = | 看一下(儿) | = | 看一看 |
| kànkan | | kànyíxià(r) | | kànyíkàn |

| 想想 | = | 想一下(儿) | = | 想一想 |
| xiǎngxiang | | xiǎngyíxià(r) | | xiǎngyìxiǎng |

| 介绍介绍 | = | 介绍一下(儿) | = | (NA) |
| jièshao jièshao | | jièshào yíxià(r) | | |

| 学习学习 | = | 学习一下(儿) | = | (NA) |
| xuéxi xuéxi | | xuéxí yíxià(r) | | |

>>Try it! With a partner, duplicate the verbs in parentheses to complete the sentences.

1. 你应该先 ＿＿＿ ，然后再决定。(想)
   Nǐ yīnggāi xiān ＿＿＿ , ránhòu zài juédìng. (xiǎng)

2. 你们不认识吗？来，我给你们 ＿＿＿ 。(介绍)
   Nǐmen bú rènshi ma? Lái, wǒ gěi nǐmen ＿＿＿ . (jièshào)

3. 这本书很好看。你想 ＿＿＿ 吗？(看)
   Zhèběn shū hěn hǎokàn. Nǐ xiǎng ＿＿＿ ma? (kàn)

4. 姐姐做的炒饭很不错，你要不要 ＿＿＿ ？(试)
   Jiějie zuòde chǎofàn hěn búcuò, nǐ yàobuyào ＿＿＿ ? (shì)

🔊 补充课文 SUPPLEMENTARY PRACTICE

Read the following passage. Then listen and repeat.

昨天¹，我和子英一起去逛街²，买衣服³。我想买一件衬衫，子英想买一条裙子或者裤子。我们到了⁴一家⁵服饰店⁶，我先挑⁷了一件黄色和一件黑色的衬衫。我试穿⁸了一下，照照镜子⁹，觉得比较喜欢黑色的，所以¹⁰我就买了那件黑衬衫。

子英也挑了一条裙子和一条裤子，然后就到试衣间¹¹穿穿，她要我帮她看看，我看了以后，觉得她穿裙子比较好看，所以她决定¹²买那条裙子，店员小姐说那条裙子十五块钱。我们买了衣服以后，就去看电影了。

Notes:
1. 昨天 [zuótiān]: yesterday
2. 逛街 [guàngjiē]: to go shopping
3. 衣服 [yīfu]: clothes
4. 了 [le]: particle indicating completed action (See Lesson 19 for more information.)
5. 家 [jiā]: measure word for shops
6. 服饰店(服飾店) [fúshìdiàn]: clothing shop
7. 挑 [tiāo]: to choose, to pick
8. 试穿(試穿) [shìchuān]: to try on
9. 照镜子(照鏡子) [zhào jìngzi]: (V.O.) to look at a reflection in a mirror
10. 所以 [suǒyǐ]: therefore
11. 试衣间(試衣間) [shìyījian]: dressing room
12. 决定(決定) [juédìng]: to decide

Pinyin version:

Zuótiān, wǒ hé Zǐyīng yìqǐ qù guàngjiē, mǎi yīfu. Wǒ xiǎng mǎi yíjiàn chènshān, Zǐyīng xiǎng mǎi yìtiáo qúnzi huòzhě kùzi. Wǒmen dàole yìjiā fúshìdiàn, wǒ xiān tiāole yíjiàn huángsè hé yíjiàn hēisè de chènshān. Wǒ shì chuān le yíxià, zhàozhao jìngzi, juéde bǐjiào xǐhuān hēisè de, suǒyǐ wǒ jiù mǎile nàjiàn hēi chènshān.

Zǐyīng yě tiāole yìtiáo qúnzi hé yìtiáo kùzi, ránhòu jiù dào shìyījiān chuānchuan, tā yào wǒ bāng tā kànkan, wǒ kànle yǐhòu, juéde tā chuān qúnzi bǐjiào hǎokàn, suǒyǐ tā juédìng mǎi nàtiáo qúnzi, diànyuán xiǎojiě shuō nàtiáo qúnzi shíwǔ kuài qián. Wǒmen mǎile yīfú yǐhòu, jiù qù kàn diànyǐng le.

Read the following statements and choose whether they are true or false.

1. The speaker tried on a yellow shirt and a red shirt.   True   False

2. The speaker bought a black skirt.   True   False

3. Of the things 子英 tried on, the skirt looked better on her.   True   False

4. 子英 bought a skirt for 50 dollars.   True   False

5. The speaker and 子英 went to see a movie before shopping.   True   False

练习 ACTIVITIES

 I. Listening Exercises

13-1 Listen and write the Pinyin for the sentences you hear. Then check your answers with a partner or the class.

1. _____

2. _____

3. _____

4. _____

5. _____

13-2 Work in groups of three or four. Take turns reading the lines of the following poem, paying special attention to the tones and rhythm.

<table>
<tr><td align="center">**Jué Jù**
(Dù Fǔ)</td><td align="center">**绝句**
(杜甫)</td></tr>
<tr><td>Liǎngge huánglí míng cuìliǔ,</td><td>两个黄鹂鸣翠柳，</td></tr>
<tr><td>Yìháng báilù shàng qīngtiān.</td><td>一行白鹭上青天。</td></tr>
<tr><td>Chuāng hán Xīlǐng qiānqiū xuě,</td><td>窗含西岭千秋雪，</td></tr>
<tr><td>Mén bó Dōngwú wànlǐ chuán.</td><td>门泊东吴万里船。</td></tr>
</table>

A Quatrain
(Du, Fu)

Two golden orioles are singing in the green willow trees,
White egrets are flying in a line in the blue sky.
Looking out of my window I see the snow-capped Western Mountains,
At my door are moored eastward-bound ships that have traveled thousands of miles.

II. Character Exercises

13-3   Match each Chinese word or phrase with its English meaning. Then check your answers with a partner or the class.

___ 1. 黄裙子
huáng qúnzi

a. red skirt

___ 2. 黑裤子
hēi kùzi

b. to help

___ 3. 红裙子
hóng qúnzi

c. black pants

___ 4. 穿裤子
chuān kùzi

d. pretty good

___ 5. 让
ràng

e. yellow skirt

___ 6. 帮
bāng

f. to wear pants

___ 7. 不错
búcuò

g. to let, to allow

___ 8. 比较
bǐjiào

h. relatively, comparatively

13-4   Work with a partner or in small groups. Write the radical and its meaning for each of the following characters. Then write as many characters with the same radical as you can. (Refer to the list of radicals on page 255 for help.)

Example: 吗 [ma]   口 mouth   呢 吃 喝 和 _____

1. 衫 [shān]   _____   _____

2. 钱 [qián]   _____   _____

3. 件 [jiàn]   _____   _____

4. 试 [shì]   _____   _____

5. 觉 [jué]   _____   _____

6. 块 [kuài]

III. Grammar Exercises

13-5   Look at the following example. With a partner, take turns extending the following words into phrases and then sentences. See how long you can keep extending the sentences.

Example: A: 好看
hǎokàn

B: 裙子好看
qúnzi hǎokàn

A: 红裙子好看
hóng qúnzi hǎokàn

B: 这条红裙子好看
zhètiáo hóng qúnzi hǎokàn

A: 你穿这条红裙子好看。
Nǐ chuān zhètiáo hóng qúnzi hǎokàn.

B: 我觉得你穿这条红裙子好看。
Wǒ juéde nǐ chuān zhètiáo hóng qúnzi hǎokàn.

A: 我觉得你穿这条红裙子比较好看。
Wǒ juéde nǐ chuān zhètiáo hóng qúnzi bǐjiào hǎokàn.

1. 店   2. 帮   3. 裤   4. 黄   5. 错   6. 票   7. 试   8. 块
   diàn   bāng   kù   huáng   cuò   piào   shì   kuài

13-6   With a partner, take turns using words from the boxes to ask and answer questions. Look carefully at the sentences to see which words fit most appropriately.

Example: A: 你想买什么？   Nǐ xiǎng mǎi shénme?

B: 我想买一件T-恤衫。   Wǒ xiǎng mǎi yíjiàn tīxùshān.

1. A: 你想买什么？
   Nǐ xiǎng mǎi shénme?

   B: 我想买一 ___ ____ 。
   Wǒ xiǎng mǎi yí ___ ____ .

件	条	双
jiàn	tiáo	shuāng
T-恤衫	毛衣	裤子
tīxùshān	máoyī	kùzi
裙子	鞋子	
qúnzi	xiézi	

2.　A: 你想做什么？
　　　Nǐ xiǎng zuò shénme?

　　B: 我想 ___ ____ 或者 ____ 。
　　　Wǒ xiǎng ___ ____ huòzhě ____ .

看	中国电影	
kàn	Zhōngguó diànyǐng	
	美国电影	
	Měiguó diànyǐng	
吃	炒面	饺子
chī	chǎomiàn	jiǎozi
去 中国饭馆		日本饭馆
qù Zhōngguó fànguǎn		Rìběn fànguǎn

3.　A: 你觉得这 ___ ____ 怎么样？
　　　Nǐ juéde zhè ___ ____ zěnmeyàng?

　　B: 我觉得这 _____ 很 ____ 。
　　　Wǒ juéde zhè _____ hěn ____ .

盘	炒饭	好吃
pán	chǎofàn	hǎochī
个	汉字[1]	好写
gè	Hànzì	hǎoxiě
部[2]	电影	好玩
bù	diànyǐng	hǎowán
条	裙子	好看
tiáo	qúnzi	hǎokàn

Notes:
1. 汉字(漢字) [Hànzì]: Chinese characters
2. 部 [bù]: measure word for 电影(電影)

13-7 With a partner, use the prompts in parentheses to complete the following sentences with a duplicated verb phrase.

1. 这件衬衫我穿太大了，你 _____ 吧 。(to have a try)
　 Zhèjiàn chènshān wǒ chuān tàidà le, nǐ _____ ba.

2. 这是谁的车？我来 _____ 车号 。(to have a look)
　 Zhè shì shéide chē? Wǒ lái _____ chēhào.

3. 这是我的室友 。来，你们 _____ 。(to get to know each other)
　 Zhè shì wǒde shìyǒu. Lái, nǐmen _____ .

4. 你知道这本书吗？我来给你 _____ 。(to give you a little introduction)
　 Nǐ zhīdào zhèběn shū ma? Wǒ lái gěi nǐ _____ .

13-8 With a partner, take turns asking and answering the following questions. Use 或者 when answering the questions.

1. 你想买什么?
   Ní xiǎng mǎi shénme?

2. 你喜欢哪件衬衫?
   Nǐ xǐhuān nǎjiàn chènshān?

3. 你说我穿什么好看?
   Nǐ shuō wǒ chuān shénme hǎokàn?

4. 你今天晚上想吃什么?
   Nǐ jīntiān wǎnshang xiǎngchī shénme?

IV. Communicative Activities

13-9 Play "Guess Who!" (猜猜他是谁? [Cāicai tā shì shéi?])

Form groups of three or four. Secretly decide on a group member to describe for the other groups to guess. Each member of the group then says one or two sentences to describe the person, and the other groups try to guess who the person is. You can encourage others to guess by saying "你们猜猜他是谁?" [Nǐmen cāicai tā shì shéi?] (Can you guess who it is?)

Example: 他今天穿一件白衬衫，一条黑裤子……
           Tā jīntiān chuān yíjiàn bái chènshān, yìtiáo hēi kùzi . . .

           你们猜猜他是谁?
           Nǐmen cāicai tā shì shéi?

13-10 In pairs, role-play the following situation.

Situation: You are at a clothing shop and see some things you would like to try on. You ask the salesperson if you can try them on. The salesperson says yes. You ask the salesperson to bring another size. You ask the salesperson what they think about the color. The salesperson asks if you would like to buy it. If you like it, ask how much. If you don't, try something else on!

Words and expressions to use:

试试	觉得	怎么样	有没有	大的/小的
shìshi	juéde	zěnmeyàng	yǒuméiyǒu	dàde/xiǎode

还是	或者	比较	多少钱?	
háishì	huòzhě	bǐjiào	duōshǎoqián?	

文化知识 Culture Link

文化点滴 CULTURE NOTES

中国的传统服饰 Traditional Chinese Clothing

When thinking about traditional Chinese clothing, many people think of the traditional dress for women, 旗袍 [qípáo] (the Qipao), or the traditional jacket, 唐装 [tángzhuāng] (the Tangzhuang), which is worn by both genders. Also common is the traditional suit, which consists of loose pants and a shirt of the same material and is worn by both men and women. Chinese clothing has a rich history with a great variety of styles.

Around the 17th century, noble Manchurian men and women wore long, loose, tube-shaped robes. Each dynasty had different preferences in style, and each generation continued to make changes to the style, such as with sleeves or sleeveless, high or low collar, and dress length. The style of traditional Chinese dress that became popular in the 1930s is the Qipao we associate with Chinese culture today.

The material used for traditional clothing is usually silk with either patterned fabric or picturesque embroidery on it. Traditional clothing, such as the Qipao or Tangzhuang, is often worn for special occasions such as weddings or cultural festivals. The less formal traditional suit is made with less expensive fabrics and can be worn on more casual everyday occasions. While traditional styles are still worn, Western-style clothing is much more common in China today.

Do you know...

- what a Qipao and Tangzhuang are?
- if traditional or Western-style clothing is more common in China today?
- why red is such a popular color in clothing for Chinese people?

Read and find out!

When traveling in China, one may also discover very colorful and distinct clothing worn by different ethnic groups in China. The unique clothing styles often have their own special meanings, such as the preference of the 白族 [Báizú] (Bai people) for white clothing. Sometimes the clothing worn can help identify a group. An example of this is the different color designations used by the Chinese to distinguish subgroups of the 苗族 [Miáozú] (Miao people). These color designations are determined by the most common color worn by the women of the group. Thus there are the Red Miao, the White Miao, and the Green Miao, among others.

The color of clothing has additional significance throughout China. Red is commonly worn as it is considered a very lucky color. Yellow has associations with gold and at one time was considered a royal color worn only by the emperor. Green has positive associations with spring and the jade stone (also considered lucky). White, however, is associated with mourning because people traditionally wore white to funerals. Due to increased Western influence, however, modern brides feel free to wear a white dress to their wedding. Of course, for such special occasions, a woman may still opt to wear a bright red Qipao!

Bai women wearing traditional clothes. Do you think their preference for the color relates to their group's name?

A young boy dressed in a traditional jacket for a cultural festival. What is the significance of the color red in Chinese culture?

Discuss the following with a group or your class.

1. Besides red, what other colors do you think Chinese people like to wear on happy occasions? Do different colors have different meanings in your culture?

2. Have you ever seen any unique clothes worn by Chinese minorities? If so, describe them to your classmates.

3. Have you seen any movies where people wear traditional Chinese clothes? What kind of clothing did you see? Was it a Qipao or a Tangzhuang? Was it worn for a special occasion or in an everyday setting?

🔊 趣味中文 FUN WITH CHINESE

人靠衣装，马靠鞍。
Clothes make the man.

rén	kào	yīzhuāng,	mǎ	kào	ān
人	靠	衣装，	马	靠	鞍
people	rely on	clothes	horse	rely on	saddle

Work in small groups or with your class.

1. Practice reading the saying aloud, paying attention to the pronunciation and rhythm.
2. Do you believe in 人靠衣装，马靠鞍? What similar sayings do you know of in other languages or cultures?

◀)) 行动吧！LET'S GO!

钱币表达方法 Ways to Express Money in Chinese

Spoken form:

SIMPLIFIED	TRADITIONAL	PINYIN		
块	塊	kuài	N.	dollar
毛	毛	máo	N.	(10毛 = 1块) (similar to a dime)
分	分	fēn	N.	(100分 = 10毛 = 1块) (similar to a penny)

Written form:

SIMPLIFIED	TRADITIONAL	PINYIN		
元	元	yuán	N.	dollar
角	角	jiǎo	N.	(10角 = 1元) (similar to a dime)
分	分	fēn	N.	(100分 = 10角 = 1元) (similar to a penny)

Answer the following questions with your partner or group.

1. How would you say the following prices in Chinese? Use the chart above and words for money.

   a. 100元   b. 15元8角   c. 28元5角7分   d. 33元6角

2. After paying, if change is due, the salesperson will give you change, or 找钱 [zhǎoqián] (V.O.: to give change). The salesperson may say something like "找你十块钱" [Zhǎo nǐ shíkuài qián] (Here's 10 dollars change).

   How would you say, "Here's 8 dollars change"? How would you say, "Here's 5 毛 change"?

   ___ 你 8 ___ ___ 。

   ___ ___ 5毛 。

3. You would like to 换钱 [huànqián] (exchange money) at the 银行 [yínháng] (bank). The person ahead of you exchanged $200 USD. They said "我想换钱。我要换 200 块美金."

   How could you tell the bank teller that you would like to exchange money? How might you say you would like to exchange $100 USD?

   我想 ___ ___ 。

   我要 ___ 100 ___ 美金 。

14

生日和庆祝
Birthdays and Celebrations

*Friends wish each other a happy birthday by saying "生日快乐!"
[shēngrì kuàilè] (Happy birthday!).*

CONNECTIONS AND COMMUNITIES PREVIEW

Discuss the following questions with a partner or your class. What similarities and differences do you think there might be between Chinese culture and your own culture?

1. How do you celebrate birthdays in your culture/community?

2. Is there any special astrological system in your culture to refer to people born at a different time?

教学目标 OBJECTIVES

- Say the days of the week
- Extend and accept invitations
- Talk about birthdays

🔊 生词 VOCABULARY

核心词 Core Vocabulary

	SIMPLIFIED	TRADITIONAL	PINYIN		
1.	岁	歲	suì	N.	age, years
2.	有空	有空	yǒukòng	V.O.	to have free time
3.	星期	星期	xīngqī	N.	week
	星期六	星期六	xīngqīliù	N.	Saturday
4.	过	過	guò	V.	to pass (time), to celebrate (birthday, holiday), to cross, to live
5.	生日	生日	shēngrì	N.	birthday
6.	为	為	wèi	Prep.	for (to do something for someone; used before the object of one's act of service)
7.	舞会	舞會	wǔhuì	N.	dance party
	舞	舞	wǔ	N.	dance
8.	请	請	qǐng	V.	to invite
9.	参加	參加	cānjiā	V.	to participate, to join
10.	一定	一定	yídìng	Aux.	certainly, surely
11.	做	做	zuò	V.	to make, to do
12.	蛋糕	蛋糕	dàngāo	N.	cake
13.	送	送	sòng	V.	to give (as a present), to send
14.	棒	棒	bàng	Adj.	wonderful

	SIMPLIFIED	TRADITIONAL	PINYIN		
15.	不客气	不客氣	búkèqi		you're welcome
16.	多大	多大	duōdà		how old
17.	地图	地圖	dìtú	N.	map

补充词 Supplementary Vocabulary

	SIMPLIFIED	TRADITIONAL	PINYIN		
1.	日历	日曆	rìlì	N.	calendar
2.	月历	月曆	yuèlì	N.	monthly calendar
3.	庆生	慶生	qìngshēng	V.O.	to celebrate a birthday
4.	礼物	禮物	lǐwù	N.	gift
5.	吹	吹	chuī	V.	to blow
6.	蜡烛	蠟燭	làzhú	N.	candle
7.	晚会	晚會	wǎnhuì	N.	party (evening party)
8.	跳舞	跳舞	tiàowǔ	V.O.	to dance
	跳	跳	tiào	V.	to jump
9.	听	聽	tīng	V.	to listen
10.	音乐	音樂	yīnyuè	N.	music
11.	唱歌	唱歌	chànggē	V.O.	to sing a song
	歌	歌	gē	N.	song
12.	祝你生日快乐。	祝你生日快樂。	Zhù nǐ shēngrì kuàilè.		Happy birthday to you.

语文知识 LANGUAGE LINK

Read and listen to the following sentence patterns. These patterns use vocabulary, expressions, and grammar that you will study in more detail in this lesson. After reading the sentence patterns, read and listen to the Language in Use section that follows.

句型 Sentence Patterns

A: 今天是星期几？
Jīntiān shì xīngqī jǐ?

B: 今天是星期六。
Jīntiān shì xīngqī liù.

A: 你今年多大？
Nǐ jīnnián duōdà?

B: 我今年二十岁。
Wǒ jīnnián èrshí suì.

A: 你的生日是几月几号？
Nǐ de shēngrì shì jǐ yuè jǐ hào?

B: 我的生日是十月三号。
Wǒ de shēngrì shì shí yuè sān hào.

🔊 **课文 Language in Use: 我今年二十岁**

方子英： 爱红，二月十八日你有没有空？
Àihóng, èr yuè shíbā rì nǐ yǒuméiyǒu kòng?

毛爱红： 二月十八日那天是星期几？
Èr yuè shíbā rì nàtiān shì xīngqī jǐ?

方子英： 星期六。
Xīngqī liù.

毛爱红： 我有空。有什么事儿吗？
Wǒ yǒu kòng. Yǒu shénme shèr ma?

方子英： 那天我过生日，
Nàtiān wǒ guò shēngrì,

我男朋友要为我开一个
wǒ nánpéngyou yào wèi wǒ kāi yíge

生日舞会，我想请你参加。
shēngrì wǔhuì, wǒ xiǎng qǐng nǐ cānjiā.

开舞会 [kāi wǔhuì]
开 here means "to hold" (a party or meeting). 开舞会 means "to hold a dance party." For parties, the following terms are also commonly used: 晚会 [wǎnhuì] and 派对 [pàiduì].

毛爱红： 谢谢你，我一定去。
Xièxie nǐ, wǒ yídìng qù.

还有谁会去？
Hái yǒu shéi huì qù?

请 [qǐng]
Though 请 is also used to mean "please," here it is used to mean "invite." It can be used to mean "to treat" (请客 [qǐngkè]) (as in to treat someone to dinner) also.

方子英： 我们想请我们的同学
Wǒmen xiǎng qǐng wǒmende tóngxué

和朋友都参加。
hé péngyou dōu cānjia.

毛爱红： 我会做蛋糕。我送你一个生日
Wǒ huì zuò dàngāo. Wǒ sòng nǐ yíge shēngrì

蛋糕，怎么样？
dàngāo, zěngmeyàng?

方子英：　太棒了！谢谢你！
　　　　　Tàibàngle! Xièxie nǐ!

毛爱红：　不客气。你今年多大？
　　　　　Búkèqi. Nǐ jīnnián duōdà?

方子英：　我今年二十岁。你呢？
　　　　　Wǒ jīnnián èrshí suì. Nǐ ne?

　　　　　你的生日是几月几号？
　　　　　Nǐde shēngrì shì jǐ yuè jǐ hào?

毛爱红：　我的生日是十月三号，
　　　　　Wǒde shēngrì shì shíyuè sānhào,

　　　　　我今年二十二岁。你的舞会
　　　　　wǒ jīnnián èrshíèr suì. Nǐde wǔhuì

　　　　　在哪儿开？
　　　　　zài nǎr kāi?

方子英：　在我男朋友的家，这是他的
　　　　　Zài wǒ nánpéngyou de jiā, zhè shì tāde

　　　　　地址。你知道怎么去吗？
　　　　　dìzhǐ. Nǐ zhīdào zěnme qù ma?

毛爱红：　没问题！我有地图。星期六
　　　　　Méi wèntí! Wǒ yǒu dìtú. Xīngqīliù

　　　　　下午五点见！
　　　　　xiàwǔ wǔdiǎn jiàn!

方子英：　再见！
　　　　　Zàijiàn!

太棒了 [tàibàngle]

太棒了 is a phrase meaning "Great!" or "Terrific!" 棒 here is an adjective meaning "good," or "great." It is similar to "太好了！"

不客气 [búkèqi]

不客气 is a phrase meaning "You are welcome." It is similar to 不谢 [búxiè].

多大 [duōdà]

多大 is generally used to ask the age of adults and children over ten years old. For children under ten years old, 几岁 [jǐ suì] is commonly used to ask how old they are. For older people, it is more appropriate to ask "您多大年纪？" [niánjì] (age).

地址/住址 [dìzhǐ/zhùzhǐ]

Both 地址 and 住址 are commonly used to mean "address."

语法 GRAMMAR

I. Days of the Week

To say the days of the week in Chinese, add 星期 [xīngqī] to the number that represents the day of the week. Note that 星期日/星期天 [xīngqī rì/xīngqī tiān] are used instead of a number for Sunday.

Monday	Tuesday	Wednesday	Thursday	Friday	Saturday	Sunday
星期一 [xīngqī yī]	星期二 [xīngqī èr]	星期三 [xīngqī sān]	星期四 [xīngqī sì]	星期五 [xīngqī wǔ]	星期六 [xīngqī liù]	星期日 [xīngqī rì] 星期天 [xīngqī tiān]

礼拜 [lǐbài] is also commonly used instead of 星期 [xīngqī] to indicate the days of the week.

礼拜一 lǐbài yī	Monday

礼拜五 lǐbài wǔ	Friday

礼拜天 lǐbài tiān	Sunday

To ask "Which day of the week?" you can use either 星期几 [xīngqī jǐ] or 礼拜几 [lǐbài jǐ].

周 [zhōu] is also used in describing the week. You can use it to say weekdays Monday through Friday. To refer to the weekend, 周末 [zhōumò] is used.

Monday	Tuesday	Wednesday	Thursday	Friday	Saturday	Sunday
周一 [zhōu yī]	周二 [zhōu èr]	周三 [zhōu sān]	周四 [zhōu sì]	周五 [zhōu wǔ]	周六 [zhōu liù] 周末 [zhōumò] weekend	周日 [zhōu rì]

Note that the week starts on Monday in Chinese culture.

II. Referring to Days, Weeks, Months, and Years

To refer to times such as *yesterday*, *today*, *tomorrow*, *last year*, *this year*, and *next year*, add the appropriate words to 天 [tiān] and 年 [nián] as shown below.

前天 [qiántiān] *the day before yesterday*	昨天 [zuótiān] *yesterday*	今天 [jīntiān] *today*	明天 [míngtiān] *tomorrow*	后天 [hòutiān] *the day after tomorrow*
前年 [qiánnián] *the year before last year*	去年 [qùnián] *last year*	今年 [jīnnián] *this year*	明年 [míngnián] *next year*	后年 [hòunián] *the year after next year*

To refer to time periods such as *this week*, *last week*, *this month*, or *next month*, add the appropriate word to the word for week or month as shown below. (Note that 上个 [shàngge] means "previous" and 下个 [xiàge] means "next.")

上上个星期 [shàngshàngge xīngqī] *the week before last week*	上个星期 [shàngge xīngqī] *last week*	这个星期 [zhège xīngqī] *this week*	下个星期 [xiàge xīngqī] *next week*	下下个星期 [xiàxiàge xīngqī] *the week after next week*
上上个月 [shàngshàngge yuè] *the month before last month*	上个月 [shàngge yuè] *last month*	这个月 [zhègge yuè] *this month*	下个月 [xiàge yuè] *next month*	下下个月 [xiàxiàgge yuè] *the month after next month*

>>Try it!   With a partner, ask and answer the following questions with the appropriate expressions for days of the week and time periods.

1. A: 今年你的生日是星期几?
   Jīnnián nǐde shēngrì shì xīngqī jǐ?

   B: 今年我的生日是 _____ 。
   Jīnnián wǒde shēngrì shì _____ .

2. A: 这个周末你有空吗?
   Zhège zhōumò nǐ yǒukòng ma?

   B: 这个 _____ 。
   Zhège _____ .

3. A: 下个月你会不会来上课？

   Xiàge yuè nǐ huìbuhuì lái shàngkè?

   B: _____ 。

4. A: _____ 我们一起去看电影好不好？

   _____ wǒmen yìqǐ qù kàn diànyǐng hǎobuhǎo?

   B: 对不起，_____ 我有事儿。下次吧。

   Duìbuqǐ, _____ wǒ yǒu shèr. Xiàcì ba.

III. The Preposition 为

为 [wèi] is a preposition meaning "for." With its object, it forms a prepositional phrase (P.P.), which occurs before a verb phrase (V.P.).

Subj.	P.P.	V.P.	
他	为我	开一个晚会。	He is having a party for me.
Tā	wèi wǒ	kāi yíge wǎnhuì.	
(He)	(for me)	(holds a party)	

>>**Try it!** With a partner, take turns asking and answering the following questions with 为.

1. A: 你会为我买东西¹吗？

   Nǐ huì wèi wǒ mǎi dōngxi ma?

   B: 对不起，我不能 _____ 买东西。

   Duìbuqǐ, wǒ bùnéng _____ mǎi dōngxi.

2. A: 你想为妈妈做一个生日蛋糕吗？

   Nǐ xiǎng wèi māma zuò yíge shēngrì dàngāo ma?

   B: _____ 。

3. A: 你男/女朋友会为你做饭吗？

   Nǐ nán/nǚ péngyou huì wèi nǐ zuòfàn ma?

   B: _____ 。

Note:
1. 东西(東西) [dōngxi]: things, stuff

🔊 补充课文 SUPPLEMENTARY PRACTICE

Read the following passage. Then listen and repeat.

二月十八日   星期六

　　今天我很高兴[1]，我过了[2]一个很棒的二十岁生日。我男朋友在他家为我开了一个庆生会[3]，他还请了很多朋友来参加，他们都送我很多礼物[4]，爱红还为我做了一个生日蛋糕，太棒了！

　　每个人都祝我生日快乐，为我唱[5]生日快乐歌[6]，我许[7]了一个愿，吹[8]了蜡烛[9]，然后切[10]蛋糕给大家吃。

　　我们一起唱卡拉OK[11]，听音乐[12]，跳舞[13]……很好玩！

Notes:

1. 高兴(高興) [gāoxìng]: happy
2. 了 [le]: particle indicating completion (See Lesson 19 for more information.)
3. 庆生会(慶生會) [qìngshēnghuì]: birthday party
4. 礼物(禮物) [lǐwù]: gift
5. 唱 [chàng]: to sing
6. 生日快乐歌(生日快樂歌) [shēngrì kuàilè gē]: happy birthday song
7. 许愿(許願) [xǔyuàn]: to make a wish
8. 吹 [chuī]: to blow
9. 蜡烛(蠟燭) [làzhú]: candle
10. 切 [qiē]: to cut, to slice
11. 卡拉OK [kǎlā ōukēi]: karaoke
12. 听音乐(聽音樂) [tīng yīnyuè]: to listen to music
13. 跳舞 [tiàowǔ]: to dance

Pinyin version:

Èr yuè shíbā rì   Xīngqī liù

Jīntiān wǒ hěn gāoxìng, wǒ guòle yíge hěn bàng de èr shí suì shēngrì. Wǒ nánpéngyou zài tājiā wèi wǒ kāile yíge qìngshēng huì, tā hái qǐng le hěnduō péngyou lái cānjiā, tāmen dōu sòng wǒ hěn duō lǐwù, Àihóng hái wèi wǒ zuòle yíge shēngrì dàngāo, tài bàng le!

　　Měige rén dōu zhù wǒ shēngrì kuàilè, wèi wǒ chàng shēngrì kuàilè gē, wǒ xǔle yíge yuàn, chuīle làzhú, ránhòu qiē dàngāo gěi dàjiā chī.

　　Wǒmen yìqǐ chàng kǎlā ōukēi, tīng yīnyuè, tiàowǔ . . . hěn hǎowán!

Choose the correct answer for the following questions about the passage above.

1. 她今年多大？
   Tā jīnnián duōdà?

   a. 十八岁   b. 二十岁   c. 二十一岁   d. 二十八岁
      shíbā suì   èrshí suì   èrshí yī suì   èrshí bā suì

2. 谁为她开生日会?
   Shéi wèi tā kāi shēngrì huì?

   a. 她朋友   b. 爱红   c. 她男朋友   d. 她同学
      tā péngyou   Àihóng   tā nánpéngyou   tā tóngxué

3. 她的生日是哪一天?
   Tāde shēngrì shì nǎ yì tiān?

   a. 一月二十日   b. 二月二十日   c. 六月十八日   d. 二月十八日
      yīyuè èrshí rì   èryuè èrshí rì   liùyuè shíbā rì   èryuè shíbā rì

4. 她的生日会在哪儿开?
   Tāde shēngrì huì zài nǎr kāi?

   a. 在她家   b. 在她朋友家   c. 在她男朋友家   d. 在爱红家
      zài tā jiā   zài tā péngyou jiā   zài tā nánpéngyou jiā   zài Àihóng jiā

练习 ACTIVITIES

I. Listening Exercises

14-1 Listen and write the Pinyin for the phrases you hear. Then check your answers with a partner or the class.

1. _____   2. _____   3. _____   4. _____

5. _____   6. _____   7. _____   8. _____

14-2 Listen and write the Pinyin for the words you hear. Then check your answers with a partner or the class.

Àimíng: Zhège _____ shì wǒde _____ . Wǒ yào kāi yígè _____ .
            Nǐ néng lái ma?

Xiǎoyīng: Tài hǎo le! Wǒ _____ qù. Nǐ jīnnián _____ ?

Àimíng: Wǒ èrshíyī _____ . Nǐde shēngrì shì _____ ?

Xiǎoyīng: Wǒde shēngrì shì _____ . Wǒ jīnnián _____ suì.

14-3   Work in small groups. Take turns reading the lines of the following poem, paying special attention to the tones and rhythm.

Xiāng Sī (Wáng Wéi)	**相思** （王维）	**Remembrance** (Wang, Wei)
Hóngdòu shēng nánguó,	红豆生南国，	The red bean grows in the southern lands,
Chūn lái fā jǐ zhī.	春来发几枝。	In spring its slender twigs bloom.
Yuàn jūn duō cǎi xié,	愿君多采撷，	Gather more of them, I hope,
Cǐ wù zuì xiāngsī.	此物最相思。	Loving remembrance they evoke.

II. Character Exercises

14-4   Work with a partner. Find words that have the following radicals in the Language in Use dialogue, and write them next to the radical.

1. 宀 _____   2. 土 _____   3. 木 _____

4. 米 _____   5. 月 _____   6. 力 _____

7. 门 _____   8. 辵(辶) _____   9. 厶 _____

14-5   Match each Chinese word with its English meaning. Then check your answers with a partner or the class.

___ 1. 地址   a. to participate
    dìzhǐ

___ 2. 参加   b. map
    cānjiā

___ 3. 舞会   c. week
    wǔhuì

___ 4. 蛋糕   d. dance party
    dàngāo

___ 5. 不客气   e. birthday
    búkèqi

___ 6. 星期   f. cake
    xīngqī

___ 7. 生日   g. address
    shēngrì

___ 8. 地图   h. you are welcome
    dìtú

III. Grammar Exercises

14-6   Look at the following example. With a partner, take turns extending the words below into phrases and then sentences. See how long you can keep extending the sentences.

Example:

A: 舞会   wǔhuì

B: 生日舞会   shēngrì wǔhuì

A: 我的生日舞会   wǒde shēngrì wǔhuì

B: 参加我的生日舞会   cānjiā wǒde shēngrì wǔhuì

A: 请你参加我的生日舞会。   Qǐng nǐ cānjiā wǒde shēngrì wǔhuì.

B: 我想请你参加我的生日舞会。
Wǒ xiǎng qǐng nǐ cānjiā wǒde shēngrì wǔhuì.

1. 岁	2. 空	3. 星	4. 过	5. 为	6. 做	7. 送	8. 棒
suì	kōng	xīng	guò	wèi	zuò	sòng	bàng

14-7   With a partner, take turns using words from the boxes to ask and answer questions. Look carefully at the sentences to see which words fit most appropriately.

Example: A: 老师的生日是几月几号星期几?
Lǎoshīde shēngrì shì jǐ yuè jǐ hào xīngqī jǐ?

B: 我想老师的生日是<u>四月二十八号</u>, <u>星期一</u>。
Wǒ xiǎng lǎoshīde shēngrì shì <u>sìyuè èrshíbā hào</u>, <u>xīngqī yī</u>.

1. A: 老师的生日是几月几号
Lǎoshīde shēngrì shì jǐ yuè jǐ hào

星期几?
xīngqī jǐ?

B: 我想老师的生日
Wǒ xiǎng lǎoshīde shēngrì

是 _____, ____。
shì _____, ____ .

十一月十三号	星期二
shíyīyuè shísānhào	xīngqī èr
一月二十九号	星期三
yīyuè èrshíjiǔ hào	xīngqī sān
九月三十号	星期五
jiǔyuè sānshíhào	xīngqī wǔ
八月七号	星期天
bāyuè qīhào	xīngqī tiān

2. A: 你要怎么为你的好朋友
Nǐ yào zěnme wèi nǐde hǎopéngyou

庆祝[1]生日？
qìngzhù shēngrì?

B: 我要为他 __ _____ 。
Wǒ yào wèi tā __ _____ .

买 mǎi	一件衬衫 yíjiàn chènshān
做 zuò	一个蛋糕 yíge dàngāo
唱 chàng	一首[2]生日歌 yìshǒu shēngrì gē
做 zuò	两个中国菜 liǎngge Zhōngguócài

Notes:
1. 庆祝(慶祝) [qìngzhù]: to celebrate
2. 首 [shǒu]: measure word for songs

14-8 Read 子英's to-do list below. In pairs, ask and answer questions about each item on 子英's list.

Example: A: 子英今天要做什么？
Zǐyīng jīntiān yào zuò shénme?

B: 她要为她男朋友开一个晚会。
Tā yào wèi tā nánpéngyou kāi yíge wǎnhuì.

子英's to do list:

1. Hold a party for her boyfriend

2. Write an email to her roommate

3. Make a birthday cake for her younger sister

4. Buy a movie ticket for Dazhong's girlfriend

IV. Communicative Activities

14-9 With a partner, role-play the following situation. Feel free to include previously learned information in your role-play.

Situation: Next Saturday is your birthday. You want to have a birthday party and invite all your friends.

You call a friend you met at the beginning of the semester. Tell your friend when your birthday is and that you would like to invite him/her to come to your party that evening. Ask if he/she is able to come. Be sure your friend knows where you live!

Your friend is happy to be invited and assures you they will come to your party. Your friend asks what time the party starts and what the address is.

14-10 Predict the future! Work in groups of three or four. Take turns being the fortune teller who predicts what will happen to the other group members. Use time expressions and other expressions you have learned before. Be creative!

Example: 明天会有一个穿红裤子的人问你图书馆在哪儿。
        Míngtiān huì yǒu yíge chuān hóng kùzi de rén wèn nǐ túshūguǎn zài nǎr.

        明天不要开车！在家里休息比较好！
        Míngtiān búyào kāichē! Zài jiālǐ xiūxi bǐjiào hǎo!

Some expressions you could use:

明年	下下个月	后天
míngnián	xiàxià ge yuè	hòutiān
得	要/不要	应该
děi	yào/búyào	yīnggāi
去中国	在……的时候	或者
qù Zhōngguó	zài . . . de shíhòu	huòzhě
等一下	然后	以后
děng yíxià	ránhòu	yǐhòu
碰到	奇怪	新
pèngdào (come across)	qíguài (strange)	xīn (new)

文化知识 Culture Link

文化点滴 CULTURE NOTES

十二生肖 The Chinese Zodiac

The 十二生肖 [Shí'èr shēngxiào] (Chinese Zodiac) refers to the 12 农历年 [nónglì nián] (lunar years) in a cycle of the Chinese lunar calendar, and to the animals that each correspond to a year, namely the rat, ox, tiger, rabbit, dragon, snake, horse, sheep, monkey, rooster, dog, and boar. Since the lunar calendar does not exactly match the Gregorian, or Western calendar, the Chinese Zodiac cannot be directly matched with Western calendar years. This is because the lunar calendar year often begins after January 1st on the Western calendar. For example, the Western calendar year 2010 is referred to as the year of the tiger, but the first month of 2010 is actually still in the lunar year of the ox since the new lunar year doesn't start until February 14th.

No one really knows for certain the origin of the Chinese Zodiac system or how it evolved. One hypothesis says that the ancient Chinese (about 4,000 years ago) invented a system for recording days and months, which later developed into the Chinese Zodiac. Another story says that the ancestors divided one 24-hour day into 12 equal two-hour periods, with the first

Do you know ...

- what the twelve animals of the Chinese Zodiac are?
- what calendar the Chinese Zodiac is associated with?
- what this year's animal sign is?

Read and find out!

period starting from 11:00 P.M. to 1:00 A.M. Each period was named after the animal that is most active during that time period. For example, the rat took the first position because it is most active around midnight during the first time period. Other explanations for the system exist, but it is debatable how accurate and complete they are.

People born in a certain lunar year are believed to share characteristics or personality traits with the animal that represents that year in the Chinese Zodiac system. Often, instead of directly asking your age, Chinese people will ask your 生肖 [shēngxiào] (animal sign), from which they can deduce not only your age, but also ascribe to you the qualities of the animal that represents that year. Because of this belief, animal signs play a big role in marriage proposals in China. People often try to find a partner who is a good zodiac match. Some very superstitious couples may even purposely schedule pregnancies in the hope that their children will be born with the characteristics of the chosen year's representative animal.

CHINESE ZODIAC

鼠 [shǔ] Rat

Born: 1924, 1936, 1948, 1960, 1972, 1984, 1996, 2008

Characteristics: charming, bright, creative, and thrifty

牛 [niú] Ox

Born: 1925, 1937, 1949, 1961, 1973, 1985, 1997, 2009

Characteristics: steadfast, dependable, and methodical

虎 [hǔ] Tiger

Born: 1926, 1938, 1950, 1962, 1974, 1986, 1998, 2010

Characteristics: dynamic, warm, sincere, and a leader

兔 [tù] Rabbit

Born: 1927, 1939, 1951, 1963, 1975, 1987, 1999, 2011

Characteristics: humble, artistic, and clear-sighted

龙 [lóng] Dragon

Born: 1916, 1928, 1940, 1952, 1964, 1976, 1988, 2000, 2012

Characteristics: flamboyant, lucky, and imaginative

蛇 [shé] Snake

Born: 1917, 1929, 1941, 1953, 1965, 1977, 1989, 2001, 2013

Characteristics: discreet, refined, and intelligent

马 [mǎ] Horse

Born: 1918, 1930, 1942, 1954, 1966, 1978, 1990, 2002, 2014

Characteristics: social, competitive, and stubborn

羊 [yáng] Sheep

Born: 1919, 1931, 1943, 1955, 1967, 1979, 1991, 2003, 2015

Characteristics: artistic, fastidious, and indecisive

猴 [hóu] Monkey

Born: 1920, 1932, 1944, 1956, 1968, 1980, 1992, 2004, 2016

Characteristics: witty, popular, good-humored, and versatile

鸡 [jī] Rooster

Born: 1921, 1933, 1945, 1957, 1969, 1981, 1993, 2005, 2017

Characteristics: aggressive, alert, and a perfectionist

狗 [gǒu] Dog

Born: 1922, 1934, 1946, 1958, 1970, 1982, 1994, 2006, 2018

Characteristics: honest, conservative, sympathetic, and loyal

猪 [zhū] Boar

Born: 1923, 1935, 1947, 1959, 1971, 1983, 1995, 2007, 2019

Characteristics: caring, industrious, and home-loving

Discuss the following with a group or your class.

1. What is your animal sign? Do you think the characteristics of your animal sign accurately describe your personality?
2. Do you know of similar systems in other cultures which describe people's personality based on when they were born? Do you believe in any of these systems? Why or why not?

趣味中文 FUN WITH CHINESE

女大十八变。

A girl changes quickly from childhood to adulthood.

nǚ	dà	shíbā	biàn
女	大	十八	变
girl	big/grow up	eighteen	change

Chinese people usually use 女大十八变 to show admiration or surprise at seeing a girl change and grow up, becoming a young lady.

Work in small groups or with your class.

1. Practice reading the saying aloud, paying attention to the pronunciation and rhythm.
2. Do you know of any sayings in your culture or others about growing up or getting older? What are they?

🔊 行动吧！LET'S GO!

庆祝贺词 Common Phrases for Congratulations and Best Wishes

Read the following phrases, which are used by Chinese to congratulate and give best wishes. Many of these sayings are often printed on red envelopes, which are given (with money inside) for birthdays, weddings, or New Year's. Some of these sayings are also put on red signs that are displayed during the new year holiday.

生日快乐(生日快樂) [shēngrì kuàilè]: Happy birthday.

新年好 [xīnnián hǎo]: Happy New Year.

新年快乐(新年快樂) [xīnnián kuàilè]: Happy New Year.

万事如意(萬事如意) [wànshì rúyì]: Hope everything will go smoothly.

吉祥如意 [jíxiáng rúyì]: May you be lucky and may things turn out as you wish.

祝你好运(祝你好運) [zhù nǐ hǎoyùn]: Wishing you good luck.

金玉满堂(金玉滿堂) [jīnyù mǎntáng]: May gold and jade fill your house.

恭喜发财(恭喜發財) [gōngxǐ fācái]: Wishing you good fortune.

Answer the following questions with your partner or group.

1. Look at the list of wishes and the pictures above. Which sayings from the list can you find in the pictures? (Hint: There are four sayings. One saying has the words in a slightly different order. In another saying you can see three of the four words.)
2. What are some different occasions on which you might use these phrases?
3. Do you have similar expressions in your language and culture?

复习 Review

LESSON 12 TO LESSON 14

I.   Conversation Review

1. With a partner, take turns asking and answering questions, using the prompts below. Ask for more details or information if needed.

Example: A: 你能不能跟我一起去参加舞会？
　　　　　　Nǐ néngbunéng gēn wǒ yìqǐ qù cānjiā wǔhuì?

　　　　　B: 舞会是什么时候？
　　　　　　Wǔhuì shì shénme shíhòu?

　　　　　A: 星期六晚上。
　　　　　　Xīngqīliù wǎnshang.

　　　　　B: 应该没问题！
　　　　　　Yīnggāi méiwèntí!

- 下课以后有没有空？要做什么？
  xiàkè yǐhòu yǒuméiyǒu kòng? yào zuò shénme?

- 觉得学生应该做什么？
  juéde xuésheng yīnggāi zuò shénme?

- 从 ＿＿＿ 到 ＿＿＿，应该怎么去？
  cóng ＿＿＿ dào ＿＿＿, yīnggāi zěnme qù?

- 不太会开车的人要做什么？可以多做什么？
  bú tài huì kāichē de rén yào zuò shénme? kěyǐ duō zuò shénme?

- 可以借你的车吗？
  kěyǐ jiè nǐde chē ma?

- 你帮我看看，你觉得 ＿＿＿ 还是 ＿＿＿ 好看？
  Nǐ bāng wǒ kànkan. Nǐ juéde ＿＿＿ háishì ＿＿＿ hǎokàn?

- 喜欢穿什么样的衣服?
  xǐhuān chuān shénmeyàng de yīfu?

- 会不会为男/女朋友 ＿＿＿＿＿＿?
  huìbuhuì wèi nán/nǚpéngyou ＿＿＿＿＿＿ ?

- 能不能跟我一起 ＿＿＿＿＿＿＿?
  néngbunéng gēn wǒ yìqǐ ＿＿＿＿＿＿＿ ?

- 生日是几月几号?
  shēngrì shì jǐ yuè jǐ hào?

- 我想吃 ＿＿＿＿＿ 或者 ＿＿＿＿＿＿。你觉得哪一个比较好?
  Wǒ xiǎng chī ＿＿＿＿＿ huò zhě ＿＿＿＿＿＿ . Nǐ juéde nǎ yíge bǐjiào hǎo?

2. With a partner, role-play the following situation.

Situation: You and a friend are talking about what to do this weekend. You are thinking about going shopping, going out to eat, and seeing a movie. You also have some obligations such as picking up your younger sister from the airport and making a birthday cake for your mother. You can't spend too much money because you want to go to China from June to July this year. Discuss plans with your friend, including how much things may cost, when both of you have free time, and what clothing you would like to buy.

Words and expressions to use:

周末	有没有空?	觉得	比较	穿
zhōumò	yǒuméiyǒu kòng?	juéde	bǐjiào	chuān

要	得	会	应该	能	可以
yào	děi	huì	yīnggāi	néng	kěyǐ

为 somebody +V.P.	多少钱?	贵	便宜
wèi	duōshǎoqián?	guì	piányi

II. Writing and Character Review

1. Radical practice game. Form groups of three or four. Write the following radicals on separate squares of paper.

土   走 (辶)   人 (亻)   衣 / 衤   木

Turn all the squares over so that the blank sides face up. As you take turns, flip over one of the paper squares and say a character you have learned that has the same radical in it. Write the character on a piece of paper so the group can keep track of which characters have already been said. (Once a character has been said, it cannot be used again.)

Keep playing until you have come up with as many characters as you can think of. Then compare your group's list with other groups. Did you find all the same characters for the radicals?

2. Race to write! Divide into two teams. Spend a few minutes looking over the characters you learned in Lessons 12–14. Then your teacher will call out a word, and a member from each team will race to write the character on the board. The first person who writes the word correctly will gain a point for their team. See which team can get 10 points first!

3. Create a weekly spending record. Use the following example along with the given suggestions or your own ideas to make a list of your expenses for the week. Write the date, the name of the day of the week, what you bought, and how much it cost. Be sure to use measure words when needed.

Example:

日期 rìqī	星期几 xīngqī jǐ	买什么 mǎi shénme	多少钱 duōshǎoqián
二月九日	星期一	一瓶水 一碗汤	两块钱 五块钱

Some of the things you may have bought include:

    beverages (tea, soda, bottled water, etc.)

    dinner at a restaurant (Japanese, French, Chinese, etc.)

    1 airplane ticket

    2 movie tickets

    a plate of dumplings

    a pair of black pants, a green shirt

    a cake for a friend's birthday

III. Comprehensive Review

1. With a partner, look at your spending records from the writing activity 3 above. Discuss the following with your partner.

   - 从星期 ___ 到星期 ___ 用了多少钱?
     cóng xīngqī ___ dào xīngqī ___ yòngle duōshǎoqián?

   - 常常买什么? 每天都买吗?
     chángcháng mǎi shénme? měitiān dōu mǎi ma?

   - 下个月能用多少钱?
     xiàge yuè néng yòng duōshǎoqián?

   - 没有钱的时候, 应该做什么?
     méiyǒu qián de shíhòu, yīnggāi zuò shénme?

2. Work with a partner or in small groups. Three friends, 爱红, 本乐, and 子英, are preparing for a friend's birthday party. Discuss the following clues and use the chart below to figure out what each person does before and during the party.

Clues:

1. 爱红不会开车。子英很喜欢开车, 可是她没有车。
   Àihóng búhuì kāichē. Zǐyīng hěn xǐhuān kāichē, kěshì tā méiyǒu chē.

2. 本乐也没有车, 可是他今天会跟他姐姐借车。
   Běnlè yě méiyǒu chē, kěshì tā jīntiān huì gēn tā jiějie jièchē.

3. 子英喜欢吃东西, 可是不喜欢做饭。本乐做的蛋糕不太好吃。
   Zǐyīng xǐhuān chī dōngxi, kěshì bù xǐhuān zuòfàn. Běnlè zuòde dàngāo bú tài hǎochī.

4. 本乐先从宿舍到电影院[1]买电影票, 然后去机场接人。
   Běnlè xiān cóng sùshè dào diànyǐngyuàn mǎi diànyǐngpiào, ránhòu qù jīchǎng jiē rén.

5. 子英想买一条红裙子。她觉得裙子应该是一个很好的礼物。
   Zǐyīng xiǎng mǎi yìtiáo hóng qúnzi. Tā juéde qúnzi yīnggāi shì yíge hěnhǎode lǐwù.

6. 本乐很会唱歌, 他一定会唱歌给大家听。
   Běnlè hěn huì chànggē, tā yídìng huì chànggē gěi dàjiā tīng.

7. 爱红不忙, 能去跳舞。
   Àihóng bù máng, néng qù tiàowǔ.

Note:
1. 电影院 [diànyǐngyuàn]: movie theater

	做饭	开车接人	买礼物	为她做蛋糕	送裙子	请她看电影	唱歌	跳舞	做服务员
爱红									
本乐									
子英									

With your partner or group, answer the following questions, using the information above.

1. 谁可以做什么？谁会送什么礼物？在舞会，谁会做什么？
   Shéi kěyǐ zuò shénme? Shéi huì sòng shénme lǐwù? Zài wǔhuì, shéi huì zuò shénme?

2. 你觉得本乐应该帮爱红做蛋糕吗？
   Nǐ juéde Běnlè yīnggāi bāng Àihóng zuò dàngāo ma?

3. 明天应该是谁去看电影？
   Míngtiān yīnggāi shì shéi qù kàn diànyǐng?

4. 一张电影票是十块钱。本乐买两张要多少钱？
   Yìzhāng diànyǐngpiào shì shíkuài qián. Běnlè mǎi liǎngzhāng yào duōshǎo qián?

5. 本乐先从宿舍到哪儿去？
   Běnlè xiān cóng sùshè dào nǎr qù?

6. 你觉得他们的舞会好玩儿吗？想不想参加？
   Nǐ juéde tāmende wǔhuì hǎowár ma? Xiǎngbuxiǎng cānjiā?

地点和位置
Location and Position

A typical guestroom with bathroom in an apartment building in Hong Kong.

CONNECTIONS AND COMMUNITIES PREVIEW

Discuss the following questions with a partner or your class. What similarities and differences do you think there might be between Chinese culture and your own culture?

1. When choosing a house or arranging furniture, are there any rules or taboos in your culture/community?

2. Do people believe in fate or destiny in your culture?

教学目标 OBJECTIVES

- Describe location with position words
- Ask where something is located
- Describe rooms in a house

生词 VOCABULARY

核心词 Core Vocabulary

SIMPLIFIED	TRADITIONAL	PINYIN		
1. 前边	前邊	qiánbiān	N.	in front of
2. 参观	參觀	cānguān	V.	to visit
3. 欢迎	歡迎	huānyíng	V.	to welcome
4. 里边	裏邊	lǐbiān	N.	inside
里	裏	lǐ	N.	inside
5. 厨房	廚房	chúfáng	N.	kitchen
6. 公用	公用	gōngyòng	Adj.	for public use, communal
7. 旁边	旁邊	pángbiān	N.	beside, nearby
8. 进	進	jìn	V.	to enter
9. 客厅	客廳	kètīng	N.	living room
10. 走	走	zǒu	V.	to walk
11. 对面	對面	duìmiàn	N.	opposite
12. 餐厅	餐廳	cāntīng	N.	dining room
13. 洗澡间	洗澡間	xǐzǎojiān	N.	bathroom, restroom
14. 卧室	臥室	wòshì	N.	bedroom
15. 中间	中間	zhōngjiān	N.	middle
16. 桌子	桌子	zhuōzi	N.	table
17. 上边	上邊	shàngbiān	N.	on top of, above, over
18. 学习	學習	xuéxí	V.	to study, to learn
19. 后边	後邊	hòubiān	N.	behind, at the back
20. 公园	公園	gōngyuán	N.	park
21. 真	真	zhēn	Adv.	really

专名 Proper Nouns

	SIMPLIFIED	TRADITIONAL	PINYIN		
1.	田进	田進	Tián Jìn	N.	(name) Jin Tian
2.	梁园生	梁園生	Liáng Yuánshēng	N.	(name) Yuansheng Liang
3.	包志中	包志中	Bāo Zhìzhōng	N.	(name) Zhizhong Bao

补充词 Supplementary Vocabulary

	SIMPLIFIED	TRADITIONAL	PINYIN		
1.	左边	左邊	zuǒbiān	N.	on the left
2.	右边	右邊	yòubiān	N.	on the right
3.	下边	下邊	xiàbiān	N.	under
4.	间	間	jiān	M.W.	measure word for rooms
5.	门	門	mén	N.	door
6.	书桌	書桌	shūzhuō	N.	desk
7.	窗户	窗戶	chuānghù	N.	window
8.	椅子	椅子	yǐzi	N.	chair
9.	衣橱	衣櫥	yīchú	N.	wardrobe
10.	床	床	chuáng	N.	bed
11.	厕所	廁所	cèsuǒ	N.	bathroom, toilet
12.	杂志	雜誌	zázhì	N.	magazine
13.	乱	亂	luàn	Adj.	messy
14.	整齐	整齊	zhěngqí	Adj.	tidy
15.	干净	乾淨	gānjìng	Adj.	clean
16.	脏	髒	zāng	Adj.	dirty

语文知识 LANGUAGE LINK

Read and listen to the following sentence patterns. These patterns use vocabulary, expressions, and grammar that you will study in more detail in this lesson. After reading the sentence patterns, read and listen to the Language in Use section that follows.

句型 Sentence Patterns

A: 宿舍里边有没有厨房?
Sùshè lǐbiān yǒuméiyǒu chúfáng?

B: 有厨房，是公用的。
Yǒu chúfáng, shì gōngyòng de.

A: 客厅的对面是什么?
Kètīng de duìmiàn shì shénme?

B: 客厅的对面是餐厅。
Kètīng de duìmiàn shì cāntīng.

A: 图书馆在哪儿?
Túshūguǎn zài nǎr?

B: 图书馆在宿舍前边。
Túshūguǎn zài sùshè qiánbiān.

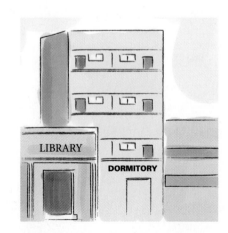

🔊 **课文 Language in Use: 图书馆在宿舍前边**

Situation: 今天是宿舍参观日，在学生宿舍。
Jīntiān shì sùshè cānguān rì, zài xuéshēng sùshè.

田进：　你们好！欢迎你们来看我的宿舍。请跟我来。
　　　　Nǐmen hǎo! Huānyíng nǐmen lái kàn wǒde sùshè. Qǐng gēn wǒ lái.

梁园生：田进，你的宿舍里边有没有厨房？
　　　　Tián Jìn, nǐde sùshè lǐbiān yǒuméiyǒu chúfáng?

田进：　有厨房，是公用的。
　　　　Yǒu chúfáng, shì gōngyòng de.

包志中：你的房间在哪儿？
　　　　Nǐde fángjiān zài nǎr?

田进：　我的房间在旁边，从这儿走。来，请进。
　　　　Wǒde fángjiān zài pángbiān, cóng zhèr zǒu. Lái, qǐngjìn.

　　　　这是客厅，客厅的对面是一个餐厅。
　　　　Zhèshì kètīng, kètīng de duìmiàn shì yíge cāntīng.

梁园生：洗澡间呢？
　　　　Xǐzǎojiān ne?

田进：　洗澡间在客厅和卧室的
　　　　Xǐzǎojiān zài kètīng hé wòshì de

　　　　中间。你看，这是我的卧室。
　　　　zhōngjiān. Nǐ kàn, zhèshì wǒde wòshì.

洗澡间 [xǐzǎojiān], 洗手间 [xǐshǒujiān], and 厕所 [cèsuǒ]
洗澡 means "to bathe." 间 means "room." Thus 洗澡间 refers to the bathroom.
洗手间 [xǐshǒujiān], which literally means "wash hands room," and 厕所 [cèsuǒ] (bathroom, toilet) are also common terms for the restroom or bathroom.

包志中：桌子上边的中文书都是你的吗？
　　　　Zhuōzi shàngbiān de Zhōngwén shū dōushì nǐde ma?

田进：　有的是我的，有的是我
　　　　Yǒude shì wǒde, yǒude shì wǒ

　　　　朋友的。
　　　　péngyoude.

有的 [yǒude]
有的 means "some (of the N.)." Thus, 有的 (书) means "some (of the books)."

包志中： 你常在宿舍学习吗？
　　　　 Nǐ cháng zài sùshè xuéxí ma?

田进： 　 不，我不常在宿舍学习，我常去图书馆学习。
　　　　 Bù, wǒ bù cháng zài sùshè xuéxí, wǒ cháng qù túshūguǎn xuéxí.

梁园生： 图书馆在哪儿?
　　　　 Túshūguǎn zài nǎr?

田进： 　 图书馆在宿舍前边。图书馆的
　　　　 Túshūguǎn zài sùshè qiánbiān. Túshūguǎnde

　　　　 后边还有一个公园。
　　　　 hòubiān háiyǒu yíge gōngyuán.

　　　　 我常去那儿打球。
　　　　 Wǒ cháng qù nàr dǎqiú.

梁园生，包志中： 你们的宿舍真不错！
　　　　　　　　 Nǐmende sùshè zhēn búcuò!

语法 GRAMMAR

I. Position Words

Position words are used to specify relative location. The following are examples of position words. (Note that these can use either the suffix 边 [biān], which means "side," or 面 [miàn], which means "face.")

前边/前面 qiánbiān/qiánmiàn	front	后边/后面 hòubiān/hòumiàn	back
上边/上面 shàngbiān/shàngmiàn	top	下边/下面 xiàbiān/xiàmiàn	under, beneath
里边/里面 lǐbiān/lǐmiàn	inside	外边/外面 wàibiān/wàimiàn	outside

While the above examples have two forms, the following position words have only one form.

左边 [zuǒbiān]	left	右边 [yòubiān]	right
旁边 [pángbiān]	beside	中间 [zhōngjiān]	middle
对面 [duìmiàn]	opposite		

In Chinese, the word order for specifying a location is different from that of English. The reference point, or landmark, is stated first and then the location is specified.

图书馆	在	宿舍的	前边。	The library is in front of the dorm.
Túshūguǎn	zài	sùshè de	qiánbiān.	(Literally: The library is at the
		(reference point)	*(location)*	dormitory's front.)

When giving the reference point, the word 的 can also be omitted, giving either 宿舍前边 or 宿舍的前边.

Note that the position word 里边 is never used with a geographical name, building name, or the name of an organization.

他正在房间里边学中文。
Tā zhèngzài fángjiān lǐbiān xué Zhōngwén.

He is in his room studying Chinese.

他在北京学中文。
Tā zài Běijīng xué Zhōngwén.

He studies Chinese in Beijing.

他在银行工作。
Tā zài yínháng gōngzuò.

He works in a bank.

>>Try it!   **With a partner, take turns completing the following sentences with things found in the classroom.**

1. _____ 在 _____ 的前边。
   _____ zài _____ de qiánbiān.

2. _____ 在 _____ 的后边。
   _____ zài _____ de hòubiān.

3. _____ 在 _____ 的上面。
   _____ zài _____ de shàngbiān.

4. _____ 在 _____ 的旁边。
   _____ zài _____ de pángbiān.

5. _____ 在 _____ 的里边。
   _____ zài _____ de lǐbiān.

II. Expressing Location and Existence with 在, 有, and 是

在 [zài], 有 [yǒu], and 是 [shì] are commonly used to indicate location and existence. Note how the different sentence patterns below affect the sentence focus. (Note that *Place* refers to the reference point and position word together.)

Pattern	Focus	Example
N. (definite)[1] + 在 + Place	location	图书馆在宿舍(的)前边。 Túshūguǎn zài sùshè (de) qiánbiān. (The library is in front of the dorm.)
Place + 有 + N. (indefinite)[2]	existence	宿舍(的)前边有一个图书馆。 Sùshè (de) qiánbiān yǒu yíge túshūguǎn. (There is a library in front of the dorm.)
Place + 是 + N. (definite or indefinite)	identification	宿舍(的)前边是图书馆。 Sùshè (de) qiánbiān shì túshūguǎn. (In front of the dorm is the library.)

Notes:
1. A definite noun is a specific noun (e.g., the library).
2. An indefinite noun is a general noun (e.g., a library).

The following are examples of how 有, 是, and 在 change the focus of questions.

Example	English	Situation
这儿有厕所吗? Zhèr yǒu cèsuǒ ma?	Is there a bathroom here?	e.g., when traveling and asking someone whether there is a bathroom
厕所在哪儿? Cèsuǒ zài nǎr?	Where is the bathroom?	e.g., at a friend's house, asking for the location of the bathroom
这儿是厕所吗? Zhèr shì cèsuǒ ma?	Is this the bathroom?	e.g., to identify whether this is or isn't a bathroom

>>**Try it!** With a partner, first identify the focus of the sentence (existence, location, or identification). Then take turns changing the sentence to have a different focus.

1. 这儿有电话吗?
   Zhèr yǒu diànhuà ma?

2. 那儿是你的大学吗?
   Nàr shì nǐde dàxué ma?

3. 这是他家吗?
   Zhè shì tā jiā ma?

4. 请问,机场在哪儿?
   Qǐng wèn, jīchǎng zài nǎr?

补充课文 SUPPLEMENTARY PRACTICE

Read the following passage. Then listen and repeat.

今天下午我和包志中去看田进。田进住在学校的宿舍里,他常常说他的宿舍很不错,所以¹我们今天去看看,他真高兴²。

田进的卧室不大,可是很明亮³。客厅很大。卧室和客厅的中间有一个洗澡间。厨房在卧室的旁边,客厅的对面是餐厅。厨房和餐厅都是公用的,虽然⁴不大,可是很干净。

田进的书桌上有很多书,有的是他的,有的是他朋友的。他不常在宿舍看书,他喜欢去图书馆学习。图书馆就在宿舍的前边。图书馆的后边还有一个很大的公园,每天有很多人在那儿锻炼⁵,打太极拳⁶。田进有时候⁷也喜欢去那儿打球。

田进很喜欢他的宿舍,我和包志中也都觉得他的宿舍真的很不错。

Notes:
1. 所以 [suǒyǐ]: therefore, so
2. 高兴(高興) [gāoxìng]: happy
3. 明亮 [míngliàng]: bright
4. 虽然……可是……(雖然…… 可是……) [suīrán . . . kěshì . . .]: although . . . but . . .
5. 锻炼(鍛煉) [duànliàn]: to exercise
6. 打太极拳(打太極拳) [dǎ tàijíquán]: to practice tai chi
7. 有时候(有時候) [yǒushíhòu]: sometimes

Pinyin version:

Jīntiān xiàwǔ wǒ hé Bāo Zhìzhōng qù kàn Tián Jìn. Tián Jìn zhù zài xuéxiào de sùshè lǐ, tā chángcháng shuō tāde sùshè hěn búcuò, suǒyǐ wǒmen jīntiān qù kànkan, tā zhēn gāoxìng.

Tián Jìn de wòshì búdà, kěshì hěn míngliàng. Kètīng hěndà. Wòshì hé kètīng de zhōngjiān yǒu yíge xǐzǎojiān. Chúfáng zài wòshì de pángbiān, kètīng de duìmiàn shì cāntīng. Chúfáng hé cāntīng dōushì gōngyòng de, suīrán bú dà, kěshì hěn gānjìng.

Tián Jìn de shūzhuō shàng yǒu hěnduō shū, yǒude shì tāde, yǒude shì tā péngyou de. Tā bù cháng zài sùshè kànshū, tā xǐhuān qù túshūguǎn xuéxí. Túshūguǎn jiùzài sùshè de qiánbiān. Túshūguǎn de hòubiān háiyǒu yíge hěndà de gōngyuán, měitiān yǒu hěnduō rén zài nàr duànliàn, dǎ tàijíquán. Tián Jìn yǒushíhòu yě xǐhuān qù nàr dǎqiú.

Tián Jìn hěn xǐhuān tāde sùshè, wǒ hé Bāo Zhìzhōng yě dōu juéde tāde sùshè zhēnde hěn búcuò.

Read the following statements and choose whether they are true or false.

1. Tian Jin lives in the dorm.	True	False
2. The kitchen is shared with other people.	True	False
3. Tian Jin often goes to study at the library.	True	False
4. There is a park in front of the library.	True	False
5. People usually only exercise in the park during the weekend.	True	False

练习 ACTIVITIES

 I.   Listening Exercises

15-1 Listen and choose the Pinyin with the correct tone for each item you hear. Then check your answers with a partner or the class.

1. a. gòngyòng chǔfàng
   b. gōngyōng chùfáng
   c. gōngyòng chúfáng

2. a. kètīng/cāntīng
   b. kétīng/càntīng
   c. kètíng/cántīng

3. a. túshūguán
   b. túshūguǎn
   c. tǔshúguàn

4. a. hǒubiàn
   b. hòubiān
   c. hōubián

5. a. cánguàn
   b. cànguàn
   c. cānguān

6. a. dìzhǐ
   b. dīzhǐ
   c. dǐzhì

15-2 Look again at the Language in Use dialogue. Listen to the following questions about the dialogue and write your answers in Pinyin. Then check your answers with a partner or the class.

1. _____

2. _____

3. _____

4. _____

5. _____

15-3 Work in groups of three or four. Take turns reading the lines of the following poem, paying special attention to the tones and rhythm.

<table>
<tr><td align="center">Wàng Lúshān Pùbù
(Lǐ Bó/Lǐ Bái)[1]</td><td align="center">望庐山瀑布
(李白)</td></tr>
<tr><td>Rì zhào xiānglú shēng zǐyān,</td><td>日照香炉生紫烟，</td></tr>
<tr><td>Yáo kàn pùbù guà qiánchuān.</td><td>遥看瀑布挂前川。</td></tr>
<tr><td>Fēi liú zhí xià sānqiān chǐ,</td><td>飞流直下三千尺，</td></tr>
<tr><td>Yí shì yínhé luò jiǔ tiān.</td><td>疑是银河落九天。</td></tr>
</table>

Viewing the Waterfall on Mount Lu
(Li, Bo/Li, Bai)

The sunshine on the incense burner produces a purple cloud,
Looking from afar the waterfall is like a huge curtain hanging high.
Its torrent rushes down three thousand feet from above,
I feel as if the Milky Way fell from the sky.

Note:
1. 李白 Lǐ Bái is pronounced as Lǐ Bó in Classical Chinese.

II. Character Exercises

15-4   Match each Chinese word with its English meaning. Then check your answers with a partner or the class.

_____ 1. 欢迎   a. living room
huānyíng

_____ 2. 公园   b. for public use
gōngyuán

_____ 3. 餐厅   c. to visit
cāntīng

_____ 4. 公用   d. dining room
gōngyòng

_____ 5. 厨房   e. kitchen
chúfáng

_____ 6. 客厅   f. park
kètīng

_____ 7. 参观   g. to welcome
cānguān

15-5   Work with a partner. Write the radical for the following characters on the first line. Then, find another character with the same radical in the Language in Use dialogue and write it on the second line. (Refer to the list of radicals on page 255 for help.)

Example: 吗   ___口___   ___呢___

1. 边 [biān]   _____ _____

2. 厨 [chú]   _____ _____

3. 洗 [xǐ]   _____ _____

4. 客 [kè]   _____ _____

III. Grammar Exercises

15-6 Look at the following example. With a partner, take turns extending the words below into phrases and then sentences. See how long you can keep extending the sentences.

Example:

A: 旁边　　　　　　　　　pángbiān

B: 在旁边　　　　　　　　zài pángbiān

A: 在客厅旁边　　　　　　zài kètīng pángbiān

B: 卧室在客厅旁边　　　　wòshì zài kètīng pángbiān

A: 我的卧室在客厅旁边。　Wǒde wòshì zài kètīng pángbiān.

B: 我的卧室在客厅和餐厅旁边。
　　Wǒde wòshì zài kètīng hé cāntīng pángbiān.

1. 前	2. 里	3. 房	4. 公	5. 间	6. 卧	7. 桌	8. 真
qián	lǐ	fáng	gōng	jiān	wò	zhuō	zhēn

15-7 With a partner, take turns using words from the boxes to ask and answer questions. Look carefully at the sentences to see which words fit most appropriately.

Example:　A: 你的<u>厨房</u>在哪儿?　　Nǐde <u>chúfáng</u> zài nǎr?

　　　　　B: 我的<u>厨房</u>在<u>客厅</u>的<u>后边</u>。Wǒde <u>chúfáng</u> zài <u>kètīng</u> de <u>hòubiān</u>.

1. A: 你的 ＿＿＿＿ 在哪儿?
　　 Nǐde ＿＿＿＿ zài nǎr?

　 B: 我的 ＿＿＿ 在 ＿＿＿ 的 ＿＿＿。
　　 Wǒde ＿＿＿ zài ＿＿＿ de ＿＿＿.

厨房 chúfáng	客厅 kètīng	后边 hòubiān
洗澡间 xǐzǎojiān	卧室 wòshì	旁边 pángbiān
书房[1] shūfáng	餐厅 cāntīng	左边 zuǒbiān
书 shū	书桌 shūzhuō	上边 shàngbiān

Note:

1. 书房(書房) [shūfáng]: study room

2. A: _____ 的 _____ 有什么?
   _____ de _____ yǒu shénme?

   B: _____ 的 _____ 有 _____ 。
   _____ de _____ yǒu _____ .

书桌 shūzhuō	上边 shàngbiān	一本书 yìběn shū
客厅 kètīng	旁边 pángbiān	一个厨房 yíge chúfáng
椅子 yǐzi	下边 xiàbiān	一个球 yíge qiú
炒饭 chǎofàn	前边 qiánbiān	一双筷子 yìshuāng kuàizi

3. A: _____ 的 _____ 是什么?
   _____ de _____ shì shénme?

   B: _____ 的 _____ 是 _____ 。
   _____ de _____ shì _____ .

中国饭馆 Zhōngguó fànguǎn	后边 hòubiān	公园 gōngyuán
停车场 tíngchēchǎng	左边 zuǒbiān	宿舍 sùshè
机场 jīchǎng	前边 qiánbiān	商店[1] shāngdiàn
宿舍和图书馆 sùshè hé túshūguǎn	中间 zhōngjiān	停车场 tíngchēchǎng

Note: 1. 商店 [shāngdiàn]: shop; store

15-8 Work with a partner. Look at the pictures and answer the questions using 有, 在, or 是 with position words.

1. 客厅里边有什么?   _____
   Kètīng lǐbiān yǒu shénme?

2. 电视的前面是什么?   _____
   Diànshì de qiánmiàn shì shénme?

3. 电话在哪儿？　　　　　　　　　_____
   Diànhuà zài nǎr?

4. 桌子上有书吗？　　　　　　　　_____
   Zhuōzi shàng yǒu shū ma?

5. 桌子的下面有什么？　　　　　　_____
   Zhuōzi de xiàmiàn yǒu shénme?

6. 小猫¹在哪儿？　　　　　　　　　_____
   Xiǎomāo zài nǎr?

Note: 1. 小猫(小貓) [xiǎomāo]: kitten

IV. Communicative Activities

15-9 With a partner, role-play the following situation.

Situation: Your friend has enrolled to study at your university and has just arrived at your place. Before your friend came, they asked you to help them find an apartment. You have found a very nice one-bedroom apartment for your friend. Your friend asks what the apartment has in it and how much it costs. Tell them everything you know about this apartment, such as the size of the the bedroom, if it is clean, if there are many windows, if there is a kitchen, etc. Use the following pictures.

Words and phrases to use:

有	是	在	前边	旁边	对面
yǒu	shì	zài	qiánbiān	pángbiān	duìmiàn

大	小	不错	干净
dà	xiǎo	búcuò	gānjìng (clean)

有没有	床	窗户
yǒuméiyǒu	chuáng (bed)	chuānghù (window)

厨房	一个月要多少钱？
chúfáng	yígeyuè yào duōshǎoqián?

15-10 Work with a partner. Take turns describing your house or dormitory while your partner draws a picture based on the information you give. In addition to saying where different rooms are, include information about what is in the room (TV, bed, books, clothes, dishes, pets, phone, etc.) Be sure to ask questions about anything you need more information about while you draw.

文化知识 Culture Link

文化点滴 CULTURE NOTES

风水 Feng Shui

风水 [fēngshuǐ] (Feng Shui) is the art or study of placement to produce harmony in living spaces. The words 风 [fēng] and 水 [shuǐ] mean "wind" and "water," respectively. They refer to the continuous interaction of these two powerful forces and how this interaction constantly changes the size, direction, and shape of the topography of the earth, its mountains, valleys, and waterways.

The goal of 风水 is to maintain harmony and balance between 阴 [yīn] and 阳 [yáng], which are opposite yet interconnected forces in the universe and in nature. Balancing these forces can bring about positive 气 [qì], which, according to Chinese culture, is the invisible flow of energy that circulates through the earth and sky, and in all life forms. It is believed that we can influence our fate and fortune by enhancing and directing the flow of 气. Thus, the practice of 风水 helps to harness this vital energy to maximize the positive effects that it bestows.

风水 originated over 4,000 years ago when farmers in southern China developed certain principles because of their dependence on the earth and the forces governing it. They learned that living in harmony with nature made life much easier. Homes were built on hills to protect them

> **Do you know...**
> - what Feng Shui is and what its goal is?
> - what Qi is?
> - what some Feng Shui remedies are?
>
> **Read and find out!**

from floods and to make it easier to defend them from attackers. Homes were also built to face south, away from the storms of yellow dust that blew down from Mongolia. Facing south into the winter sunshine kept the houses bright and warm during the cold months. In addition to its use by farmers, 风水 also played a vital role in ancient Chinese burials. It was believed that ancestors made happy with good 风水 guiding the placement of their tombs would shower blessings of prosperity, honor, long life, and healthy offspring on the living.

In Chinese culture, where family life and honor are important, good 风水 positioning in the home is believed to facilitate harmonious relationships between husband and wife, foster good health, attract abundance and prosperity, and help build good reputations. Common remedies for the home include proper placement of the bed and clearing clutter to remove blocked energy. Plants such as "lucky bamboo" are also often used as 风水 remedies. In business, following the rules of 风水 in the selection or design of an office is thought to create opportunities for growth, raise one's business profile and standing in the community, attract customers, and increase profits. It is also believed that adhering to good 风水 practices in business will help ensure loyal employees and smooth working relationships.

To Chinese communities the world over, 风水 has been a common mystical practice for centuries. It blends ancient wisdom with cultural traditions and inspires people to live in harmony with the environment for health, wealth, and happiness. 风水 has also attained popularity in many Western countries where its benefits are now being increasingly recognized.

A Feng Shui expert advised that this Hong Kong building be built with a hole in it to allow a nearby dragon spirit to pass through. What would a business person hope to get from using Feng Shui?

"Lucky bamboo" is often used as a Feng Shui remedy. What other remedies might one use?

Discuss the following with a group or your class.

1. Do you believe in 风水? Would you consult with a 风水 master when buying a house?
2. Do you think 风水 is a superstition or a science? Do you know any other culture that attempts to balance natural forces when selecting building locations, designing architecture, or doing interior design?

趣味中文 FUN WITH CHINESE

有缘千里来相会，无缘对面不相识。

If destined to meet, even those separated by a great distance will meet each other.
If not destined to meet, even those who are face to face will not know each other.

yǒu	yuán	qiān	lǐ	lái	xiāng	huì,
有	缘	千	里	来	相	会,
have	fate	thousand	kilometer	come	mutually	meet,

wú	yuán	duìmiàn	bù	xiāng	shí.
无	缘	对面	不	相	识。
no	fate	face to face	no	mutually	know.

The concept of fate, or destiny, is very important in Chinese culture. This saying shows how Chinese people emphasize the importance of their acquaintances. It is usually used to refer to couples who are meant to be together or to remind people that friends are very precious.

Work in small groups or with your class.

1. Practice reading the saying aloud, paying attention to the pronunciation and rhythm.
2. Which position word in 有缘千里来相会，无缘对面不相识 did you learn in this lesson? Write it on the line and use it in a sentence.

_____

3. Where do your classmates come from? Do you consider yourselves 有缘千里来相会?

🔊 行动吧！ LET'S GO!

北京景点地图 Map of Scenic Spots in Beijing

Look at the following map of Beijing.

Direction words:

东边(東邊) [dōngbiān]: east side
南边(南邊) [nánbiān]: south side
西边(西邊) [xībiān]: west side
北边(北邊) [běibiān]: north side
东南边(東南邊) [dōngnánbiān]: southeast side
东北边(東北邊) [dōngběibiān]: northeast side
西南边(西南邊) [xīnánbiān]: southwest side
西北边(西北邊) [xīběibiān]: northwest side

Answer the following questions with your partner or group.

Look at the direction words above. Use them to answer the following questions.

1. 长城在北京的哪一边?

   Chángchéng zài Běijīng de nǎ yì biān?

2. 故宫的南边有什么?

   Gùgōng de nánbiān yǒu shénme?

3. 颐和园在机场的东边还是西边?

   Yíhéyuán zài jīchǎng de dōngbiān háishì xībiān?

爱好和运动
Hobbies and Sports

Yao Ming, one of China's most famous basketball players.

CONNECTIONS AND COMMUNITIES PREVIEW

Discuss the following questions with a partner or your class. What similarities and differences do you think there might be between Chinese culture and your own culture?

1. What are some popular sports in your country? Are there any sports that are unique to your culture?

2. Are sports and physical exercise important in your culture? Do you think physical training methods are different in different cultures?

教学目标 OBJECTIVES

- Describe how an action is performed
- Talk about hobbies, sports, and exercise

生词 VOCABULARY

核心词 Core Vocabulary

	SIMPLIFIED	TRADITIONAL	PINYIN		
1.	篮球	籃球	lánqiú	N.	basketball
2.	得	得	de	Part.	(used between a verb or an adjective and its complement to indicate a result, possibility, or degree)
3.	俩	倆	liǎ		two people (colloquial)
4.	教练	教練	jiàoliàn	N.	coach, trainer
5.	教	教	jiāo	V.	to teach, to coach
6.	游泳	游泳	yóuyǒng	V.O.	to swim
7.	非常	非常	fēicháng	Adv.	very
8.	快	快	kuài	Adj.	fast
9.	体育馆	體育館	tǐyùguǎn	N.	gymnasium
10.	游泳池	游泳池	yóuyǒngchí	N.	swimming pool
11.	健身房	健身房	jiànshēnfáng	N.	gym (workout facility)
12.	锻炼	鍛煉	duànliàn	V.	to exercise
13.	现在	現在	xiànzài	Adv.	now
14.	昨天	昨天	zuótiān	Adv.	yesterday
15.	球赛	球賽	qiúsài	N.	ball game, match
16.	作业	作業	zuòyè	N.	homework
17.	包	包	bāo	V.	to wrap
18.	慢	慢	màn	Adj.	slow

补充词 Supplementary Vocabulary

	SIMPLIFIED	TRADITIONAL	PINYIN		
1.	社团	社團	shètuán	N.	organization
2.	俱乐部	俱樂部	jùlèbù	N.	club
3.	球季	球季	qiújì	N.	season (of a sport)
4.	运动	運動	yùndòng	V.	to exercise
				N.	sports
5.	骑自行车	騎自行車	qí zìxíngchē	V.O.	to ride a bike
6.	滑雪	滑雪	huáxuě	V.O.	to ski
7.	爬山	爬山	páshān	V.O.	to climb a mountain
8.	远足	遠足	yuǎnzú	N.	a hike, hiking
9.	棒球	棒球	bàngqiú	N.	baseball
10.	橄榄球	橄欖球	gǎnlǎnqiú	N.	football
11.	足球	足球	zúqiú	N.	soccer
12.	网球	網球	wǎngqiú	N.	tennis
13.	跑步	跑步	pǎobù	V.O.	to run
	跑	跑	pǎo	V.	to run
	步	步	bù	N.	step

语文知识 LANGUAGE LINK

Read and listen to the following sentence patterns. These patterns use vocabulary, expressions, and grammar that you will study in more detail in this lesson. After reading the sentence patterns, read and listen to the Language in Use section that follows.

句型 Sentence Patterns

A: 你游泳游得怎么样?
Nǐ yóuyǒng yóude zěnmeyàng?

B: 我游泳游得非常快。
Wǒ yóuyǒng yóude fēicháng kuài.

A: 你做饭做得好不好?
Nǐ zuòfàn zuòde hǎobuhǎo?

B: 我做饭做得不太好。
Wǒ zuòfàn zuòde bútàihǎo.

课文 Language in Use: 她打篮球打得很好

张正然: 你们俩要去哪儿?
Nǐmenliǎ yàoqù nǎr?

孙信美, 杨欢: 我们去打篮球。
Wǒmen qù dǎ lánqiú.

俩 [liǎ]
俩 means "two people" and is used with pronouns. For example, 我们俩 (us two), 你们俩 (you two), and 他们俩 (those two).

打 [dǎ]
打 is used for sports that are played with the hands. For sports which are mainly played with the foot, the verb 踢 [tī] (to kick) is used.

张正然：你们篮球打得怎么样？
Nǐmen lánqiú dǎde zěnmeyàng?

孙信美：杨欢篮球打得很好。
Yáng Huān lánqiú dǎde hěnhǎo.

我还不太会打篮球，
Wǒ hái bú tài huì dǎ lánqiú,

她是我的教练，她教得很好。
tā shì wǒde jiàoliàn, tā jiāode hěnhǎo.

杨欢：不行，我还打得不太好。
Bùxíng, wǒ hái dǎde bútàihǎo.

张正然：我不常打篮球，我常常和我
Wǒ bù cháng dǎ lánqiú, wǒ chángcháng hé wǒ

室友去游泳，他游泳游得非常快。
shìyǒu qù yóuyǒng, tā yóuyǒng yóude fēicháng kuài.

杨欢：你们常去哪儿游泳？
Nǐmen cháng qù nǎr yóuyǒng?

张正然：我们常去体育馆里边的游泳池游泳，
Wǒmen cháng qù tǐyùguǎn lǐbiān de yóuyǒngchí yóuyǒng,

我们也常去健身房锻炼。
wǒmen yě cháng qù jiànshēnfáng duànliàn.

孙信美：你现在要不要跟我们去打篮球？
Nǐ xiànzài yàobuyào gēn wǒmen qù dǎ lánqiú?

张正然：现在不行。我昨天看球赛看得太晚了，
Xiànzài bùxíng. Wǒ zuótiān kàn qiúsài kànde tàiwǎn le,

今天起得很晚，现在得去做作业。
jīntiān qǐde hěnwǎn, xiànzài děi qù zuò zuòyè.

得 [de, děi]

得 has two pronunciations that have different meanings and functions. 得 [de] is used for degree of complement sentences, whereas [děi] is an optative verb meaning "have to" or "must."

教 [jiào, jiāo]

When 教 is used as a noun, it is pronounced as [jiào], such as 教练, 教授 [jiàoshòu] (professor) or 教育 [jiàoyù] (education). When 教 is used as a verb, it is pronounced as [jiāo].

锻炼 [duànliàn]

锻炼 means "to exercise" or "to work out." In Taiwan, the term 运动 [yùndòng] is more commonly used.

杨欢：   昨天我们那儿包饺子、做中国菜。
Zuótiān wǒmen nàr bāo jiǎozi, zuò Zhōngguó cài.

你晚上到我们那儿吃饺子吧。
Nǐ wǎnshang dào wǒmen nàr chī jiǎozi ba.

张正然： 太好了！我很喜欢吃饺子。
Tàihǎo le! Wǒ hěn xǐhuān chī jiǎozi.

你们包饺子包得快不快？
Nǐmen bāo jiǎozi bāode kuàibukuài?

孙信美： 我们包得很慢。
Wǒmen bāode hěnmàn.

杨欢：   信美很会做饭。她做饭做得很好。
Xìngměi hěn huì zuòfàn. Tā zuòfàn zuòde hěnhǎo.

语法 GRAMMAR

I. Degree of Complement Sentences

A degree of complement sentence tells how an action is performed (how fast, how well, how soon, etc.). In these kinds of sentences, the verb is followed by the particle 得 [de] plus the information describing how the action is performed (usually formed by an adverb and adjective together). Sentence patterns for this kind of sentence are as follows:

Single verb: Subject + V. + 得 + Adv. + Adj.

你游得怎么样？   How well do you swim?
Nǐ yóude zěnmeyàng?

我游得很快。   I swim very fast.
Wǒ yóude hěnkuài.

我游得不快。   I don't swim fast.
Wǒ yóude bú kuài.

Verb + Object (V.O.): Subject + V.O. + V. + 得 + Adv. + Adj.

他打篮球打得好不好？
Tā dǎ lánqiú dǎde hǎobuhǎo?

Does he play basketball well?

他打篮球打得很好。
Tā dǎ lánqiú dǎde hěnhǎo

He plays basketball very well.

他打篮球打得不太好。
Tā dǎ lánqiú dǎde bútài hǎo.

He doesn't play basketball very well.

In degree of complement sentences, the object can also be placed at the beginning of a sentence for emphasis.

饺子我包得很慢。
Jiǎozi wǒ bāode hěnmàn.

篮球他打得非常好。
Lánqiú tā dǎde fēicháng hǎo.

>>**Try it!** With a partner, take turns asking and answering the following questions, using 得 with verbs and verb-objects to show degrees of action.

1. A: 他说法文说 ＿ 怎么样？
   Tā shuō Fǎwén shuō ___ zěnmeyàng?

   B: 他说法文说得 ＿＿＿＿。
   Tā shuō Fǎwén shuō de ＿＿＿＿ .

2. A: 小狗吃 ＿ 快不快？
   Xiǎogǒu chī ___ kuàibukuài?

   B: 小狗吃得 ＿＿＿＿。
   Xiǎogǒu chī de ＿＿＿＿ .

3. A: 老师教书[1]教 ＿ 好不好？
   Lǎoshī jiāoshū jiāo ___ hǎobuhǎo?

   B: 老师教书教得 ＿＿＿＿。
   Lǎoshī jiāoshū jiāo de ＿＿＿＿ .

4. A: 你妈妈做饭做 ＿ 怎么样？
   Nǐ māma zuòfàn zuò ___ zěnmeyàng?

   B: 我妈妈做饭做得 ＿＿＿＿。
   Wǒ māma zuòfàn zuò de ＿＿＿＿ .

5. A: 你开车开得 ＿＿＿＿ ？
   Nǐ kāichē kāi de ＿＿＿ ?

   B: 我 ＿＿＿＿＿＿。
   Wǒ ＿＿＿＿＿ .

6. A: 你昨天睡觉睡得 ＿＿＿＿ ？
   Nǐ zuótiān shuìjiào shuì de ＿＿＿ ?

   B: 我昨天 ＿＿＿＿＿＿。
   Wǒ zuótiān ＿＿＿＿＿ .

Note:
1. 教书(教書) [jiāoshū]: to teach

补充课文 SUPPLEMENTARY PRACTICE

Read the following passage. Then listen and repeat.

大家好！我叫孙信美。我和杨欢是好朋友。我们俩都喜欢游泳，常常一起去体育馆里边的游泳池游泳。我不太会游泳，现在正在学。杨欢游泳游得非常好，她也是我的游泳教练。她教我教得很好，所以我学得很快。

杨欢有一个男朋友。他不常游泳，可是他特别[1]喜欢打篮球。我们学校[2]有一个很好的健身房，他常常跟他的室友一起去那儿打篮球。他的室友篮球打得非常好，他还是学校篮球队[3]的队长[4]。他们常常一起出去[5]参加比赛[6]。

我们四个人都是体育活动[7]爱好者[8]，常常去健身房锻炼。我们有时候[9]也一起吃饭。杨欢包饺子包得又[10]快又好，我包饺子包得很慢，可是我做中国菜做得特别好吃，他们都喜欢吃我做的菜。

Notes:
1. 特别 [tèbié]: especially, particularly
2. 学校(學校) [xuéxiào]: school
3. 队(隊) [duì]: team
4. 队长(隊長) [duìzhǎng]: team leader
5. 出去 [chūqù]: to go out
6. 比赛(比賽) [bǐsài]: contest
7. 活动(活動) [huódòng]: activity
8. 爱好者(愛好者) [àihàozhě]: one who loves (a sport, a hobby, etc.)
9. 有时候(有時候) [yǒushíhòu]: sometimes
10. 又……又…… [yòu . . . yòu . . .]: both . . . and . . . (used for emphasis)

Pinyin version:

Dàjiā hǎo! Wǒ jiào Sūn Xìnměi. Wǒ hé Yáng Huān shì hǎo péngyou. Wǒmen liǎ dōu xǐhuān yóuyǒng, chángcháng yìqǐ qù tǐyùguǎn lǐbiān de yóuyǒngchí yóuyǒng. Wǒ bú tài huì yóuyǒng, xiànzài zhèngzài xué. Yáng Huān yóuyǒng yóude fēicháng hǎo, tā yě shì wǒde yóuyǒng jiàoliàn. Tā jiāo wǒ jiāode hěnhǎo, suǒyǐ wǒ xuéde hěnkuài.

Yáng Huān yǒu yíge nánpéngyou. Tā bùcháng yóuyǒng, kěshì tā tèbié xǐhuān dǎ lánqiú. Wǒmen xuéxiào yǒu yíge hěnhǎo de jiànshēnfáng, tā chángcháng gēn tāde shìyǒu yìqǐ qù nàr dǎ lánqiú. Tāde shìyǒu lánqiú dǎde fēicháng hǎo, tā hái shì xuéxiào lánqiúduì de duìzhǎng. Tāmen chángcháng yìqǐ chūqù cānjiā bǐsài.

Wǒmen sìge rén dōu shì tǐyù huódòng àihàozhě, chángcháng qù jiànshēnfáng duànliàn. Wǒmen yǒushíhòu yě yìqǐ chīfàn. Yáng Huān bāo jiǎozi bāode yòu kuài yòu hǎo, wǒ bāo jiǎozi bāode hěnmàn, kěshì wǒ zuò Zhōngguó cài zuòde tèbié hǎochī, tāmen dōu xǐhuān chī wǒ zuò de cài.

Choose the correct answer for the following questions.

1. 孙信美正在学 ＿＿＿ 。
   Sūn Xìnměi zhèngzài xué ＿＿＿ .

   a. 锻炼   b. 教练   c. 打篮球   d. 游泳
      duànliàn   jiàoliàn   dǎ lánqiú   yóuyǒng

2. 谁是孙信美的教练?
   Shéi shì Sūn Xìnměi de jiàoliàn?

   a. 杨欢   b. 杨欢的男朋友
      Yáng Huān   Yáng Huān de nánpéngyou

   c. 男朋友的室友   d. 孙信美没有教练
      nánpéngyou de shìyǒu   Sūn Xìnměi méiyǒu jiàoliàn

3. 杨欢的男朋友常打篮球吗?
   Yáng Huān de nánpéngyou cháng dǎ lánqiú ma?

   a. 不，他不喜欢打篮球。   b. 是，他常打篮球。
      Bù, tā bù xǐhuān dǎ lánqiú.   Shì, tā cháng dǎ lánqiú.

   c. 不，他不常打篮球。   d. 不，他不会打篮球。
      Bù, tā bù cháng dǎ lánqiú.   Bù, tā búhuì dǎ lánqiú.

4. 谁喜欢锻炼?
   Shéi xǐhuān duànliàn?

   a. 孙信美   b. 杨欢   c. 杨欢的男朋友   d. 他们都喜欢
      Sūn Xìnměi   Yáng Huān   Yáng Huān de nánpéngyou   Tāmen dōu xǐhuān

5. 杨欢会做什么菜?
   Yáng Huān huì zuò shénme cài?

   a. 美国菜   b. 饺子   c. 韩国炒面   d. 日本菜
      Měiguó cài   jiǎozi   Hánguó chǎomiàn   Rìběn cài

练习 ACTIVITIES

I.   Listening Exercises

16-1   Listen and choose the Pinyin with the correct tone for each word you hear. Then check your answers with a partner or the class.

1. a. dǎ lánqiú
   b. dà lànqiú
   c. dá lānqiú

2. a. bāo jiàozi
   b. bāo jiǎozi
   c. bǎo jiǎozi

3. a. kán qiùsài
   b. kān qiùsài
   c. kàn qiúsài

4. a. jiāo yóuyǒng
   b. jiáo yōuyòng
   c. jiào yòuyōng

5. a. tìyùguán
   b. tǐyúguǎn
   c. tǐyùguǎn

6. a. zuō zuóyè
   b. zuò zuòyè
   c. zuò zuǒyè

16-2   Listen and complete the sentences. Then check your answers with a partner or the class.

1. Nǐmen _____ zhème kuài, yào qù nǎr?

2. Yáng Huān _____ fēicháng hǎo.

3. Zhāng Zhèngrán yóuyǒng _____ .

4. Wǒ zuótiān wǎnshang _____ .

5. Shéi zuò fàn _____ ?

16-3   Work in groups of three or four. Take turns reading the lines of the following poem, paying special attention to the tones and rhythm.

Fēngqiáo Yè Bó
(Zhāng Jì)

枫桥夜泊
(张继)

Yuè luò wū tí shuāng mǎn tiān,
Jiāng fēng yúhuǒ duì chóu mián.
Gūsū chéngwài Hánshānsì,
Yè bàn zhōngshēng dào kèchuán.

月落乌啼霜满天，
江枫渔火对愁眠。
姑苏城外寒山寺，
夜半钟声到客船。

Night Docking at Maple Bridge
(Zhang, Ji)

The moon is setting, the magpie chirping, and the sky full of frost,
Accompanied by the water of the Maple River and fishing candles I sleep with
    worries on my mind.
Outside Suzhou is the Hanshan Temple,
At midnight the sound of its bell reaches my boat.

II. Character Exercises

16-4   Match each Chinese word with its English meaning. Then check your answers with a partner or the class.

____ 1. 作业   a. slow
        zuòyè

____ 2. 快   b. exercise
        kuài

____ 3. 体育馆   c. coach
        tǐyùguǎn

____ 4. 游泳池   d. fast
        yóuyǒngchí

____ 5. 教练   e. ball game
        jiàoliàn

____ 6. 慢   f. gymnasium
        màn

____ 7. 锻炼   g. homework
        duànliàn

____ 8. 球赛   h. swimming pool
        qiúsài

16-5   Work with a partner. Write the radical and its meaning for each of the following characters. Write at least two other characters with the same radical. (Refer to the list of radicals on page 255 for help.)

Example: 快 [kuài] _____忙　想_____

1. 游 [yóu] _____

2. 慢 [màn] _____

3. 锻 [duàn] _____

4. 篮 [lán] _____

5. 俩 [liǎ] _____

6. 赛 [sài] _____

III. Grammar Exercises

16-6   Look at the following example. With a partner, take turns extending the following words into phrases and then sentences. See how long you can keep extending the sentences.

Example:

A: 快   kuài ·

B: 非常快   fēicháng kuài

A: 说得非常快   shuōde fēicháng kuài

B: 王老师说得非常快。   Wáng lǎoshī shuōde fēicháng kuài.

A: 王老师说中文说得非常快。
   Wáng lǎoshī shuō Zhōngwén shuōde fēicháng kuài.

B: 王老师和方老师中文都说得非常快。
   Wáng lǎoshī hé Fāng lǎoshī Zhōngwén dōu shuōde fēicháng kuài.

1. 俩   2. 教   3. 游   4. 体   5. 健   6. 锻   7. 赛   8. 包
   liǎ   jiāo   yóu   tǐ   jiàn   duàn   sài   bāo

16-7   With a partner, take turns using words from the boxes to complete and practice the dialogues. Look carefully at the sentences to see which words fit most appropriately.

Example: A: 他<u>游泳游</u>得怎么样？   Tā <u>yóuyǒng yóu</u> de zěnmeyang?

             B: 他<u>游泳游</u>得很<u>好</u>。   Tā <u>yóuyǒng yóu</u> de <u>hěnhǎo</u>.

1. A: 他 _____ 得怎么样？
      Tā _____ de zěnmeyàng?

   B: 他 _____ 得很 ___ 。
      Tā _____ de hěn ___ .

教书[1] jiāoshū	不错 bú cuò
做饭 zuòfàn	好 hǎo
包饺子 bāo jiǎozi	快 kuài
吃饭 chīfàn	高兴[2] gāoxìng

Note:
1. 教书 (教書) [jiāoshū]: to teach
2. 高兴 (高興) [gāoxìng]: happy

2. A: 你的 ___ ___ 得 _____ 吗？
   Nǐ de ___ ___ de _____ ma?

   B: 我的 ___ ___ 得很 ___ 。
   Wǒde ___ ___ de hěn ___ .

生日 shēngrì	过 guò	好 hǎo
中文 Zhōngwén	说 shuō	棒 bàng
功课 gōngkè	做 zuò	好 hǎo
篮球 lánqiú	打 dǎ	棒 bàng

16-8 Use the prompts in parentheses to create degree of complement sentences with 得.
Then check your answers with a partner.

Example: 他说中文 (fast)   他说中文说得很快。/中文他说得很快。
             Tā shuō Zhōngwén

1. 我妈妈做饭 (well)   _____
   Wǒ māma zuòfàn

2. 杨欢打篮球 (well)   _____
   Yáng Huān dǎ lánqiú

3. 你们做作业 (fast)   _____
   Nǐmen zuò zuòyè

4. 我锻炼 (little)   _____
   Wǒ duànliàn

5. 谁包饺子 (slow)   _____
   Shéi bāo jiǎozi

16-9   With a partner, take turns asking and answering questions about the pictures with 得.

1.

游泳 [yóuyǒng]: to swim

2.

打篮球 [dǎ lánqiú]: to play basketball

3.

打棒球 [dǎ bàngqiú]: to play baseball

4.
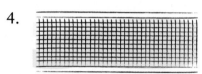

打排球 [dǎ páiqiú]: to play volleyball

5.

踢足球 [tī zúqiú]: to kick a soccer ball

6.

跑步 [pǎobù]: to run

IV. Communicative Activities

16-10   Work in small groups. Ask each other questions to find out the following information. Then compare your group's answers with other groups' answers.

Information to find out:

Do they eat quickly or slowly?
Do they drive fast or slow?
Who can swim? How well do they swim?
How well do they play basketball?

Words and expressions to use:

V. (V.O.) + 得	慢/快
de	màn/kuài

非常	好/不好
fēicháng	hǎo/bùhǎo

怎么样	真
zěnmeyàng	zhēn

16-11 Work with a partner. Create a dialogue between two friends who are chatting about the hobbies and sports they participate in. In addition to words you learned in this lesson, try to use information you have learned in previous lessons.

Words and expressions to use:

球赛	篮球	排球
qiúsài	lánqiú	páiqiú (volleyball)

足球	棒球	乒乓球[1]
zúqiú (soccer)	bàngqiú (baseball)	pīngpāngqiú (table tennis; ping pong)

高尔夫球	健身房	游泳
gāo'ěrfūqiú (golf)	jiànshēnfáng	yóuyǒng

锻炼	体育馆	社团
duànliàn	tǐyùguǎn	shètuán (organization, club)

Note:

1. 乒乓球 is also called 桌球 [zhuōqiú] in Taiwan

文化知识 Culture Link

文化点滴 CULTURE NOTES

中国功夫 Chinese Martial Arts (Kung Fu)

When people think of martial arts, many of them think of 中国功夫 [Zhōngguó Gōngfū] (Kung Fu). Kung Fu has become very popular worldwide as a form of exercise and self-improvement, as well as a form of entertainment. Those who practice Kung Fu believe it helps them improve their self-defense ability, train their body, maintain their health, and cultivate their mind. During the 20th century the popularity of Kung Fu spread around the world as Chinese martial artists and actors such as 李小龙 [Lǐ Xiǎolóng] (Bruce Lee), 成龙 [Chéng Lóng] (Jackie Chan), and 李连杰 [Lǐ Liánjié] (Jet Li) starred in many Chinese Kung Fu movies in Hollywood and became international stars.

Kung Fu is also commonly known as 武术 [wǔshù] (martial arts skills) or 武艺 [wǔyì] (martial arts). Legend has it that Chinese martial arts originated during the reign of the 黄帝 [Huángdì] (Yellow Emperor) around 5,000 years ago as a form of physical training for the military. During its long historical development, Kung Fu has incorporated various combat skills and elements of Chinese philosophies such as Taoism, Buddhism, and Confucianism. It is

Do you know...
- when and how Kung Fu began?
- what some different Kung Fu styles are?
- what some famous Kung Fu movies are?

Read and find out!

now commonly classified into several styles: Internal and External, Southern and Northern, 少林派 [Shàolín pài] (Shaolin), 武当派 [Wǔdāng pài] (Wudang), and 峨嵋派 [Éméi pài] (Emei). The famous Shaolin style evolved from the self-defense skills of the monks at the Shaolin Temple on 嵩山 [Sōngshān] (Songshan mountain) in the Henan province of Central China.

Kung Fu often appears in Chinese literature and has developed its own genre, 武侠小说 [wǔxiá xiǎoshuō] (martial arts and chivalry novels). Famous writers of this genre, such as 古龙 [Gǔ Lóng] and 金庸 [Jīn Yōng], have written many bestselling novels that feature complex human relationships, gratitude and resentment, heroes and heroines, romance, and history. Their novels have attracted many devoted Chinese martial arts fans, and many of these stories have been adapted into Peking Opera, puppet theater, Chinese TV series, movies, comic books, and computer games.

Every year, thousands of people from different parts of the world come to China, Taiwan, and Hong Kong to learn Kung Fu. Below are some selected movies in which you can see Kung Fu in action!

Some 中国功夫 *movies:*

Hero (英雄 [Yīngxióng])

Crouching Tiger, Hidden Dragon (卧虎藏龙 [Wòhǔ cánglóng])

House of Flying Daggers (十面埋伏 [Shímiàn máifú])

The Game of Death (死亡的游戏 [Sǐwáng de yóuxì]) (featuring Bruce Lee)

Drunken Master (醉拳 [Zuìquán]) (featuring Jackie Chan)

Shaolin Temple (少林寺 [Shàolínsì]) (featuring Jet Li)

A group of children practice Kung Fu in front of the Temple of Heaven in Beijing. What are some different styles of Kung Fu?

Martial arts master Bruce Lee starred in many Kung Fu movies. Besides movies, what other genre features stories about Kung Fu heroes?

Discuss the following with a group or your class.

1. Do you or any of your friends practice martial arts? If so, what kinds of martial arts do you or your friends practice?
2. Have you seen any martial arts movies? Which martial arts movies do you like?

趣味中文 FUN WITH CHINESE

高人一等

To regard someone/oneself as better than others.

gāo	rén	yì	děng
高	人	一	等
tall/high	people	number one	level

Work in small groups or with your class.

1. Practice reading the saying aloud, paying attention to the pronunciation and rhythm.
2. Do you know of any similar sayings in other languages or cultures?

行动吧! LET'S GO!

比赛结果 Competition Results (Game Results)

孙信美 and 杨欢 recently participated in their school's sports week, competing with students from other schools in different races and games. Read the results of some of the events that 孙信美 and 杨欢 participated in.

北京高校[1]运动会比赛结果[2]			
游泳: 蝶泳[3](女100米[4])		田径[5]: 马拉松[6]	
名次[7]	姓名	名次	姓名
第一名[8]	杨欢	第一名	张英红
第二名	毛爱红	第二名	于英
第三名	方小文	第三名	杨欢
……		……	
第十七名	孙信美	第八名	孙信美
……		……	
乒乓球[9]		足球	
名次	姓名	名次	学校
第一名	孙信美	第一名	北京大学
第二名	杨欢	第二名	清华大学
第三名	方小文	第三名	交通大学

Notes:
1. 高校 [gāoxiào]: college, university
2. 比赛结果(比賽結果) [bǐsài jiéguǒ]: competition/race results
3. 蝶泳 [diéyǒng]: butterfly stroke
4. 米 [mǐ]: meter
5. 田径(田徑) [tiánjìng]: track and field
6. 马拉松(馬拉松) [mǎlāsōng]: marathon
7. 名次 [míngcì]: placement, rank
8. 第一名 [dìyīmíng]: first place
9. 乒乓球 [pīngpāngqiú]: table tennis; ping pong. 乒乓球 is also called 桌球 [zhuōqiú] in Taiwan

Answer the following questions with your partner or group.

1. 孙信美和杨欢马拉松跑得怎么样? 她们是第几名[1]?
   Sūn Xìnměi hé Yáng Huān mǎlāsōng pǎode zěnmeyàng? Tāmen shì dìjǐmíng?

2. 杨欢游泳游得怎么样? 孙信美呢? 孙信美游得快不快?
   Yáng Huān yóuyǒng yóude zěnmeyàng? Sūn Xìnměi ne? Sūn Xìnměi yóude kuàibukuài?

3. 杨欢乒乓球打得好不好? 孙信美呢?
   Yáng Huān pīngpāngqiú dǎde hǎobuhǎo? Sūn Xìnměi ne?

4. 北京大学足球踢[2]得怎么样? 北京大学是第几名?
   Běijīng dàxué zúqiú tīde zěnmeyàng? Běijīng dàxué shì dìjǐmíng?

Notes:
1. 第几名 (第幾名) [dìjǐmíng]: which place
2. 踢 [tī]: to kick

17

天气和四季
Weather and Seasons

Peonies bloom in the garden of the Forbidden City in spring. The 牡丹 *[mǔdān] (peony) is a national favorite flower in Mainland China.*

CONNECTIONS AND COMMUNITIES PREVIEW

Discuss the following questions with a partner or your class. What similarities and differences do you think there might be between Chinese culture and your own culture?

1. What is the climate of your hometown like? What type of weather do you like the most and why?

2. What are the main holidays in your culture/community? How does your community celebrate these holidays?

教学目标 OBJECTIVES

- Describe the weather

- Talk about the four seasons

- Say that something will happen in the near future

生词 VOCABULARY

核心词 Core Vocabulary

	SIMPLIFIED	TRADITIONAL	PINYIN		
1.	春天	春天	chūntiān	N.	spring
2.	久	久	jiǔ	Adv.	for a long time
3.	时间	時間	shíjiān	N.	time
4.	过	過	guò	V.	to pass
5.	放	放	fàng	V.	to have, to start (a vacation)
6.	春假	春假	chūnjià	N.	spring break
7.	气候	氣候	qìhòu	N.	climate
8.	夏	夏	xià	N.	summer
9.	秋	秋	qiū	N.	autumn
10.	冬	冬	dōng	N.	winter
11.	其中	其中	qízhōng	Prep.	among (whom, which)
12.	最	最	zuì	Adv.	(indicates the superlative degree)
13.	暖和	暖和	nuǎnhuo	Adj.	warm
14.	短	短	duǎn	Adj.	short
15.	有时候	有時候	yǒushíhou	Adv.	sometimes
16.	热	熱	rè	Adj.	hot
17.	华氏	華氏	huáshì	N.	Fahrenheit
18.	百	百	bǎi	Num.	hundred
19.	度	度	dù	N.	degree
20.	极	極	jí	Adv.	extremely

	SIMPLIFIED	TRADITIONAL	PINYIN		
21.	刮风 风	颳風 風	guāfēng fēng	V.O. N.	to blow (wind) wind
22.	下雨 雨	下雨 雨	xiàyǔ yǔ	V.O. N.	to rain rain
23.	冷	冷	lěng	Adj.	cold
24.	下雪 雪	下雪 雪	xiàxuě xuě	V.O. N.	to snow snow
25.	见面 面	見面 面	jiànmiàn miàn	V.O. N.	to meet each other face

专名 Proper Nouns

	SIMPLIFIED	TRADITIONAL	PINYIN		
1.	小玲	小玲	Xiǎolíng	N.	(name) Xiaoling

补充词 Supplementary Vocabulary

	SIMPLIFIED	TRADITIONAL	PINYIN		
1.	放假	放假	fàngjià	V.O.	to have a holiday or vacation
2.	寒假	寒假	hánjià	N.	winter vacation
3.	暑假	暑假	shǔjià	N.	summer vacation
4.	假期	假期	jiàqī	N.	vacation
5.	四季	四季	sìjì	N.	four seasons
6.	天气	天氣	tiānqì	N.	weather
7.	晴	晴	qíng	Adj.	clear, sunny
8.	阴	陰	yīn	Adj.	cloudy, overcast
9.	凉	涼	liáng	Adj.	cool

SIMPLIFIED	TRADITIONAL	PINYIN		
10. 摄氏	攝氏	shèshì	N.	Celsius, Centigrade
11. 长	長	cháng	Adj.	long
12. 气温	氣溫	qìwēn	N.	temperature

语文知识 LANGUAGE LINK

Read and listen to the following sentence patterns. These patterns use vocabulary, expressions, and grammar that you will study in more detail in this lesson. After reading the sentence patterns, read and listen to the Language in Use section that follows.

句型 Sentence Patterns

A: 春天就要来了。
Chūntiān jiùyào lái le.

B: 太好了！我们快要放春假了。
Tài hǎo le! Wǒmen kuàiyào fàng chūnjià le.

A: 春夏秋冬，其中你最喜欢哪一个？
Chūn xià qiū dōng, qízhōng nǐ zuì xǐhuān nǎ yíge?

B: 我最喜欢春天。你呢？
Wǒ zuì xǐhuān chūntiān. Nǐ ne?

A: 这儿的夏天热不热？
Zhèr de xiàtiān rèburè?

B: 这儿的夏天热极了！
Zhèr de xiàtiān rè jí le!

🔊 **课文 Language in Use: 春天就要来了!**

小玲,
Xiǎolíng,

好久不见!
Hǎojiǔ bújiàn!

你现在怎么样? 时间过得
Nǐ xiànzài zěnmeyàng? Shíjiān guòde

<table>
<tr><td>**好久不见** [hǎojiǔ bújiàn]</td></tr>
<tr><td>好久不见 is a common phrase meaning "long time no see." It is usually used by acquaintances to greet each other when they haven't seen each other for a while.</td></tr>
</table>

真快, 春天就要来了, 我们也快要
zhēnkuài, chūntiān jiùyào lái le, wǒmen yě kuàiyào

放春假了。
fàng chūnjià le.

我们这儿的气候春夏秋冬都有。
Wǒmen zhèr de qìhòu chūn xià qiū dōng dōuyǒu.

其中我最喜欢春天, 很暖和,
Qízhōng wǒ zuì xǐhuān chūntiān, hěn nuǎnhuo,

可是很短。夏天有时候很热,
kěshì hěnduǎn. Xiàtiān yǒushíhou hěn rè,

最热的时候, 会到华氏一百度,
zuì rè de shíhou, huì dào huáshì yìbǎi dù,

热极了。秋天有时候会刮风、下雨。
rè jí le. Qiūtiān yǒushíhou huì guāfēng, xiàyǔ.

这儿的冬天非常冷, 常常
Zhèr de dōngtiān fēicháng lěng, chángcháng

下雪。
xiàxuě.

<table>
<tr><td>**和** [hé/huo]</td></tr>
<tr><td>When 和 is pronounced as [hé] (or [hàn], in Taiwan), it means "and." When used in 暖和, it is pronounced as [huo].</td></tr>
</table>

<table>
<tr><td>**华氏** [huáshì]</td></tr>
<tr><td>华氏 refers to the Fahrenheit system. 摄氏 [shèshì] refers to the Celsius system, which is used in Mainland China, Taiwan, and Hong Kong.</td></tr>
</table>

<table>
<tr><td>**The Verb 刮** [guā]</td></tr>
<tr><td>The verb 刮 has two traditional forms: 刮 and 颳. In traditional forms, 颳風 [guāfēng] "blowing wind" can also be written as 刮風 [guāfēng]. The difference between the two forms is that while 颳 is only used in the context of blowing wind, 刮 as a verb can have several meanings, including "to blow (wind)," "to pare," "to shave," or "to scrape."

刮大风 [guā dàfēng] (a large wind is blowing)
刮胡子 [guā húzi] (to shave)
刮掉 [guādiào] (to scrape off)</td></tr>
</table>

放春假的时候我想去你那儿玩玩，
Fàng chūnjià de shíhou wǒ xiǎng qù nǐ nàr wánwan,

我们很快就要见面了！
wǒmen hěnkuài jiùyào jiànmiàn le!

祝　　好!
Zhù　　Hǎo!

大中
Dàzhōng

二〇一〇年三月十日
èr líng yī líng nián sān yuè shí rì

语法 GRAMMAR

I. 就要/快要......了

Both 就要 [jiùyào] ...... 了 [le] and 快要 [kuàiyào] ...... 了 [le] are patterns that are used to indicate that a certain action or event is about to happen.

春天就要来了。　　　　　　Spring is coming soon.
Chūntiān jiùyào lái le.

我们快要见面了。　　　　　We are going to see each other soon.
Wǒmen kuàiyào jiànmiàn le.

> **>>Try it!** With a partner, practice creating sentences with 就要......了 or 快要......了.

1. 学校 _____ 放春假 ___ 。
   Xuéxiào _____ fàng chūnjià ____ .

2. 我们这儿很冷! 冬天 _____ 来 ___ !
   Wǒmen zhèr hěnlěng! Dōngtiān _____ lái ____ !

3. 我 _____ 去中国 ___ 。
   Wǒ _____ qù Zhōngguó ____ .

4. 姐姐今年 _____ 二十一岁 ___ 。
   Jiějie jīnnián _____ èrshíyī suì ____ .

II. 最

最 [zuì], "the most," is used for the superlative. It occurs before a verb or an adjective.

我最喜欢秋天。   I like autumn the most.
Wǒ zuì xǐhuān qiūtiān.

他游泳游得最快。   He is the fastest swimmer.
Tā yóuyǒng yóude zuì kuài.

她最好看。   She is the prettiest.
Tā zuì hǎokàn.

>> **Try it!**   **With a partner, take turns completing the following sentences with 最 and your own ideas.**

1. 我最喜欢吃 _____ 。
   Wǒ zuì xǐhuān chī _____ .

2. 我 ___ 想去 _____ 。
   Wǒ ___ xiǎng qù _____ .

3. 冬天是 _____ 的时候。
   Dōngtiān shì _____ de shíhòu.

4. 他开车开得 _____ 。
   Tā kāichē kāi de _____ .

III. Adjective + 极了

极了 [jíle] is an intensifier. It occurs after an adjective to indicate a very high degree of the adjective.

热极了!   It is extremely hot!
Rè jí le!

冷极了!   It is extremely cold!
Lěng jí le!

我忙极了!   I am extremely busy!
Wǒ máng jí le!

晚会好极了! The party went very well!
Wǎnhuì hǎo jí le!

>>**Try it!**   With a partner, complete the following sentences with 极了, adjectives, or your own ideas.

1. 妈妈做的蛋糕好吃 ＿＿＿ ！
   Māma zuòde dàngāo hǎochī ＿＿＿ !

2. 妹妹穿的衣服都 ＿＿＿ 极了！
   Mèimei chuānde yīfu dōu ＿＿＿ jí le!

3. ＿＿＿＿ 快极了！
   ＿＿＿＿ kuài jí le!

4. ＿＿＿ 热极了！
   ＿＿＿ rè jí le!

🔊 补充课文 SUPPLEMENTARY PRACTICE

Read the following dialogue. Then listen and repeat.

小玲： 喂，大中，是你吗？

大中： 小玲啊[1]，是我。好久不见，你现在怎么样？

小玲： 还不错。时间过得真快，现在是三月，我们就要放春假了。

大中： 是啊，春天就要来了，我们这儿的天气也快要暖和了。

小玲： 我们这儿很暖和。今天是华氏六十二度，听说[2]明天要到七十度。

大中： 真的吗？那太好了！我们这儿今天还是三十五度。这儿冬天很长[3]，也很冷，还常常下雪。我们的秋天很美[4]，也很舒服[5]，不太冷，也不太热，可是太短了。

小玲： 我们这儿春夏秋冬四季[6]分明[7]，其中我最喜欢春天，这儿的春天非常美，不常刮风、也很少下雨。冬天不太冷，可是夏天很热，有时候温度[8]会到华氏一百度，热极了。对了，放春假的时候你能来我这儿玩吗？

大中： 好啊！我也很想去看看你，我们可以一起出去[9]玩玩。

小玲： 太好了！我真高兴[10]，我们很快就要见面了！

Notes:

1. 啊 [a]: an interjection indicating recognition or agreement
2. 听说 (聽說) [tīngshuō]: "I've heard," "It's been said that . . ."
3. 长 (長) [cháng]: long
4. 美 [měi]: beautiful
5. 舒服 [shūfu]: comfortable
6. 四季 [sìjì]: four seasons
7. 分明 [fēnmíng]: distinctively different

8. 温度(溫度) [wēndù]: temperature
9. 出去 [chūqù]: to go out
10. 高兴(高興) [gāoxìng]: happy

Pinyin version:

Xiǎolíng: Wéi, Dàzhōng, shì nǐ ma?

Dàzhōng: Xiǎolíng a, shì wǒ. Hǎojiǔbújiàn, nǐ xiànzài zěnmeyàng?

Xiǎolíng: Hái búcuò. Shíjiān guòde zhēn kuài, xiànzài shì sānyuè, wǒmen jiùyào fàng chūnjià le.

Dàzhōng: Shì a, chūntiān jiùyào lái le, wǒmen zhèr de tiānqì yě kuàiyào nuǎnhuo le.

Xiǎolíng: Wǒmen zhèr hěn nuǎnhuo. Jīntiān shì huáshì liùshí èr dù, tīngshuō míngtiān yào dào qīshí dù.

Dàzhōng: Zhēnde ma? Nà tàihǎo le! Wǒmen zhèr jīntiān háishì sānshí wǔ dù. Zhèr dōngtiān hěn cháng, yě hěn lěng, hái chángcháng xiàxuě. Wǒmen de qiūtiān hěnměi, yě hěn shūfu, bú tài lěng, yě bú tài rè, kěshì tài duǎn le.

Xiǎolíng: Wǒmen zhèr chūn xià qiū dōng sìjì fēnmíng, qízhōng wǒ zuì xǐhuān chūntiān, zhèr de chūntiān fēicháng měi, bù cháng guāfēng, yě hěn shǎo xiàyǔ. Dōngtiān bú tài lěng, kěshì xiàtiān hěn rè, yǒushíhòu wēndù huì dào huáshì yìbǎi dù, rè jí le. Duì le, fàng chūnjià de shíhòu nǐ néng lái wǒ zhèr wán ma?

Dàzhōng: Hǎo a! Wǒ yě hěnxiǎng qù kànkan nǐ, wǒmen kěyǐ yìqǐ chūqù wánwan.

Xiǎolíng: Tàihǎo le! Wǒ zhēn gāoxìng, wǒmen hěnkuài jiùyào jiànmiàn le!

Read the following statements and choose whether they are true or false.

1. 小玲 and 大中 met each other yesterday.	True False
2. It is currently March.	True False
3. It snows a lot in 大中's city.	True False
4. In 小玲's city, the summers are not very hot.	True False
5. 小玲 and 大中 plan to see each other during spring break.	True False

练习 ACTIVITIES

I. Listening Exercises

17-1 Listen and choose whether the Pinyin is correct (对 [duì]) or incorrect (不对 [búduì]). If it is incorrect, write the correct Pinyin on the line. Then check your answers with a partner or the class.

1. cūntiān 对 不对 _____	2. shíjiā 对 不对 _____
3. fàngjià 对 不对 _____	4. qìhòu 对 不对 _____
5. jízhōng 对 不对 _____	6. shíhòu 对 不对 _____
7. huáshì 对 不对 _____	8. xiàoyǔ 对 不对 _____

17-2   Listen and complete the sentences. Then check your answers with a partner or the class.

1. Hěnkuài _____ kǎoshì le, wǒ máng _____ le.

2. Wǒ _____ méiyǒu huíjiā le, fàng _____ de _____ wǒ xiǎng huíjiā kànkan.

3. Běijīng de_____ chūn xià qiū dōng dōu yǒu, _____ wǒ bǐjiào xǐhuān _____ .

4. Xiānggǎng de_____ hěn _____ , yǒushíhòu fēicháng _____ , hái huì _____ , _____ .

5. _____ jiùyào lái le, _____ jiùyào _____ le.

17-3   Work in groups of three or four. Take turns reading the lines of the following poem, paying special attention to the tones and rhythm.

Zǎo Fā Báidìchéng
(Lǐ Bó/Lǐ Bái)

Zhāo cí Báidì cǎiyún jiān,

Qiānlǐ jiānglíng yírì huán.

Liǎng'àn yuánshēng tí bú zhù,

Qīngzhōu yǐ guò wàn chóng shān.

早发白帝城
(李白)

朝辞白帝彩云间，

千里江陵一日还。

两岸猿声啼不住，

轻舟已过万重山。

Departing Baidi at Dawn
(Li, Bo/Li, Bai)

At dawn I depart Baidi amid the colorful clouds,
After a day I reach Jiangling, a thousand miles away.
On the riverbanks monkey calls ring endlessly,
My little boat has already passed ten thousand mountains.

II. Character Exercises

17-4   Write the Chinese characters for the following adjectives. Then check your answers with a partner.

1. warm _____   2. hot _____   3. cold _____

4. long (time) _____   5. short _____   6. fast _____

7. slow _____   8. difficult _____   9. many _____

10. few _____   11. big _____   12. small _____

17-5 Work with a partner. Write the radical and its meaning for each of the following characters. Discuss with your partner how the radical relates to the word's meaning. (Refer to the list of radicals on page 255 for help.)

1. 热 _____
   rè

2. 冷 _____
   lěng

3. 雪 _____
   xuě

4. 冬 _____
   dōng

5. 暖 _____
   nuǎn

6. 温 _____
   wēn

III. Grammar Exercises

17-6 Look at the following example. With a partner, take turns extending the following words into phrases and then sentences. See how long you can keep extending the sentences.

Example: A: 就   jiù

           B: 就要   jiùyào

           A: 就要到了   jiùyào dào le

           B: 就要到上海了   jiùyào dào Shànghǎi le

           A: 飞机就要到上海了。   Fēijī jiùyào dào Shànghǎi le.

           B: 飞机很快就要到上海了。   Fēijī hěnkuài jiùyào dào Shànghǎi le.

1. 春	2. 久	3. 气	4. 其	5. 暖	6. 短	7. 热	8. 风
chūn	jiǔ	qì	qí	nuǎn	duǎn	rè	fēng

17-7 With a partner, take turns using words from the boxes to complete and practice the dialogues. Look carefully at the sentences to see which words fit most appropriately.

Example: A: 我们什么时候去<u>学开车</u>?
Wǒmen shénme shíhou qù <u>xué kāichē</u>?

B: 现在就要去了。
Xiànzài jiùyào qù le.

1. A: 我们什么时候
Wǒmen shénme shíhou

去 _____?
qù _____ ?

B: _____ 。

中国饭馆 Zhōngguó fànguǎn	马上¹就要去了。 Mǎshàng jiùyào qù le.
看电影 kàn diànyǐng	现在就要去了。 Xiànzài jiùyào qù le.
参加舞会 cānjiā wǔhuì	快要去了。 Kuàiyào qù le.
买衬衫 mǎi chènshān	

Note:
1. 马上(馬上) [mǎshàng]: immediately

2. A: 谁 _____ 得最 ___ ?
Shéi _____ de zuì ___ ?

B: 他 _____ 得最 ___ 。
Tā _____ de zuì ___ .

Hint: be sure to use V. (V.O.) + 得

包饺子 bāo jiǎozi	慢 màn
做蛋糕 zuò dàngāo	好 hǎo
学习 xuéxí	久 jiǔ
吃饭 chīfàn	少 shǎo

17-8 Match the beginning of each sentence to its ending. Then check your answers with a partner.

___ 1. 天气热极了，
Tiānqì rè jí le,

___ 2. 这儿的裙子都很好看，
Zhèr de qúnzi dōu hěn hǎokàn,

___ 3. 他们认识的时间很短，
Tāmen rènshi de shíjiān hěnduǎn,

___ 4. 她的中国菜做得很不错，
Tāde Zhōngguócài zuò de hěn búcuò,

___ 5. 就要放春假了，
Jiùyào fàng chūnjià le,

A. 其中我最喜欢红色的那条。
qízhōng wǒ zuì xǐhuān hóngsè de nàtiáo.

B. 有时候她会请我们去她家吃饭。
yǒushíhòu tā huì qǐng wǒmen qù tā jiā chīfàn.

C. 我想坐飞机去中国玩儿。
wǒ xiǎng zuò fēijī qù Zhōngguó wár.

D. 夏天就要到了。
xiàtiān jiùyào dào le.

E. 才不到一个月。
cái bùdào yíge yuè.

IV. Communicative Activities

17-9 In pairs, role-play the following situation.

Situation: You and your roommate are going to a party together. Your friend will arrive soon to pick you up, but your roommate is still trying to decide what to wear for the party. Your roommate asks your opinion on different clothes and asks what time your friend will arrive. Your roommate asks who will be at the party. You help your roommate pick out clothes to wear for the party, according to the weather, and suggest that you should both hurry. Your friend is arriving soon. You tell your roommate who might be at the party and that it should be fun.

Words and expressions to use:

就/快要......了
jiù/kuàiyào . . . le

应该
yīnggāi

快一点儿
kuài yìdiǎr

这件/条还是那件/条好看......
zhè jiàn/tiáo háishì nà jiàn/tiáo hǎokàn . . .

我觉得
wǒ juéde

比较/最
bǐjiào/zuì

美女/帅哥
měinǚ/shuàigē (beautiful woman/handsome guy)

热/冷/暖和
rè/lěng/nuǎnhuo

17-10 Weather report! (天气报告 [tiānqì bàogào]) With a partner, prepare a weather report to present to the class. Decide on the location, the season, and the weather for your report. Decide if there will be any extreme temperatures, if it is raining, sunny, snowing, etc., or if the weather will change soon. Give advice on activities that people may or may not be able to enjoy due to the weather. Present your weather report to the class.

Words and expressions to use:

热/冷/暖和
rè/lěng/nuǎnhuo

极了
jí le

最
zuì

非常
fēicháng

就/快要......了
jiù/kuàiyào . . . le

春/夏/秋/冬
chūn/xià/qiū/dōng

下雨/下雪/刮风
xiàyǔ/xiàxuě/guāfēng

文化知识 Culture Link

文化点滴 CULTURE NOTES

中国的主要节庆 The Main Chinese Festivals

The three main Chinese festivals are 春节 [Chūnjié] (Chinese New Year), 端午节 [Duānwǔjié] (the Dragon Boat Festival), and 中秋节 [Zhōngqiūjié] (the Mid-Autumn Festival). These festivals are celebrated on the lunar calendar dates of January 1, May 5, and August 15, respectively. As their dates are celebrated according to the Chinese lunar calendar, their corresponding Western dates vary from year to year.

Chinese New Year preparations begin well in advance and include such activities as making 年糕 [niángāo] (New Year cakes), cleaning the house, and planning the family reunion dinner. Schools have their winter break during the New Year celebration, and almost all businesses take the week off. The family reunion dinner is held on New Year's Eve, and then the New Year is welcomed by setting off fireworks. Children wear new clothes for the first day of the year and receive 红包 [hóngbāo] (red envelopes) with cash inside for good fortune. The second day of the New Year is a traditional time for married women to visit their parents and family. During the New Year holiday Chinese people also take time to visit temples, visit friends and relatives, and go sightseeing. The atmosphere of the New Year

Do you know...

- what the three main festivals in China are and when they occur?
- what "hong bao" (红包 [hóngbāo]) are and what they are used for?
- what some traditional foods are for the three main Chinese holidays?

Read and find out!

lasts until January 15th of the lunar calendar, when 元宵节 [Yuánxiāojié] (the Lantern Festival) occurs. The Lantern Festival is celebrated at night by hanging lanterns and having a lantern parade.

端午节 is also called 龙舟节 [Lóngzhōujié] (the Dragon Boat Festival). The story of this festival comes from that of a famous Chinese scholar named 屈原 [Qū Yuán] (Qu Yuan) who served the king of 楚 [Chǔ] (Chu). Though Qu Yuan was loyal and gave good advice to the king, the king didn't listen and the kingdom was destroyed. Qu Yuan was so upset by the fall of the kingdom that he took his own life by jumping into a river. Some people searched for his body in boats, beating drums to scare away the fish. Others made special treats of sticky rice wrapped in bamboo leaves (called 粽子 [zòngzi]) and threw them into the river, in hopes that the fish would eat the 粽子 instead of Qu Yuan's body. Today, Chinese people still observe these traditions during the Dragon Boat Festival by eating 粽子 and racing dragon boats.

The Mid-Autumn Festival is also sometimes called the Moon Festival. Families usually celebrate this festival by gathering together, eating 月饼 [yuèbǐng] (mooncakes)

123

round-shaped pastries), and watching the bright moon. Among the legends behind the Moon Festival are the famous stories of 嫦娥 [Cháng É], a woman who took her husband's immortality pill and flew to the moon, 吴刚 [Wú Gāng] a man who was sent by the gods to the moon to continue chopping a tree forever as punishment for his impatience, and 玉兔 [Yù Tù] (the Jade Rabbit) whose self-sacrifice inspired the gods to allow him to live forever on the moon. It is thought that all three of these figures can be seen on the moon when the moon is at its brightest in mid-autumn.

Lion dances are often performed to celebrate the Chinese New Year. What other traditions are observed during Chinese New Year?

粽子 [zòngzi] is a traditional holiday food served during the 端午节 [Duānwǔjié]. What other foods are eaten during Chinese festivals?

Discuss the following with a group or your class.

1. Do you know of any other traditional Chinese festivals besides the three mentioned in the reading? Do you know of any foods people eat or traditions people observe for these holidays?

2. Do you know any greetings that one can say during the Chinese New Year? (Hint: Turn to the Let's Go! section in Lesson 14 for some expressions.)

3. In your culture, do you have special festivals or holidays? What are some traditions and foods associated with these festivals or holidays?

趣味中文 FUN WITH CHINESE

> 雨过天晴
>
> The sun will come out again.

yǔ	guò	tiān	qíng
雨	过	天	晴
rain	pass	sky	clear, sunny

The saying 雨过天晴 literally means "the sun shines again after the rain." It is also commonly used as a metaphor to describe a situation in which troubles or hardships have been overcome and the situation has improved.

Work in small groups or with your class.

1. Practice reading the saying aloud, paying attention to the pronunciation and rhythm.

2. Which character in 雨过天晴 did you learn in this lesson? Practice using it in a few sentences.

3. Do you know of any similar sayings in other languages?

🔊 行动吧！LET'S GO!

天气预报 Weather Forecast

书文 is visiting 上海 for a week. Here is the weather forecast he found in the newspaper. Read the forecast and then answer the questions that follow.

周	天气 [tiānqì] weather	最高气温 [zuìgāo qìwēn] high temperature	最低气温 [zuìdī qìwēn] low temperature	风力 [fēnglì] wind	紫外线 [zǐwàixiàn] ultraviolet rays ● ● ● ●
周二	晴	🌡 22 度	🌡 19 度	微风[3] 〰	● 中[5]弱[6]
周三	晴	🌡 26 度	🌡 23 度	轻[4] ✓	● 中强[7]
周四	多云[2]	🌡 23 度	🌡 20 度	轻 ✓	● 弱
周五	雨	🌡 31 度	🌡 25 度	轻 ✓	● 中强
周六	雨	🌡 21 度	🌡 18 度	轻 ✓	● 弱
周日	晴	🌡 26 度	🌡 23 度	微风 〰	● 强

一周天气预报[1]

Notes:

1. 预报(預報) [yùbào]: forecast
2. 云(雲) [yún]: cloud
3. 微风(微風) [wēifēng]: breeze
4. 轻(輕) [qīng]: light, gentle
5. 中 [zhōng]: middle, medium
6. 弱 [ruò]: weak
7. 强 [qiáng]: strong

Discuss the following questions with a partner or your group.

1. 星期三书文要穿外套吗？
   Xīngqī sān Shūwén yào chuān wàitào ma?

2. 哪天要带雨伞？(带 [dài]: bring; 雨伞 [yǔsǎn]: umbrella)
   Nǎ tiān yào dài yǔsǎn?

3. 哪一天的温度最高？哪一天的温度最低？(高: high; 低: low)
   Nǎ yìtiān de wēndù zuì gāo? Nǎ yì tiān de wēndù zuì dī?

4. 星期五会有大风吗？
   Xīngqī wǔ huì yǒu dàfēng ma?

18

旅行和交通
Travel and Transportation

A new Maglev train departing from Shanghai. China has one of the largest train networks in the world, reaching almost every city and town.

CONNECTIONS AND COMMUNITIES PREVIEW

Discuss the following questions with a partner or your class. What similarities and differences do you think there might be between Chinese culture and your own culture?

1. What are the most popular/ convenient means of transportation to get around in your community?

2. Have you been to any other cities or countries? What interesting things have you noticed while traveling in other cities/countries?

教学目标 OBJECTIVES

- Describe means of transportation
- Talk about travel plans

生词 VOCABULARY

核心词 Core Vocabulary

	SIMPLIFIED	TRADITIONAL	PINYIN		
1.	火车	火車	huǒchē	N.	train
2.	旅行	旅行	lǚxíng	V.	to travel
3.	离	離	lí	V.	to be away from
4.	学校	學校	xuéxiào	N.	school
5.	远	遠	yuǎn	Adj.	far
6.	只要	只要	zhǐyào	Adv.	only
7.	分钟	分鐘	fēnzhōng	N.	minute
8.	骑	騎	qí	V.	to ride
9.	自行车	自行車	zìxíngchē	N.	bicycle
10.	公共汽车	公共汽車	gōnggòngqìchē	N.	bus
11.	走路	走路	zǒulù	V.O.	to walk
	路	路	lù	N.	road
12.	近	近	jìn	Adj.	near
13.	西部	西部	xībù	N.	the West
14.	先	先	xiān	Adv.	first
15.	风景	風景	fēngjǐng	N.	scenery
16.	船	船	chuán	N.	ship
17.	南部	南部	nánbù	N.	the South
18.	听说	聽說	tīngshuō	V.	to hear of, it is said that . . .
	听	聽	tīng	V.	to hear
19.	海边	海邊	hǎibiān	N.	seaside

	SIMPLIFIED	TRADITIONAL	PINYIN		
20.	景色	景色	jǐngsè	N.	scenery, view
21.	一共	一共	yígòng	Adv.	altogether, in all
22.	租	租	zū	V.	to rent, to hire, to lease

专名 Proper Nouns

	SIMPLIFIED	TRADITIONAL	PINYIN		
1.	季长风	季長風	Jì Chángfēng	N.	(name) Changfeng Ji
2.	白秋影	白秋影	Bái Qiūyǐng	N.	(name) Qiuying Bai
3.	加拿大	加拿大	Jiānádà	N.	Canada

补充词 Supplementary Vocabulary

	SIMPLIFIED	TRADITIONAL	PINYIN		
1.	海滩	海灘	hǎitān	N.	seashore
2.	东	東	dōng	N.	east
3.	北	北	běi	N.	north
4.	旺季	旺季	wàngjì	N.	busy season
5.	淡季	淡季	dànjì	N.	off-season
6.	单车 (脚踏车)	單車 (腳踏車)	dānchē (jiǎotàchē)	N.	bicycle
7.	汽车	汽車	qìchē	N.	car
8.	摩托车 (机车)	摩托車 (機車)	mótuōchē (jīchē)	N.	scooter, motorcycle
9.	出租汽车 (计程车)	出租汽車 (計程車)	chūzūqìchē (jìchéngchē)	N.	taxi

	SIMPLIFIED	TRADITIONAL	PINYIN		
10.	火车	火車	huǒchē	N.	train
11.	公车 (巴士)	公車 (巴士)	gōngchē (bāshì)	N.	bus
12.	车站	車站	chēzhàn	N.	stop, station
13.	捷运	捷運	jiéyùn	N.	MRT (Mass Rapid Transportation) in Taiwan
14.	地铁	地鐵	dìtiě	N.	subway
15.	马路	馬路	mǎlù	N.	road, street
16.	地下道	地下道	dìxiàdào	N.	underground walkway
17.	隧道	隧道	suìdào	N.	tunnel
18.	码头	碼頭	mǎtóu	N.	wharf, dock, pier
19.	司机	司機	sījī	N.	driver

语文知识 LANGUAGE LINK

Read and listen to the following sentence patterns. These patterns use vocabulary, expressions, and grammar that you will study in more detail in this lesson. After reading the sentence patterns, read and listen to the Language in Use section that follows.

句型 Sentence Patterns

A: 你家离学校远不远？
　　Nǐ jiā lí xuéxiào yuǎnbuyuǎn?

B: 不太远。开车只要五分钟。
　　Bú tài yuǎn. Kāichē zhǐyào wǔ fēnzhōng.

A: 你每天怎么来学校？
Nǐ měitiān zěnme lái xuéxiào?

B: 我常骑自行车，
Wǒ cháng qí zìxíngchē,

有时候坐公共汽车。
yǒushíhou zuò gōnggòng qìchē.

A: 你们怎么去旅行？
Nǐmen zěnme qù lǚxíng?

B: 我们先坐火车，然后坐船去加拿大，
Wǒmen xiān zuò huǒchē, ránhòu zuò chuán qù Jiānádà,

再从加拿大坐飞机回来。
zài cóng Jiānádà zuò fēijī huílai.

课文 Language in Use: 我们要坐火车去旅行

季长风: 秋影，你住在校外吗？离学校远不远？
Qiūyǐng, nǐ zhù zài xiàowài ma? Lí xuéxiào yuǎnbuyuǎn?

白秋影: 不太远，开车只要五分钟。
Bú tài yuǎn, kāichē zhǐyào wǔ fēnzhōng.

季长风: 你每天怎么来学校？
Nǐ měitiān zěnme lái xuéxiào?

白秋影: 我常骑自行车，下雨下雪
Wǒ cháng qí zìxíngchē, xiàyǔ xiàxuě

的时候就坐公共汽车，
de shíhou jiù zuò gōnggòng qìchē,

有时候我也走路，
yǒushíhou wǒ yě zǒulù,

可以锻炼锻炼。你呢？
kěyǐ duànlian duànlian. Nǐ ne?

自行车 [zìxíngchē]

自行车 means "bicycle." A more colloquial form used mostly in Taiwan is 脚踏车 [jiǎotàchē]. 单车 [dānchē] is also used in Mainland China and Hong Kong.

The bicycle is currently the most common means of transportation in China.

公共汽车 [gōnggòngqìchē]

公共汽车 is used to describe a public bus. In Taiwan, it is more commonly called 公车 or 巴士 [bāshì].

季长风：我住在宿舍，离学校很近，我每天走路来学校。
Wǒ zhùzài sùshè, lí xuéxiào hěnjìn, wǒ měitiān zǒulù lái xuéxiào.

白秋影：对了，这个春假你要做什么？
Duìle, zhège chūnjià nǐ yào zuò shénme?

季长风：我要跟我的室友一起去西部旅行。
Wǒ yào gēn wǒde shìyǒu yìqǐ qù xībù lǚxíng.

白秋影：你们怎么去？
Nǐmen zěnme qù?

季长风：我们想先坐火车去，
Wǒmen xiǎng xiān zuò huǒchē qù,

路上可以看看风景。
lùshang kěyǐ kànkan fēngjǐng.

路上 [lùshang]
路上 is an idiomatic expression commonly used to mean "on the way."

然后坐船去加拿大，
Ránhòu zuò chuán qù Jiānádà,

再从加拿大坐飞机回来。你呢？
zài cóng Jiānádà zuò fēijī huílai. Nǐ ne?

白秋影：我很想我爸爸、妈妈和妹妹，我要先回家。
Wǒ hěn xiǎng wǒ bàba, māma hé mèimei, wǒ yào xiān huíjiā.

然后再跟朋友开车去玩儿。
Ránhòu zài gēn péngyou kāichē qù wár.

季长风：你们要去哪儿玩儿？
Nǐmen yào qù nǎr wár?

白秋影：我们想去南部玩儿。听说那儿的海边
Wǒmen xiǎng qù nánbù wár. Tīngshuō nàr de hǎibiān

景色很美。
jǐngsè hěn měi.

季长风： 你们有几个人去？
Nǐmen yǒu jǐge rén qù?

白秋影： 我们一共有五个人去，我们想租一辆车。
Wǒmen yígòng yǒu wǔge rén qù, wǒmen xiǎng zū yíliàng chē.

语法 GRAMMAR

I. 离

The verb 离 [lí] means "to be away from." It is used in the following pattern.

A + 离 + B + adjective phrase

| 宿舍 | 离 | 学校 | 很近。 | The dorm is very close to the school. |
| Sùshè | lí | xuéxiào | hěnjìn. | |

| 中国 | 离 | 美国 | 很远。 | China is very far from the U.S. |
| Zhōngguó | lí | Měiguó | hěnyuǎn. | |

Note that while English modifiers of distance such as "very close" and "very far" are placed between the names of two places, Chinese modifiers of distance are placed at the end of the sentence, as shown in the examples above.

When using 离 in questions, note that adjective phrases, such as those with the adverb 很 are not used. In questions with 离 only the adjective is used.

宿舍离学校近吗？   Is the dorm near the school?
Sùshè lí xuéxiào jìn ma?

中国离美国远吗？   Is China far from the U.S.?
Zhōngguó lí Měiguó yuǎn ma?

>>**Try it!**   With a partner, complete the following sentences with 离 and adjective phrases. Be sure to use the correct format for any questions.

1. 图书馆 ____ 这里 _____ 。
   Túshūguǎn ____ zhèlǐ _____ .

2. 游泳池 ____ 体育馆 _____ 。
   Yóuyǒngchí ____ tǐyùguǎn _____ .

3. 韩国 ____ 日本 _____ 。
   Hánguó ____ Rìběn _____ .

4. A: 机场 ____ 你家 _____ 吗?
      Jīchǎng ____ nǐ jiā _____ ma?

   B: _____ 。

II. 先……再……然后

Both 先 [xiān] and 再 [zài] are adverbs, while 然后 [ránhòu] is a conjunction. All three words are used to show events in a sequence. When describing events in a sequence, use 先 [xiān] first and then 然后 [ránhòu] or 再 [zài].

> 我先去见老师，然后去看你。
> Wǒ xiān qù jiàn lǎoshī , ránhòu qù kàn nǐ.
> (I will first go to see the teacher and then go to see you.)

If there are more than two actions involved, another 再 or 然后 is used as well. The order can be either "先……, 再……, 然后……" or "先……, 然后……再……." For example, for the sentence "Xiaomei will go to Beijing first, then to Hong Kong, and then to Taiwan to visit her Grandma," the Chinese sentence can be either

> 小美要先去北京，再去香港，然后去台湾看奶奶。
> Xiǎoměi yào xiān qù Běijīng, zài qù Xiānggǎng, ránhòu qù Táiwān kàn nǎinai.

or 小美要先去北京，然后去香港，再去台湾看奶奶。
> Xiǎoměi yào xiān qù Běijīng, ránhòu qù Xiānggǎng, zài qù Táiwān kàn nǎinai.

> **Try it!** With a partner, complete the following with 先, 再, and 然后 to show sequences of events.

1. 妈妈说要 ＿＿ 吃饭，＿＿ 走一走 。
   Māma shuō yào ＿＿ chīfàn, ＿＿ zǒuyìzǒu.

2. 他们会 ＿＿ 去海边，＿＿ 游泳 。
   Tāmen huì ＿＿ qù hǎibiān, ＿＿ yóuyǒng.

3. 我们要 ＿＿ 吃饺子，＿＿ 吃炒饭，＿＿ 吃蛋糕 。
   Wǒmen yào ＿＿ chī jiǎozi, ＿＿ chī chǎofàn, ＿＿ chī dàngāo.

4. 今天我想 ＿＿＿＿＿， ＿＿＿＿＿ 。
   Jīntiān wǒ xiǎng ＿＿＿＿＿, ＿＿＿＿＿ .

III. 坐, 骑, and 开

The three verbs 坐 [zuò], 骑 [qí], and 开 [kāi] are used with different kinds of vehicles, as shown below:

Verb	Vehicle Used With	Translation
坐 to go by, to take, to ride in	汽车 [qìchē]	to go by car
	出租汽车 [chūzūqìchē]	to take (ride in) a taxi/cab
	公共汽车 [gōnggòngqìchē]	to take (ride in) a (public) bus
	火车 [huǒchē]	to take (ride in) a train
	飞机 [fēijī]	to take (fly in) an airplane
	船 [chuán]	to go by boat
骑 to ride	自行车 [zìxíngchē]	to ride a bike
	马 [mǎ]	to ride a horse
开 to drive	车 [chē]	to drive a car

补充课文 SUPPLEMENTARY PRACTICE

Read the following passage. Then listen and repeat.

四月十日　　　星期六

今天下午我去看大中。他住在校外的公寓[1]里，他的公寓离学校很近，开车只要五分钟。他常骑自行车去学校，有时候也走路，他觉得走路可以锻炼身体[2]，下雨下雪的时候他就坐公共汽车。

大中跟他的室友正在上网。因为[3]他们想在放假的时候一起去西部旅行，所以[4]他们想看看网上[5]有没有便宜[6]的火车票和飞机票。他们想先坐飞机到旧金山[7]，在旧金山玩两天，然后坐火车去西雅图[8]，在路上可以看看风景，在西雅图玩两天，然后坐船去加拿大，再从加拿大坐飞机回来。

我好久没有回家了，我很想家。放假以后我要先回家，看看我的爸爸、妈妈和妹妹，然后我想租一辆车，跟我的朋友一起开车去南部的海边玩儿。听说那儿的风景很美[9]，还可以游泳、晒太阳[10]，所以我想在那儿好好地玩儿几[11]天再回家。

Notes:

1. 公寓 [gōngyù]: apartment
2. 身体(身體) [shēntǐ]: body
3. 因为(因為) [yīnwèi]: because
4. 所以 [suǒyǐ]: therefore, so
5. 网上(網上) [wǎngshàng]: online
6. 便宜 [piányi]: (pronounced as [piányí] in Taiwan): inexpensive, cheap
7. 旧金山(舊金山) [Jiùjīnshān]: San Francisco
8. 西雅图(西雅圖) [Xīyǎtú]: Seattle
9. 美 [měi]: beautiful
10. 晒太阳(曬太陽) [shài tàiyáng]: to get a suntan
11. 几(幾) [jǐ]: an indefinite pronoun used here to indicate "some"

Pinyin version:

Sìyuè Shírì　　　Xīngqī Liù

Jīntiān xiàwǔ wǒ qù kàn Dàzhōng. Tā zhùzài xiàowàide gōngyù lǐ, tāde gōngyù lí xuéxiào hěnjìn, kāichē zhǐyào wǔ fēnzhōng. Tā cháng qí zìxíngchē qù xuéxiào, yǒushíhòu yě zǒulù, tā juéde zǒulù kěyǐ duànliàn shēntǐ, xiàyǔ xiàxuě de shíhòu tā jiù zuò gōnggòngqìchē.

Dàzhōng gēn tāde shìyǒu zhèngzài shàngwǎng. Yīnwèi tāmen xiǎng zài fàngjià de shíhòu yìqǐ qù xībù lǚxíng, suǒyǐ tāmen xiǎng kànkan wǎngshàng yǒuméiyǒu piányi de huǒchēpiào hé fēijīpiào. Tāmen xiǎng xiān zuò fēijī dào Jiùjīnshān, zài Jiùjīnshān wán liǎngtiān, ránhòu zuò huǒchē qù Xīyǎtú, zài lùshang kěyǐ kànkan fēngjǐng, zài Xīyǎtú wán liǎngtiān, ránhòu zuò chuán qù Jiānádà, zài cóng Jiānádà zuò fēijī huílái.

Wǒ hǎojiǔ méiyǒu huíjiā le, wǒ hěn xiǎng jiā. Fàngjià yǐhòu wǒ yào xiān huíjiā, kànkan wǒde bàba, māma hé mèimei, ránhòu wǒ xiǎng zū yíliàng chē, gēn wǒde péngyou yìqǐ kāichē qù nánbù de hǎibiān wár. Tīngshuō nàr de fēngjǐng hěnměi, hái kěyǐ yóuyǒng, shài tàiyáng, suǒyǐ wǒ xiǎng zài nàr hǎohǎo de wár jǐtiān zài huíjiā.

Choose the correct answer for the following questions.

1. Where does 大中 live?

   a. on campus   b. in an apartment by himself off campus
   c. at home with his family   d. with a roommate off campus

2. How does he get to school when the weather is bad?

   a. by bus   b. by train
   c. on foot   d. by bike

3. How do they plan to go from San Francisco to Seattle?

   a. by plane   b. by car
   c. by boat   d. by train

4. Where does he want to go after seeing his family?

   a. the North   b. the South
   c. Canada   d. San Francisco

5. He will _____ to go to the beach.

   a. take a flight   b. take the bus
   c. rent a car   d. go by boat

练习 ACTIVITIES

I. Listening Exercises

18-1 Listen and complete the sentences with the correct Pinyin. Then check your answers with a partner or the class.

   1. Wǒ měitiān _____ lái xuéxiào.

   2. _____ wǒ yào gēn péngyou _____ qù wár.

   3. Wǒmen xià _____ xià _____ de shíhou zuò _____ qù xuéxiào.

   4. Dào _____ qù kěyǐ kàndào hěnduō _____ .

   5. Wǒ tèbié xǐhuān _____ de _____ .

18-2 Work in groups of three or four. Take turns reading the lines of the following poem, paying special attention to the tones and rhythm.

Tí Xīlínbì
(Sū Shì)

Héng kàn chéng lǐng cè chéng fēng,

Yuǎn jìn gāo dī gè bùtóng.

Bù shí Lúshān zhēn miànmù,

Zhǐ yuán shēn zài cǐ shān zhōng.

题西林壁
(苏轼)

横看成岭侧成峰，

远近高低各不同。

不识庐山真面目，

只缘身在此山中。

Inscription on the Xilin Cliff
(Su, Shi)

Looking across we see a mountain ridge and sidewise, a peak,
The cliff looks very different from all directions.
The true face of Mount Lushan cannot be seen,
Just because you are in the mountains.

II. Character Exercises

18-3 Work with a partner. Write the radical and its meaning for the following characters. Discuss how the radical relates to the meaning of the character. (Refer to the list of radicals on page 255 for help.)

1. 海 _____

2. 远 _____

3. 骑 _____

4. 路 _____

5. 船 _____

18-4 Write the Chinese characters for the following phrases. Then check your answers with a partner.

1. zhù zài xiào wài _____

2. zū yíliàng chē _____

3. zuò fēijī _____

4. qí zìxíngchē _____

5. zuò chuán qù wán _____

6. xībù fēngjǐng _____

7. lí xuéxiào hěnjìn _____

8. kāichē lǚxíng _____

9. hǎibiān jǐngsè _____

10. zuò huǒchē _____

III. Grammar Exercises

18-5 Look at the following example. With a partner, take turns extending the words below into phrases and then sentences. See how long you can keep extending the sentences.

Example: A: 火   huǒ

B: 火车   huǒchē

A: 坐火车   zuò huǒchē

B: 从上海坐火车   cóng Shànghǎi zuò huǒchē

A: 从上海坐火车去北京
cóng Shànghǎi zuò huǒchē qù Běijīng

B: 我们想从上海坐火车去北京玩儿 。
Wǒmen xiǎng cóng Shànghǎi zuò huǒchē qù Běijīng wár.

1. 旅   2. 离   3. 远   4. 只   5. 骑   6. 汽   7. 景   8. 船
   lǚ   lí   yuǎn   zhǐ   qí   qì   jǐng   chuán

18-6 With a partner, take turns using words from the boxes to complete and practice the dialogues. Look carefully at the sentences to see which words fit most appropriately.

Example: A: 机场离体育馆远吗?
Jīchǎng lí tǐyùguǎn yuǎn ma?

B: 机场离体育馆远极了!
Jīchǎng lí tǐyùguǎn yuǎn jí le!

1. A: _____ 离 _____ 远吗?
_____ lí _____ yuǎn ma?

B: _____ 离 _____ _____ 。
_____ lí _____ _____ .

他家	海边	很远
tā jiā	hǎibiān	hěnyuǎn
停车场	图书馆	很近
tíngchēchǎng	túshūguǎn	hěnjìn
加拿大	日本	远极了
Jiānádà	Rìběn	yuǎn jí le

2. A: 你会做什么？
   Nǐ huì zuò shénme?

   B: 我会先＿＿＿＿，
   Wǒ huì xiān ＿＿＿＿，

   再＿＿＿，然后＿＿＿。
   zài ＿＿＿, ránhòu ＿＿＿.

去健身房 qù jiànshēnfáng	去游泳池 qù yóuyǒngchí	洗澡 xǐzǎo
去图书馆 qù túshūguǎn	去书店 qù shūdiàn	回宿舍 huí sùshè
喝汤 hētāng	吃饺子 chī jiǎozi	吃蛋糕 chī dàngāo

18-7 With a partner, complete the dialogues with 坐 [zuò], 开 [kāi], 骑 [qí], or 租 [zū].

1. A: 你每天怎么来学校？
   Nǐ měitiān zěnme lái xuéxiào?

   B: 我每天 ＿＿ 公共汽车来学校。
   Wǒ měitiān ＿＿＿ gōnggòngqìchē lái xuéxiào.

2. A: 你 ＿＿ 车 ＿＿ 得快吗？
   Nǐ ＿＿＿ chē ＿＿＿ de kuài ma?

   B: 我 ＿＿ 车 ＿＿ 得不太快！
   Wǒ ＿＿＿ chē ＿＿＿ de bútàikuài!

3. A: 他会不会 ＿＿ 自行车？
   Tā huìbuhuì ＿＿＿ zìxíngchē?

   B: 会。他 ＿＿ 得很好。
   Huì. Tā ＿＿＿ de hěnhǎo.

4. A: 你觉得 ＿＿ 火车怎么样？
   Nǐ juéde ＿＿＿ huǒchē zěnmeyàng?

   B: ＿＿ 火车比较慢，可是很舒服。
   ＿＿＿ huǒchē bǐjiào màn, kěshì hěn shūfu.

5. A: 我们可以用你的车吗？
   Wǒmen kěyǐ yòng nǐde chē ma?

   B: 我的车太小了。你们应该 ＿＿ 一辆面包车[1]。
   Wǒde chē tài xiǎo le. Nǐmen yīnggāi ＿＿＿ yíliàng miànbāochē.

Note:

1. 面包车(麵包車) [miànbāochē]: van (van is called 休旅车 [xiūlǚchē] in Taiwan)

IV. Communicative Activities

18-8 In pairs, role-play the following situation.

> *Situation:* In one month, your summer vacation will begin. You and your friend discuss a trip you may take to Canada. Your discussion should include the length of the trip, the route, mode of travel, weather, what you will do there, and anything else you can think of.

18-9 Ask the travel agent! In small groups, role-play travel agents giving a presentation on a vacation destination.

Each group chooses a different travel destination. Think of a travel itinerary and work out a detailed plan, including where to go, when to go, how to go, and why. Present the travel plan to the class as if you were travel agents trying to promote the location and the trip. Try to refer to your or someone else's past travel experiences when presenting the information. After each group presents their travel information, the class can take a vote on where they would like to travel!

Words and expressions to use:

离......远/近	先......然后......再......	东/南/西/北部
lí . . . yuǎn/jìn,	xiān . . . ránhòu . . . zài . . .	dōng/nán/xī/běi bù
只要	一共	听说
zhǐyào	yígòng	tīngshuō
觉得	风景/景色	坐(船/火车/飞机/etc.)
juéde	fēngjǐng/jǐngsè	zuò (chuán/huǒchē/fēijī/etc.)
海边	租	
hǎibiān	zū	

文化知识 Culture Link

文化点滴 CULTURE NOTES

在中国：坐火车或者坐船旅行 Traveling by Train or Boat in China

China is the third largest country in the world, behind Russia and Canada, and has a great variety in its geographic terrain, a rich cultural history, and many unique places with their own traditions, cuisines, and local culture. Among the many travel options sightseers have in China, taking a train or a boat are quite popular and have historical traditions.

Train travel is popular not only among tourists but among locals as well. Though early railroads were constructed in the late 1890s and early 1900s, they weren't developed heavily until after the establishment of the People's Republic of China in 1949. From the 1950s to 1970s, the railroad was greatly expanded and today almost every province is connected to the railroad network of more than 76,000 km total track length. The most recent additions to China's railroad system are the high-altitude railway to Tibet 青藏铁路 [Qīngzàng tiělù] (the Qinghai-Tibet railway) and the high-speed modern train using magnetic levitation (the Maglev) in Shanghai (上海磁浮 [Shànghǎi cífú]).

One popular train trip for tourists is the historic 丝绸之路 [Sīchóuzhīlù] (Silk Road) in northern China. Traveling toward the west, the route starts in 西安 [Xī'ān] (Xi'an), known for its famous

Do you know...

- how common train or boat travel is in China?
- what the longest river in China is?
- what some popular train trips or boat trips are in China?

Read and find out!

兵马俑 [bīngmǎ yǒng] (Terracotta Warriors), and passes through cities such as 兰州 [Lánzhōu] (Lanzhou), the transportation hub of the Silk Road, and 敦煌 [Dūnhuáng] (Dunhuang), with nearby ancient grottoes and Buddha caves. The train continues past mountains and desert landscape as it approaches the western cities 乌鲁木齐 [Wūlǔmùqí] (Urumqi) and 喀什 [Kāshí] (Kashgar), known for their exotic bazaars and Islamic mosques.

Traveling by boat in China is not as common as traveling by train. The waterways today are used mainly for commercial and cargo shipping, fishing, and tourist cruises. There are some boat services used by locals to islands such as 海南岛 [Hǎinándǎo] (Hainan island) in the south or 普陀山 [Pǔtuóshān] (Putuoshan) in the 东海 [Dōnghǎi] (East China Sea). For tourists, popular boat trips are the 长江 [Chángjiāng] (Yangtze River) cruise, the 漓江 [Líjiāng] (Li River) cruise, and traveling the 大运河 [Dàyùnhé] (Grand Canal) from 杭州 [Hángzhōu] (Hangzhou) to 苏州 [Sūzhōu] (Suzhou) on a tourist boat.

The Yangtze River is China's longest river and winds like a dragon through central China. People have traveled this river since ancient times and many people today take the Yangtze River to visit the 三峡 [Sānxiá] (Three Gorges). In southern China, the Li River passes by dramatic mountain scenery in 桂林 [Guìlín] (Guilin). The beautiful scenery is world-famous, causing many people to quote the well-known saying "桂林山水甲天下" [Guìlín shānshuǐ jiǎ tiānxià], which means "Guilin's mountains and waters are the best under heaven." The other popular boat trip travels through a section of the Grand Canal, which is the longest constructed waterway and was a major transportation channel for past dynasties. Travelers on the Grand Canal and other rivers can catch glimpses of river towns, ancient bridges, and local customs.

A train makes a stop at Yinchuan in Ningxia province, a town along the historic Silk Road. What other sights might one see traveling by train along the Silk Road?

Traveling by boat along the Li River in Guilin. What are some other popular boat trips in China?

Discuss the following with a group or your class.

1. Are there any famous or popular train/boat journeys in your country or city? Where do they go? What can you see on these trips?
2. Which place in China do you want to visit the most? Do you prefer visiting natural or historical sites?

趣味中文 FUN WITH CHINESE

读万卷书，行万里路。

Read ten thousand books, travel ten thousand miles.

dú	wàn	juàn	shū,	xíng	wàn	lǐ	lù.
读	万	卷	书，	行	万	里	路。
read	ten thousand	roll	book,	travel	ten thousand	mile	road.

This saying has three possible interpretations, as described below:

Interpretation 1: Having read ten thousand rolls of books, (is as good as) having traveled ten thousand miles.

Interpretation 2: To read ten thousand rolls of books is not as good as traveling ten thousand miles — seeing is believing.

Interpretation 3: One should seek opportunities to read and travel as much as possible.

Work in small groups or with your class.

1. Practice reading the saying aloud, paying attention to the pronunciation and rhythm.
2. Which interpretation do you agree with? Why?

🔊 行动吧! LET'S GO!

火车站 Train Station

正明 would like to see China by train. He is in the Beijing train station looking at the information board. Look at the picture and the schedule below. Then with a partner or in small groups, answer the questions that follow.

本站¹各次列车²候车地点³

车次 [chēcì] train number	终点站 [zhōngdiǎn zhàn] destination	开点 [kāidiǎn] departure time	候车地点 [hòuchē dìdiǎn] departure platform
K285	烟台⁴	16:36	二楼⁸第二候车室⁹
T47	齐齐哈尔⁵	17:30	二楼第四候车室
Z23	哈尔滨⁶	17:40	二楼第四候车室
T549	天津⁷	17:50	二楼中央¹⁰检票厅¹¹

Notes:

1. 本站 [běnzhàn]: This station
2. 各次列车(各次列車) [gècì lièchē]: train timetables
3. 候车地点(候車地點) [hòuchē dìdiǎn]: departure platforms
4. 烟台(煙台) [Yāntái]: a city in northeast China
5. 齐齐哈尔(齊齊哈爾) [Qíqíhā'ěr]: a city in northwest China
6. 哈尔滨(哈爾濱) [Hā'ěrbīn]: a city in northern China
7. 天津 [Tiānjīn]: a city in northern China
8. 二楼(二樓) [èrlóu]: the second floor
9. 候车室(候車室) [hòuchēshì]: waiting room
10. 中央 [zhōngyāng]: center
11. 检票厅(檢票廳) [jiǎnpiào tīng]: ticket office

Answer the following questions with your partner or group.

1. 去天津要坐几点的火车？在几楼等？

   Qù Tiānjīn yào zuò jǐdiǎn de huǒchē? Zài jǐlóu děng?

2. 想去齐齐哈尔的人应该坐哪个火车？什么车次？

   Xiǎng qù Qíqíhā'ěr de rén yīnggāi zuò nǎge huǒchē? Shénme chēcì?

3. 可以从这儿到哈尔滨吗？什么车次？

   Kěyǐ cóng zhèr dào Hā'ěrbīn ma? Shénme chēcì?

4. 正明要去烟台。现在是四点。他会不会等很久？

   Zhèngmíng yào qù Yāntái. Xiànzài shì sìdiǎn. Tā huìbuhuì děng hěnjiǔ?

   他要等多久？

   Tā yào děng duōjiǔ?

复习 Review

LESSON 15 TO LESSON 18

I. Conversation Review

1. Work with a partner. Take turns asking questions to find out the following information about each other.

Example: A: 你走路走得快不快？

             Nǐ zǒulù zǒude kuàibukuài?

        B: 我走路走得不快。我走得非常慢！

             Wǒ zǒulù zǒude bú kuài. Wǒ zǒude fēicháng màn!

- 家里有哪些房间？(哪些 [nǎxiē]: which)
  Jiālǐ yǒu nǎxiē fángjiān?

- 最常用的房间是哪一个房间？
  Zuì chángyòngde fángjiān shì nǎyíge fángjiān?

- 卧室的对面是什么？
  Wòshì de duìmiàn shì shénme?

- 书桌上面常常有什么？
  Shūzhuō shàngmiàn chángcháng yǒu shénme?

- 书包里边有什么？(书包 [shūbāo]: bookbag)
  Shūbāo lǐbiān yǒu shénme?

- 游泳游得怎么样？
  Yóuyǒng yóude zěnmeyàng?

- 走路走得快不快？
  Zǒulù zǒude kuàibukuài?

- 会不会打篮球？打得好不好？
  Huìbuhuì dǎ lánqiú? Dǎde hǎobuhǎo?

- 每天怎么去学校？坐公车还是开车去？骑自行车还是走路去？
  Měitiān zěnme qù xuéxiào? Zuò gōngchē háishì kāichē qù? Qí zìxíngchē háishì zǒulù qù?

- 喜欢坐飞机吗？喜欢去旅行吗？下次想去哪儿旅行？
  Xǐhuān zuò fēijī ma? Xǐhuān qù lǚxíng ma? Xiàcì xiǎng qù nǎr lǚxíng?

- 春夏秋冬四季，比较喜欢哪一个？为什么？(四季 [sìjì]: four seasons; 为什么 [wèishénme]: why)

  Chūnxiàqiūdōng sìjì, bǐjiào xǐhuān nǎ yíge? Wèishénme?

- 下雨的时候，常做什么？

  Xiàyǔ de shíhòu, cháng zuò shénme?

- 会不会包饺子？想试试吗？

  Huìbuhuì bāo jiǎozi? Xiǎng shìshi ma?

2. With a partner, role-play the following situation.

Situation: You and your friend are training for an international sports competition being held in China. One of you will compete in basketball, and one in swimming. The competition will be in summer, which is coming up soon.

Be sure to talk about the following:

- How your current skills are and how you plan to improve
- Where you go to practice, on campus or in town
- What the weather will be like in China
- If the hotel will be far from the gymnasium and swimming pool
- How you will get around in China to go to the sports event

Words and expressions to use:

在/有/是 with position words	V./V.O. + 得	就要/快要......了
zài/yǒu/shì	děi	jiùyào/kuàiyào . . . le

比较/最	......极了	离......远/近	先......再......然后
bǐjiào/zuì	. . . jíle	lí . . . yuǎn/jìn	xiān . . . zài . . . ránhòu

II. Writing and Character Review

1. Radical practice game. Form groups of three or four. Write the following radicals on separate squares of paper.

人(亻)   日   广   辵(辶)   水(氵)

Turn all the squares over so that the blank sides face up. As you take turns, flip over one of the paper squares and say a character you have learned that has the same radical in it. Write the character on a piece of paper so the group can keep track of which characters have already been said. (Once a character has been said, it cannot be used again.)

Keep playing until you have come up with as many characters as you can think of. Then compare your group's list with other groups. Did you find all the same characters for the radicals?

2. Race to write! Divide into two teams. Spend a few minutes looking over the characters you have learned in Lessons 15–18. Then your teacher will call out a word, and a member from each team will race to write the character on the board. The first person who writes the word correctly will gain a point for their team. See which team can get 10 points first!

3. Label the town map below. Use the following list of places and decide where you would like each place to be on your map. Then write the Chinese characters for each place name on the map.

Places: airport, parking lot, university, dorm, park, swimming pool, gym, Chinese restaurant, movie theater, clothing store (饭馆 [fànguǎn]: restaurant; 电影院 [diànyǐngyuàn]: movie theater; 服饰店 [fúshìdiàn]: clothing store)

1 _____   2 _____   3 _____   4 _____

5 _____   6 _____   7 _____   8 _____

9 _____   10 _____

III. Comprehensive Review

1. Work with a partner. Take turns describing the locations of places on your town map while your partner draws them on a blank sheet of paper. Use position words in your directions.

Position words:

前边	后边	左边	右边	上边	下边
qiánbiān	hòubiān	zuǒbiān	yòubiān	shàngbiān	xiàbiān

里边	外边	旁边	中间	对面
lǐbiān	wàibiān	pángbiān	zhōngjiān	duìmiàn

2. Bicycle race! With a partner or in small groups, read the following race report. The report is divided into parts. Read the first part and answer the questions with your partner or group. Then move on to the other parts.

Part 1:

田进、常风和秋影要参加一个自行车比赛[1]。常风骑得很快，秋影骑得最快，田进骑得最慢。

田进和秋影是从国外来的。田进是坐火车去的。秋影是坐飞机去的。常风住得很近，他骑自行车去。秋影的飞机会晚点[2]。比赛就要开始[3]了！

Notes:
1. 比赛(比賽) [bǐsài]: competition, race
2. 晚点(晚點) [wǎndiǎn]: delay
3. 开始(開始) [kāishǐ]: to start

Tián Jìn, Cháng Fēng hé Qiūyǐng yào cānjiā yíge zìxíngchē bǐsài. Cháng Fēng qíde hěn kuài, Qiūyǐng qíde zuìkuài, Tián Jìn qíde zuì màn.

Tián Jìn hé Qiūyǐng shì cóng guówài láide. Tián Jìn shì zuò huǒchē qù de. Qiūyǐng shì zuò fēijī qù de. Cháng Fēng zhùde hěnjìn, tā qí zìxíngchē qù. Qiūyǐng de fēijī huì wǎndiǎn. Bǐsài jiùyào kāishǐ le!

Discuss the following questions for Part 1.

- 谁离比赛地点最远？最近呢？
  Shéi lí bǐsài dìdiǎn zuì yuǎn? Zuì jìn ne?

- 你们觉得谁可以参加开始的比赛？为什么？
  Nǐmen juéde shéi kěyǐ cānjiā kāishǐde bǐsài? Wèishénme?

- 你们觉得谁会赢？ (赢 [yíng]: to win)
  Nǐmen juéde shéi huì yíng?

Part 2:

田进和常风都到了，他们开始骑。常风骑得比较快，很快就在前面。田进骑得比较慢，在后面。秋影现在才到，她开始骑自行车了。

天气不太好，下雨。常风觉得太冷了，也有一点儿累，想停一下。秋影还离前面的人很远，可是她骑得非常快，快极了！常风还在休息[1]，田进快要超过[2]常风了！

Notes:
1. 休息 [xiūxi]: to rest
2. 超过(超過) [chāoguò]: to pass

Tián Jìn hé Cháng Fēng dōu dào le, tāmen kāishǐ qí. Cháng Fēng qíde bǐjiào kuài, hěn kuài jiù zài qiánmiàn. Tián Jìn qíde bǐjiào màn, zài hòumiàn. Qiūyǐng xiànzài cái dào, tā kāishǐ qí zìxíngchē le.

Tiānqì bútài hǎo, xiàyǔ. Cháng Fēng juéde tài lěng le, yěyǒu yìdiǎr lèi, xiǎng tíng yíxià. Qiūyǐng hái lí qiánmiànde rén hěnyuǎn, kěshì tā qíde fēicháng kuài, kuàijí le! Cháng Fēng hái zài xiūxi, Tián Jìn kuàiyào chāoguò Cháng Fēng le!

Discuss the following questions for Part 2.

- 你们觉得常风离田进远吗？常风离秋影远不远？
  Nǐmen juéde Cháng Fēng lí Tián Jìn yuǎn ma? Cháng Fēng lí Qiūyǐng yuǎnbuyuǎn?

- 谁在最后面？谁在中间？谁在前面？
  Shéi zài zuì hòumiàn? Shéi zài zhōngjiān? Shéi zài qiánmiàn?

- 现在你们觉得谁会赢？为什么？
  Xiànzài nǐmen juéde shéi huì yíng? Wèishénme?

Part 3:

> 大家都在等……谁会赢呢？有人快要到了！第一¹是……田进！第二²是秋影！常风呢？常风在哪儿？
>
> *Notes:*
> 1. 第一 [dì yī]: first
> 2. 第二 [dì èr]: second
>
> Dàjiā dōuzài děng . . . Shéi huì yíng ne? Yǒurén kuàiyào dào le! Dì yī shì . . . Tián Jìn! Dì èr shì Qiūyǐng! Cháng Fēng ne? Cháng Fēng zài nǎr?

Discuss the following questions for Part 3.

- 田进是不是最慢？为什么是第一？
  Tián Jìn shìbushì zuì màn? Wèishénme shì dì yī?

- 你们觉得秋影骑得怎么样？
  Nǐmen juéde Qiūyǐng qíde zěnmeyàng?

- 你们觉得常风正在做什么？他在哪儿？
  Nǐmen juéde Cháng Fēng zhèngzài zuòshénme? Tā zài nǎr?

19

健康和医药
Health and Medicine

China does not have family doctors as many other countries do. In China, most doctors work in hospitals and see patients there.

CONNECTIONS AND COMMUNITIES PREVIEW

Discuss the following questions with a partner or your class. What similarities and differences do you think there might be between Chinese culture and your own culture?

1. Does your culture have any traditional medicine practices? Have you heard of traditional medicine in other cultures? What are some common remedies?

2. What is the medical system like in your culture or community? Is medical care affordable?

教学目标 OBJECTIVES

- Describe the symptoms of an illness
- Describe something that has happened
- Describe a changing situation

生词 VOCABULARY

核心词 Core Vocabulary

SIMPLIFIED	TRADITIONAL	PINYIN		
1. 感冒	感冒	gǎnmào	N. V.	cold, flu to catch a cold
2. 饿	餓	è	Adj. V.	hungry to starve
3. 怎么了	怎麼了	zěnmele		what happened, what's wrong
4. 好像	好像	hǎoxiàng	V.	to be like, to seem
5. 舒服	舒服	shūfu	Adj.	comfortable, well
6. 头疼 头 疼	頭疼 頭 疼	tóuténg tóu téng	V. N. V.	to have a headache head to ache
7. 发烧	發燒	fāshāo	V.O.	to have a fever
8. 咳嗽	咳嗽	késòu	V.	to cough
9. 生病 病	生病 病	shēngbìng bìng	V.O. N.	to fall ill, to get sick disease, illness
10. 考试	考試	kǎoshì	N.	exam
11. 复习	復習	fùxí	V.	to review
12. 所以	所以	suǒyǐ	Conj.	therefore, consequently
13. 医生	醫生	yīshēng	N.	doctor
14. 吃药 药	吃藥 藥	chīyào yào	V.O. N.	to take medicine medicine
15. 地	地	de	Part.	(attached to an adjective to transform the whole unit into an adverb when preceding a verb; describes manner of the verb)
16. 休息	休息	xiūxi	V.	to rest

SIMPLIFIED	TRADITIONAL	PINYIN		
17. 准备	準備	zhǔnbèi	V.	to prepare
18. 笔记	筆記	bǐjì	N.	notes
19. 感谢	感謝	gǎnxiè	V.	to thank, to be grateful
20. 送	送	sòng	V.	to deliver, to escort, to see off

专名 Proper Nouns

SIMPLIFIED	TRADITIONAL	PINYIN		
1. 欧阳迎	歐陽迎	Ōuyáng Yíng	N.	(name) Ying Ouyang
2. 唐志信	唐志信	Táng Zhìxìn	N.	(name) Zhixin Tang

补充词 Supplementary Vocabulary

SIMPLIFIED	TRADITIONAL	PINYIN		
1. 医务室 (医护室)	醫務室 (醫護室)	yīwùshì (yīhùshì)	N.	medical exam room
2. 打针	打針	dǎzhēn	V.O.	to give or receive an injection
3. 护士	護士	hùshi	N.	nurse
4. 医院	醫院	yīyuàn	N.	hospital
5. 诊所	診所	zhěnsuǒ	N.	clinic
6. 严重	嚴重	yánzhòng	Adj.	severe
7. 厉害	厲害	lìhài	Adj.	severely, very much
8. 体温	體溫	tǐwēn	N.	body temperature
9. 流感 (流行性感冒)	流感 (流行性感冒)	liúgǎn (liúxíngxìng gǎnmào)	N.	flu
10. 预防针	預防針	yùfángzhēn	N.	immunization shot
11. 流感疫苗	流感疫苗	liúgǎn yìmiáo	N.	flu shot

语文知识 LANGUAGE LINK

Read and listen to the following sentence patterns. These patterns use vocabulary, expressions, and grammar that you will study in more detail in this lesson. After reading the sentence patterns, read and listen to the Language in Use section that follows.

句型 Sentence Patterns

A: 你吃饭了吗？
   Nǐ chīfàn le ma?

B: 还没有呢。我不饿。
   Hái méiyǒu ne. Wǒ bú è.

A: 你怎么了？好像不舒服。
   Nǐ zěnme le? Hǎoxiàng bù shūfu.

B: 我感冒了。我头疼发烧，
   Wǒ gǎnmào le. Wǒ tóuténg fāshāo,

   还有一点儿咳嗽。
   háiyǒu yìdiǎr késòu.

A: 你看医生了没有？
   Nǐ kàn yīshēng le méiyǒu?

B: 看了。我也吃药了。
   Kàn le. Wǒ yě chīyào le.

   可是还没有好呢。
   Kěshì hái méiyǒu hǎo ne.

🔊 课文 Language in Use: 我感冒了

唐志信： 欧阳迎，你吃饭了吗？
Ōuyáng Yíng, nǐ chīfàn le ma?

欧阳迎： 还没有呢。我不饿。
Hái méiyǒu ne. Wǒ bú è.

唐志信： 你怎么了？好像不舒服。
Nǐ zěnme le? Hǎoxiàng bù shūfu.

欧阳迎： 我感冒了。我头疼发烧，还有一点儿咳嗽。
Wǒ gǎnmào le. Wǒ tóuténg fāshāo, háiyǒu yìdiǎr késòu.

唐志信： 你怎么生病了呢？
Nǐ zěnme shēngbìng le ne?

生病了 [shēngbìngle]
"I am sick" can be expressed by either 我病了 (I am sick) or 我生病了 (literally, "I produced sickness").

欧阳迎： 这几天我有很多考试，
Zhè jǐtiān wǒ yǒu hěnduō kǎoshì,

每天都在复习，睡觉睡得
měitiān dōu zài fùxí, shuìjiào shuì de

太少，所以就病了。
tàishǎo, suǒyǐ jiù bìng le.

这几天 [zhè jǐtiān]
几 can also be used to mean "a few." In this context it does not function as a question word. 这几天 means "the past few days."

唐志信： 你看医生了没有？
Nǐ kàn yīshēng le méiyǒu?

欧阳迎： 看了。我也吃药了。可是还没有好呢。
Kàn le. Wǒ yě chīyào le. Kěshì hái méiyǒu hǎo ne.

唐志信： 你应该在家好好地休息。
Nǐ yīnggāi zàijiā hǎohǎode xiūxi.

不应该来上课。
Bù yīnggāi lái shàngkè.

地 [dì, de]
地 [dì] can be a noun meaning "ground, earth" as in 地图 and 地址. 地 [de] can also be attached to an adjective to transform the whole unit into an adverb preceding a verb, such as 慢慢地 (slowly).

欧阳迎： 你说得很对。可是我有很多考试。
Nǐ shuō de hěnduì. Kěshì wǒ yǒu hěnduō kǎoshì.

我得好好地准备。
Wǒ děi hǎohǎode zhǔnbèi.

唐志信： 这是我上课的笔记，借给你看看。
Zhèshì wǒ shàngkè de bǐjì, jiè gěi nǐ kànkan.

欧阳迎： 非常感谢！好吧，我现在就回家休息。
Fēicháng gǎnxiè! Hǎo ba, wǒ xiànzài jiù huíjiā xiūxi.

唐志信： 好，我开车送你回去。
Hǎo, wǒ kāichē sòng nǐ huíqù.

你得好好地睡觉。
Nǐ děi hǎohǎode shuìjiào.

送 [sòng]

送 as a verb has different meanings: "to give," "to deliver," or "to escort." In Lesson 14, 送 was used to mean "to give." Here it means "to deliver" or "to escort" somebody.

语法 GRAMMAR

I. Expressing Completed Action with 了

了 [le] is a particle that is normally used to show the completion of an action or to show that a situation or state has changed.

To indicate a completed action, 了 is placed after the verb or at the end of the sentence. Note that 了 must *not* be regarded as a "past tense" marker. In Chinese, to indicate the present, past, and future tenses, time words, such as 去年, 现在, and 明天, are often used instead.

To use 了 in questions and in giving positive answers or statements, the following patterns are used.

Use	Pattern	Example
In questions	• V. + 了吗	你看医生了吗？ Nǐ kàn yīshēng le ma? (Did you go to see a doctor?)
	• V. + 了没有	你看医生了没有？ Nǐ kàn yīshēng le méiyǒu? (Did you go to see a doctor?)
In positive answers	• V. + 了	我看了医生。 Wǒ kàn le yīshēng. (I saw the doctor.)
	• sentence ends with 了	我看医生了。 Wǒ kàn yīshēng le. (I saw the doctor.)

Note that when 了 is followed by a quantified object or amount, it is preferable to place 了 after the verb and before the quantified amount.

我看了两次医生。 I saw the doctor twice.
Wǒ kàn le liǎngcì yīshēng.

我买了三本中文书。 I bought three Chinese books.
Wǒ mǎi le sānběn Zhōngwén shū.

When giving negative answers, 了 is not used, since a negative answer means that the action was not completed. To answer a question in the negative, instead of 了, we use the following patterns.

Use	Pattern	Example
To indicate that an action did not take place	没有 + V.	我没有参加旅行。 Wǒ méiyǒu cānjiā lǚxíng. (I didn't go on the trip.)
To indicate a planned action (the action has not taken place yet)	还没有……呢	我们还没有去旅行呢。 Wǒmen hái méiyǒu qù lǚxíng ne. (We haven't gone on our trip yet.)

>>**Try it!** With a partner, complete the following dialogues with 了 in questions and positive answers. Be sure to use the correct form for any negative answers.

1. A: 他回来 ___ 吗?
   Tā huílai ___ ma?

   B: 回来 ___ 。
   Huílai ___ .

2. A: 你吃饭 ___ 没有?
   Nǐ chīfàn ___ méiyǒu?

   B: 我还没有 ___ 。
   Wǒ hái méiyǒu ___ .

3. A: 你买 ___ 几瓶可乐?
   Nǐ mǎi ___ jǐpíng kělè?

   B: 我买 ___ 两瓶。
   Wǒ mǎi ___ liǎngpíng.

4. A: 你给他笔记 ___ 吗?
   Nǐ gěi tā bǐjì ___ ma?

   B: _____ 。

II. Expressing a Change of State/New Situation with 了

了 [le] is also used at the end of a sentence to express that a situation has changed.

Pattern	Example	
Sentence ends with 了	你会开车了吗? Nǐ huì kāichē le ma?	Do you know how to drive now?
	我会开车了。 Wǒ huì kāichē le.	I can drive now.
不……V. 了 (not doing V. any more)	她不跳舞[1]了。 Tā bú tiàowǔ le.	She does not dance any more.
	他不喝咖啡[2]了。 Tā bùhē kāfēi le.	He does not drink coffee any more.

Notes:
1. 跳舞 [tiàowǔ]: to dance
2. 咖啡 [kāfēi]: coffee

Note that when 了 is placed at the end of a sentence, it may be an indication of a completed action or of a situation that has changed. The meaning of the sentence would thus be determined by the context of the sentence. For example, the sentence "他去北京了" [Tā qù Běijīng le] could mean "He went to Beijing" (i.e., he did the action) or "He is in Beijing now" (but wasn't before), depending on the context.

>>**Try it!** With a partner, complete the following sentences with 了 to show a change of state or situation.

1. 春天到 ___ 。
   Chūntiān dào ___ .

2. 哥哥不学工程 ___ 。
   Gēge bù xué gōngchéng ___ .

3. 我不跟他一起住 ___ 。
   Wǒ bù gēn tā yìqǐ zhù ___ .

4. 现在我会开手排挡的车 ___ 。
   Xiànzài wǒ huì kāi shǒupáidǎng de chē ___ .

III. 的, 得, and 地

的, 得, and 地 are all pronounced as [de] but have different grammatical functions, as shown below.

Pattern	Features	Examples
的 + N.	Used with a noun to show possessive case or as a structural 的 to describe the noun that follows	我的车 wǒde chē (my car) 这是上课的笔记。 Zhèshì shàngkè de bǐjì. (These are the notes taken in class.) 他是一个认真[1]的学生。 Tā shì yíge rènzhēn de xuéshēng. (He is a conscientious student.)
V. + 得 + Adv. + Adj.	Used in degree of complement sentences to show how an action is performed	他说中文说得很快。 Tā shuō Zhōngwén shuō de hěn kuài. (He speaks Chinese very fast.) 他写汉字写得很认真。 Tā xiě Hànzì xiě de hěn rènzhēn. (He writes the characters conscientiously.)
Adj. + 地 + V.	Used in combination with an adjective, or preceding a verb to indicate the attitude or manner of an action; similar to *-ly* in English	他慢慢地吃饭。 Tā mànmànde chīfàn. (He eats slowly.) 他认真地写汉字。 Tā rènzhēnde xiě Hànzì. (He writes the characters conscientiously.)

Note:

1. 认真(認真) [rènzhēn]: conscientious, serious

补充课文 SUPPLEMENTARY PRACTICE

Read the following passage. Then listen and repeat.

　　欧阳迎是我中文班[1]的同学。她今天好像有点儿不舒服，脸色[2]不太好，中饭[3]也没有吃，她头疼发烧，还有一点儿咳嗽，原来[4]她感冒了。

　　这几天她太忙了。这个学期她有六门课，每门课都有很多功课，前几天刚[5]写了两个报告[6]，还有几个考试。每天晚上她都要开夜车[7]，复习到很晚，睡觉睡得太少，每天只睡三个小时。这两天天气也不太好，一会儿热，一会儿冷，常常下雨，所以她感冒了。

　　我想送她去医院[8]，她说前天看了医生，也吃了点儿药。医生说她应该在家里好好地休息，多喝水，多睡觉。可是她得准备考试，没有时间休息，所以她的病好得很慢。我觉得她应该好好地睡一觉。我告诉[9]她我有上课的笔记，可以借给她。然后我就开车送她回家了，我也为她买了一些[10]吃的东西[11]，她非常感谢。

Notes:
1. 班 [bān]: class
2. 脸色(臉色) [liǎnsè]: complexion
3. 中饭(中飯) [zhōngfàn]: lunch
4. 原来 [yuánlái]: it turned out that . . . , apparently
5. 刚(剛) [gāng]: just now
6. 报告(報告) [bàogào]: report
7. 开夜车(開夜車) [kāiyèchē]: to burn the midnight oil
8. 医院(醫院) [yīyuàn]: hospital
9. 告诉(告訴) [gàosu]: to tell
10. 一些 [yìxiē]: some
11. 东西(東西) [dōngxi]: things

Pinyin version:

Ōuyáng Yíng shì wǒ Zhōngwén bān de tóngxué. Tā jīntiān hǎoxiàng yǒudiǎr bùshūfu, liǎnsè bútài hǎo, zhōngfàn yě méiyǒu chī, tā tóuténg fāshāo, háiyǒu yìdiǎr késòu, yuánlái tā gǎnmào le.

　　Zhèjǐtiān tā tài máng le. Zhège xuéqī tā yǒu liùmén kè, měimén kè dōu yǒu hěnduō gōngkè, qiánjǐtiān gāng xiě le liǎngge bàogào, háiyǒu jǐge kǎoshì. Měitiān wǎnshang tā dōu yào kāiyèchē, fùxí dào hěnwǎn, shuìjiào shuìde tàishǎo, měitiān zhǐshuì sānge xiǎoshí. Zhè liǎngtiān tiānqì yě bú tài hǎo, yíhuèr rè, yíhuèr lěng, chángcháng xiàyǔ, suǒyǐ tā gǎnmào le.

Wǒ xiǎng sòng tā qù yīyuàn, tā shuō qiántiān kànle yīshēng, yě chīle diǎr yào. Yīshēng shuō tā yīnggāi zài jiālǐ hǎohǎode xiūxi, duō hēshuǐ, duō shuìjiào. Kěshì tā děi zhǔnbèi kǎoshì, méiyǒu shíjiān xiūxi, suǒyǐ tāde bìng hǎo de hěn màn. Wǒ juéde tā yīnggāi hǎohǎode shuìyíjiào. Wǒ gàosu tā wǒ yǒu shàngkè de bǐjì, kěyǐ jiè gěi tā. Ránhòu wǒ jiù kāichē sòng tā huíjiā le, wǒ yě wèi tā mǎi le yìxiē chīde dōngxi, tā fēicháng gǎnxiè.

Write the answers to the following questions in Chinese.

1. 欧阳迎怎么了? _____
   Ōuyáng Yíng zěnmele?

2. 她吃中饭了没有? _____
   Tā chī zhōngfàn le méiyǒu?

3. 这个学期她有几门课?_____
   Zhège xuéqī tā yǒu jǐmén kè?

4. 她看医生了没有? _____
   Tā kàn yīshēng le méiyǒu?

5. 她吃药了没有? _____
   Tā chīyào le méiyǒu?

练习 ACTIVITIES

I. Listening Exercises

19-1 Listen and choose whether the Pinyin is correct (对 [duì]) or incorrect (不对 [búduì]). If it is incorrect, write the correct Pinyin on the line. Then check your answers with a partner or the class.

1. gǎngmào   对   不对 _____   2. shūfù   对   不对 _____

3. tóuténg   对   不对 _____   4. késuò   对   不对 _____

5. kǒushì   对   不对 _____   6. shēngbìn   对   不对 _____

7. zhǔnbèi   对   不对 _____   8. yìshēng   对   不对 _____

19-2 Work in groups of three or four. Take turns reading the lines of the following poem, paying special attention to the tones and rhythm.

Xún Yǐnzhě Bú Yù (Jiǎ Dǎo)	寻隐者不遇 (贾岛)	Seeking the Hermit but Not Found (Jia, Dao)
Sōng xià wèn tóngzǐ,	松下问童子，	Beneath a pine tree I inquire of a young servant,
Yán shī cǎi yào qù.	言师采药去 。	He says his master has gone to collect herbs.
Zhǐ zài cǐ shān zhōng,	只在此山中，	He is somewhere in the mountains,
Yún shēn bù zhī chù.	云深不知处 。	But I can't tell where he is for the clouds are so deep.

II. Character Exercises

19-3 Match each Chinese word with its English meaning. Then check your answers with a partner.

____ 1. 感谢   a. to catch a cold
     gǎnxiè

____ 2. 感冒   b. comfortable
     gǎnmào

____ 3. 舒服   c. to review
     shūfu

____ 4. 复习   d. exam
     fùxí

____ 5. 咳嗽   e. to be grateful
     késòu

____ 6. 考试   f. to cough
     kǎoshì

19-4 Work with a partner. Write the radical and its meaning for each of the following characters. Write other characters you have learned with the same radical. (Refer to the list of radicals on page 255 for help.)

1. 咳   _____

2. 药   _____

3. 饿   _____

4. 笔   _____

5. 病   _____

III. Grammar Exercises

19-5 Look at the following example. With a partner, take turns extending the words below into phrases and then sentences. See how long you can keep extending the sentences.

Example:

A: 好好地   hǎohǎode

B: 好好地休息   hǎohǎode xiūxi

A: 应该好好地休息   yīnggāi hǎohǎode xiūxi

B: 应该在家好好地休息   yīnggāi zài jiā hǎohǎode xiūxi

A: 我觉得你应该在家好好地休息。
   Wǒ juéde nǐ yīnggāi zài jiā hǎohǎode xiūxi.

1. 感	2. 饿	3. 舒	4. 疼	5. 咳	6. 考	7. 准	8. 记
gǎn	è	shū	téng	ké	kǎo	zhǔn	jì

19-6 With a partner, take turns using words from the boxes to complete and practice the dialogues. Look carefully at the sentences to see which words fit most appropriately.

Example: A: 你<u>看球赛</u>了吗?   Nǐ <u>kàn qiúsài</u> le ma?

　　　　　　 B: 我还没有<u>看球赛</u>呢。   Wǒ hái méiyǒu <u>kàn qiúsài</u> ne.

1. A: 你 _____ 了吗?
     Nǐ _____ le ma?

   B: 我还没有 _____ 呢。
     Wǒ hái méiyou _____ ne.

跟朋友见面 gēn péngyou jiànmiàn	坐火车去玩儿 zuò huǒchē qù wár
去机场接妹妹 qù jīchǎng jiē mèimei	买衬衫 mǎi chènshān
参加晚会 cānjiā wǎnhuì	

2. A: 你 ___ _____ 了没有？

   Nǐ ___ _____ le méiyǒu?

   B: 我 ___ _____ 了。

   Wǒ ___ _____ le.

知道 zhīdào	怎么去机场 zěnme qù jīchǎng
看 kàn	电影 diànyǐng
打 dǎ	篮球 lánqiú
包 bāo	饺子 jiǎozi

3. A: ___ ___ 了吗？

   ___ ___ le ma?

   B: _____ 没有 _____。

   _____ méiyǒu _____ .

王老师 Wáng lǎoshī	教第二十课 jiāo dì èrshí kè
你爸爸 nǐ bàba	去北京 qù Běijīng
你的朋友 nǐde péngyou	吃药 chīyào
妹妹 mèimei	睡觉 shuìjiào

19-7 Complete the sentences with 的, 得, or 地. Then check your answers with a partner.

1. 那个穿红色裙子____人是我妹妹。

   Nàge chuān hóngsè qúnzi _____ rén shì wǒ mèimei.

2. 他很快____吃了饭。

   Tā hěnkuài _____ chīle fàn.

3. 这个公园____景色很美。

   Zhège gōngyuán _____ jǐngsè hěnměi.

4. 我的德文说____不好。

   Wǒde Déwén shuō _____ bùhǎo.

5. 考试以后我要好好____玩玩。

   Kǎoshì yǐhòu wǒ yào hǎohǎo _____ wánwan.

6. 小文走路走____很慢。

   Xiǎowén zǒulù zǒu _____ hěnmàn.

IV. Communicative Activities

19-8 In pairs, role-play the following situation.

Situation: Your friend has been practicing for a basketball game for several days. Because the weather has been cold and they didn't wear warm clothes after practice, they caught a cold. After greeting your friend you notice they don't look well and ask what's wrong. Your friend tells you about their symptoms and how they got sick. You show your concern and make suggestions.

Words and expressions to use:

怎么了	是不是……	……了吗/了没有?
zěnme le	shìbushì . . .	. . . le ma/le méiyǒu?

打球……得	没有很快……穿	暖和	衣服	所以
dǎqiú . . . de	méiyǒu hěnkuài . . . chuān	nuǎnhuo	yīfu	suǒyǐ

药	医生	想……	应该……
yào	yīshēng	xiǎng . . .	yīnggāi . . .

19-9 In pairs, role-play the following situation.

Situation: You have just returned home from a Chinese classmate's party, and your roommate asks about it. You tell your roommate about your new Chinese friends and things that you did at the party. Your roommate asks questions to find out more details.

Words and expressions to use:

参加	介绍	中国学生	认识
cānjiā	jièshào	Zhōngguó xuésheng	rènshi

中国朋友	中国菜	包
Zhōngguó péngyou	Zhōngguó cài	bāo

饺子	电影	了
jiǎozi	diànyǐng	le

文化知识 Culture Link

文化点滴 CULTURE NOTES

中医中药 Traditional Chinese Medicine

Traditional Chinese medicine is a unique scientific system. In ancient times, medicinal herbs and treatments were the only means to treat illnesses and protect the health of Chinese people. Today, many Chinese people still have faith in traditional Chinese medicine, even though Western medicine has been practiced in China for years. Some believe that traditional Chinese medicine can provide a permanent cure for an illness, while Western medicine merely alleviates the symptoms.

At the root of traditional Chinese medicine are the ancient Daoist theories of 阴阳 [yīnyáng] (yin-yang) and 五行 [wǔxíng] (wu xing: the five elements). The Daoist yin-yang concept says that yang predominates during the day and turns into yin after dark. The human body is regarded as the universe in miniature, thus excitement brings the human body towards the state of yang, while too much of the yin energy inevitably results in depression. When the yin and yang elements in a person's body are well balanced, the person is in good health. A person falls sick when the balance is disrupted.

Like the concept of 阴阳, the concept of 五行 is also a fundamental theoretical premise of traditional Chinese medicine. The five vital organs (the heart, liver, spleen, lungs, and kidneys) are each seen as corresponding to one of the five elements of earth, wood, metal, fire, and water. The five vital organs function in an interlocked and interconnected relationship and it is believed that a pathological change in any of the vital organs will affect the health and functioning of the other organs.

A traditional Chinese doctor will examine a patient's tongue and take their pulse. These will all show signs of any imbalances that may be present in the five organs or in the 阴阳 energy in the body. To treat any imbalances, common remedies include 针灸 [zhēnjiǔ] (acupuncture), moxibustion, 拔罐 [báguàn] (cupping), 推拿 [tuīná] (tuina) (a form of Chinese acupressure massage), and herbal medicine.

Herbal medicine has been used by Chinese people to treat diseases for over 4,000 years. The traditional Chinese pharmacy consists mainly of natural medicinal materials such as plants, animal parts, and minerals of medicinal value. So far, specialists in traditional Chinese medicine have identified the therapeutic value of more than 8,000 medicinal

Do you know...

- what is believed to happen when the balance of yin and yang in the human body is disrupted?
- what some common Chinese medicine treatments are?
- what some ways to maintain health in daily habits are?

Read and find out!

materials, of which over 6,000 are plants. Traditional medicines are often ground to a powder for oral consumption or boiled to produce a medicinal broth. In addition to herbal medicine, 食疗 [shíliáo] (the treatment of diseases by food) is often suggested as a remedy.

Traditional Chinese medicine attaches great importance to the prevention of diseases, and Chinese people believe prevention is better than cure. To live a long, healthy life, Chinese people are faithful to traditional ways of maintaining physical and mental soundness which include leading a regulated life, eating the type of diet that best fits their body conditions, and doing exercises such as 气功 [qìgōng] (*qigong*) or 太极拳 [tàijíquán] (*tai chi*), which allow the body and mind to regulate their functions and balance the body's energy or qi.

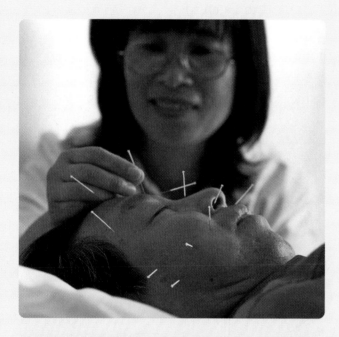

Acupuncture is popular in China. What are some other common treatments in traditional Chinese medicine?

Herbs used in Chinese medicine are weighed and got ready at a hospital. How are these medicines usually prepared and taken?

Discuss the following with a group or your class.

1. Have you ever tried Chinese medicine? What did you try? If you haven't tried Chinese medicine, would you like to?
2. Traditional Chinese medicine emphasizes the prevention of disease. Do you think Western medicine also stresses prevention?

趣味中文 FUN WITH CHINESE

良药苦口，忠言逆耳。

Good medicine is often bitter; good advice is often hard to listen to.

liáng	yào	kǔ	kǒu,	zhōng	yán	nì	ěr.
良	药	苦	口，	忠	言	逆	耳。
good	medicine	bitter	mouth,	loyal; sincere	words	against	ear.

Work in small groups or with your class.

1. Practice reading the saying aloud, paying attention to the pronunciation and rhythm.
2. Which character in 良药苦口，忠言逆耳 did you learn in this lesson? Practice using it in a sentence.
3. Do you believe the saying is true? Why or why not?

行动吧！ LET'S GO!

传统中医补品 Traditional Chinese Supplements

王中 bought some traditional Chinese herbal medicine as gifts for his relatives. Read the information and instructions for the herbal medicine below.

燕窝[1]和人参[2]的功用[3]：
养身补气[4]，提高[5]免疫力[6]

燕窝食用[7]时间：
早晚各一次[8](早饭前一个小时，
晚饭前一个小时)

人参食用时间：
下午，放入[9]开水[10]冲服[11]

Notes:

1. 燕窝(燕窩) [yànwō]: swallow's nest
2. 人参(人參) [rénshēn]: ginseng
3. 功用 [gōngyòng]: function
4. 养身补气(養身補氣) [yǎngshēn bǔqì]: to support the body and enhance "qi"
5. 提高 [tígāo]: to enhance, to promote
6. 免疫力 [miǎnyìlì]: immune system
7. 食用 [shíyòng]: written form for "eating 吃" and "taking medicine"
8. 各一次 [gè yícì]: once each time
9. 放入 [fàngrù]: to put in
10. 开水(開水) [kāishuǐ]: boiling water
11. 冲服(沖服) [chōngfú]: to steep then drink

Discuss the following questions with your partner or group.

1. 王中买了什么？有什么功用？

   Wáng Zhōng mǎi le shénme? Yǒu shénmen gōngyòng?

2. 燕窝应该什么时候吃？

   Yànwō yīnggāi shénme shíhòu chī?

3. 人参要怎么吃？

   Rénshēn yào zěnme chī?

4. 你想不想试试中药？(中药: Chinese medicine)

   Nǐ xiǎngbuxiǎng shìshi zhōngyào?

20

看房和租房
Renting an Apartment

Apartment buildings in Hong Kong. In cities in China, most people live in apartment buildings. Only the very rich live in luxury single family homes.

教学目标 OBJECTIVES

- Talk about renting an apartment
- Indicate the direction of a movement
- Specify the effects or results of an action on an object

CONNECTIONS AND COMMUNITIES PREVIEW

Discuss the following questions with a partner or your class. What similarities and differences do you think there might be between Chinese culture and your own culture?

1. Are there many different kinds of housing in your community? What are some of these different kinds?

2. Have you ever been to any other countries? What was the housing situation like there?

生词 VOCABULARY

核心词 Core Vocabulary

SIMPLIFIED	TRADITIONAL	PINYIN		
1. 把	把	bǎ	Prep.	(introduces the object of a verb)
2. 带来	帶來	dàilái	V.C.	to bring over
3. 啊	啊	a	Int.	(used at the end of a sentence to indicate surprise)
4. 搬	搬	bān	V.	to move
5. 出	出	chū	V.	to be out
6. 出去	出去	chūqù	V.C.	to go out
7. 过来	過來	guòlái	V.C.	to come over
8. 做饭	做飯	zuòfàn	V.O.	to cook
9. 没关系	沒關係	méiguānxi		no problem
10. 以前	以前	yǐqián	N.	before, previously
11. 但是	但是	dànshì	Conj.	but
12. 女朋友	女朋友	nǚpéngyou	N.	girlfriend
13. 必须	必須	bìxū	Aux.	must
14. 第一天 第	第一天 第	dìyītiān dì	N.	first day (prefix indicating an ordinal number)
15. 付	付	fù	V.	to pay
16. 房租	房租	fángzū	N.	rent
17. 楼上	樓上	lóushàng	N.	upstairs
18. 马上	馬上	mǎshàng	Adv.	immediately

专名 Proper Nouns

	SIMPLIFIED	TRADITIONAL	PINYIN		
1.	常天	常天	Cháng Tiān	N.	(name) Tian Chang
2.	夏中明	夏中明	Xià Zhōngmíng	N.	(name) Zhongming Xia
3.	谢进学	謝進學	Xiè Jìnxué	N.	(name) Jinxue Xie

补充词 Supplementary Vocabulary

	SIMPLIFIED	TRADITIONAL	PINYIN		
1.	搬家	搬家	bānjiā	V.O.	to move
2.	房东	房東	fángdōng	N.	landlord
3.	房客	房客	fángkè	N.	tenant
4.	签约	簽約	qiānyuē	V.O.	to sign a contract
5.	租屋	租屋	zūwū	V.O.	to rent a house
6.	楼下	樓下	lóuxià	N.	downstairs

语文知识 LANGUAGE LINK

Read and listen to the following sentence patterns. These patterns use vocabulary, expressions, and grammar that you will study in more detail in this lesson. After reading the sentence patterns, read and listen to the Language in Use section that follows.

句型 Sentence Patterns

A: 我把我朋友带来了。
Wǒ bǎ wǒ péngyou dàilái le.

B: 快请他进来。
Kuài qǐng tā jìnlái.

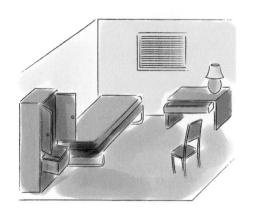

A: 我们这儿有一个人搬出去了，
Wǒmen zhèr yǒu yíge rén bān chūqù le,

你要不要搬进来？
nǐ yàobuyào bān jìnlái?

B: 太好了！我可以先过去看看吗？
Tài hǎo le! Wǒ kěyǐ xiān guòqù kànkan ma?

A: 请你下来帮我把桌子
Qǐng nǐ xiàlái bāng wǒ bǎ zhuōzi

搬上去，好吗？
bān shàngqu, hǎo ma?

B: 好的，我马上下去。
Hǎo de, wǒ mǎshàng xiàqu.

🔊 **课文 Language in Use: 我把小谢带来了……**

常天：   中明，我回来了。我把车开回来了，
Zhōngmíng, wǒ huílái le. Wǒ bǎ chē kāi huílái le,

还把小谢也带来了。
hái bǎ Xiǎo Xiè yě dàilái le.

> **小谢 [Xiǎo Xiè]**
>
> 小谢 literally means "Little Xie." In Mainland China, 老 (old) or 小 (young, little) is often used with a person's surname as a nickname. It is a friendly and informal way to address familiar people who are older or younger than you.

夏中明：   是小谢啊！快请他进来。
Shì Xiǎo Xiè a! Kuài qǐng tā jìnlái.

谢进学：   我听说你们这儿有一个人
Wǒ tīngshuō nǐmen zhèr yǒu yíge rén

搬出去了，我想搬进来，所以过来看看。
bān chūqù le, wǒ xiǎng bān jìnlái, suǒyǐ guòlái kànkan.

常天：   你不想住宿舍了，是不是？
Nǐ bù xiǎng zhù sùshè le, shìbushì?

谢进学： 是的。宿舍太小了，我想搬出来住。
Shìde. Sùshè tài xiǎo le, wǒ xiǎng bān chūlái zhù.

这儿可以不可以做饭？
Zhèr kěyǐbukěyǐ zuòfàn?

夏中明： 可以，我们有厨房。
Kěyǐ, wǒmen yǒu chúfáng.

谢进学： 太好了！我很喜欢做饭。搬出来以后就可以常常
Tài hǎo le! Wǒ hěn xǐhuān zuòfàn. Bān chūlái yǐhòu jiù kěyǐ chángcháng

做饭了。
zuòfàn le.

夏中明： 你有狗吗？我们这儿不能有狗。
Nǐ yǒu gǒu ma? Wǒmen zhèr bùnéng yǒu gǒu.

谢进学： 没关系。以前我有一只狗，
Méiguānxi. Yǐqián wǒ yǒu yìzhī gǒu,

但是宿舍不可以有狗，所以
dànshì sùshè bù kěyǐ yǒu gǒu, suǒyǐ

但是 [dànshì] and 可是 [kěshì]
Both 但是 and 可是 mean "but." 可是 is more colloquial than 但是.

我把我的狗给我女朋友了。
wǒ bǎ wǒde gǒu gěi wǒ nǚpéngyou le.

现在没有狗了。
Xiànzài méiyǒu gǒu le.

夏中明： 还有，我们必须在每个月的
Háiyǒu, wǒmen bìxū zài měigeyuè de

必须 [bìxū]
必须 is an optative verb meaning "must" or "be required to."

第一天付房租。
dìyītiān fù fángzū.

第 [dì]
第 is used for ordinal numbers. For example, 第一 (the first), 第二 (the second), 第三 (the third), and 第一天 (the first day).

谢进学： 没问题！
Méi wèntí!

常天： 喂，小谢，我在楼上，你要不要上来
Wèi, Xiǎo Xiè, wǒ zài lóushàng, nǐ yàobuyào shànglái

看看？中明，你把小谢带上来看看吧。
kànkan? Zhōngmíng, nǐ bǎ Xiǎo Xiè dài shànglái kànkan ba.

夏中明： 常天，我们现在还不能上去。
　　　　Chángtiān, wǒmen xiànzài hái bùnéng shàngqu.

　　　　你得先下来帮我把这张桌子搬上去。
　　　　Nǐ děi xiān xiàlái bāng wǒ bǎ zhèzhang zhuōzi bān shàngqu.

常天：　 好的，我马上下去。
　　　　Hǎode, wǒ mǎshàng xiàqu.

语法 GRAMMAR

I. Simple Directional Complements (Simple DC)

A directional complement is a word or phrase that follows a motion or action verb to show the direction of the motion or action. There are two kinds of directional complements: simple directional complements and compound directional complements.

Simple directional complements are formed by adding 来 [lái] or 去 [qù] to a motion verb. In this construction, 来 [lái] and 去 [qù] indicate the direction of the motion. 来 [lái] indicates a motion coming toward the speaker and 去 [qù] indicates a motion that is going away from the speaker. For example, 进来 [jìnlái] means to enter, coming toward the speaker who is inside. 进去 [jìnqù] means to enter, going in and away from the speaker who is outside. The following are some examples of simple directional complements:

(Motion verb)	上 upward	下 downward	进 enter	出 outward	回 return	过 cross	起 up	搬 move	带 take with
+ 来 (coming toward)	上来	下来	进来	出来	回来	过来	起来	搬来	带来
+ 去 (going away)	上去	下去	进去	出去	回去	过去	(NA)[1]	搬去	带去

Note:
1. 起 can only be combined with 来.

When using a simple DC with a verb that has an object, the object comes after the motion verb and before the complement. Note that the object is usually a place or a person.

Pattern: Verb + Object + 来/去

他回宿舍去了。   He went back to the dorm.
Tā <u>huí</u> sùshè <u>qù</u> le.   (The speaker is not at the dorm.)

你们都进客厅来吧!   Everyone come into the living room!
Nǐmen dōu <u>jìn</u> kètīng <u>lái</u> ba!   (The speaker is in the living room.)

>>**Try it!**   With a partner, look at the above chart of simple directional complements. Act out the motion of the simple DCs. Try to think of a situation where you would use the simple directional complement. (Try to describe the situation in Chinese if you can.)

Example: A: "我在楼上。你上来吧!"
                    (motions hand toward self)
                    Wǒ zài lóushàng. Nǐ shànglái ba!

             B: "I'm taking this book with me when I leave class. 带去"
                    (points toward the door)

II. Compound Directional Complements (Compound DC)

To form a compound directional complement, use a simple DC (as detailed above) together with an action verb. In this construction, the action verb expresses the action. The simple DC indicates the direction of the action relative to a location or the direction of motion toward or away from the speaker.

我哥哥想   搬   过来 。   My older brother is thinking about moving here.
Wǒ gēge xiǎng   bān   guòlái
              (action)   (simple DC)

The following are examples of some common action verbs and their compound directional complements:

Common action verbs:

走 [zǒu] to walk   跑 [pǎo] to run   跳 [tiào] to jump   坐 [zuò] to sit

站 [zhàn] to stand   搬 [bān] to move   带 [dài] to bring   拿 [ná] to take

Compound DCs:

上来/上去：	坐上来	坐下去	跑上来	跑下去
下来/下去：	走下来	走下去	跳下来	跳下去
进来/进去：	走进来	走进去	拿进来	拿进去
出来/出去：	搬出来	搬出去	带进来	带出去
回来/回去：	跑回来	跑回去	拿回来	拿回去
过来/过去：	带过来	带过去	搬过来	搬过去
起来：	站起来	跳起来	拿起来	

When using a compound DC with a verb that has an object, the object comes after the verb and before the simple DC. Note that the object is usually a person or a thing.

Pattern: Verb + Object + simple DC

他	要搬	桌子	过来 。	He wants to move the table over here.
Tā	yào bān	zhuōzi	guòlái.	
(Subject)	(V.)	(Object)	(simple DC)	

他	带	炒面	回来	了 。	He returned with fried noodles.
Tā	dài	chǎomiàn	huílái	le.	
(Subject)	(V.)	(Object)	(simple DC)		

Note that 起来 is an expression with idiomatic usage and does not follow the above pattern with objects after the verb. Instead, it has the following patterns:

他<u>拿起来</u>一本书 。　　He takes a book with him.
Tā <u>ná qǐlái</u> yìběn shū.

他<u>拿起书来</u> 。　　He takes a book with him.
Tā <u>ná qǐ</u> shū <u>lái</u>.

>>**Try it!** With a partner, complete the following sentences with a compound directional complement from the list of compound DCs above and the prompts in parentheses.

1. 明天会有很多学生要 ___ ___ ___ 我们的宿舍 。(move in over here)
   Míngtiān huì yǒu hěnduō xuéshēng yào ___ ___ ___ wǒmende sùshè.

2. 公车来了！快一点儿 ___ ___ ___ ！ (run over here)
   Gōngchē lái le! Kuài yìdiǎr ___ ___ ___ !

3. 外面很冷，要 ___ 外套 ___ ___ 。(bring and go out)
   Wàimiàn hěn lěng, yào ___ wàitào ___ ___ .

4. 妹妹 ___ 了一只狗 ___ ___ 。(bring and come back)
   Mèimei ___ le yìzhī gǒu ___ ___ .

III. 把 Sentences

把 [bǎ] sentences are used to indicate the effects of an action upon its object. The structure used is as follows: Subject + 把 + Object + Verb + complement.

把 is used most often with action verbs. When 把 is used with action verbs, the object of the verb must be definite and the verb must incorporate a complement. Some of the common complements involved with 把 structures are as follows:

- degree of complement: 他把这个字写得很好 。[Tā bǎ zhège zì xiěde hěnhǎo.] (He wrote this character very well.)
- 了, used as a complement to show a completed action: 我把汤喝了 。[Wǒ bǎ tāng hē le.] (I drank the soup.)
- directional complement: 我要把那张桌子搬过去 。[Wǒ yào bǎ nàzhāng zhuōzi bān guòqù.] (I want to move that table out.)

(Note that there are other complements used with 把, such as resultative complements, which show the results of an action, and duration/frequency complements, which show how long/how often an action occurs. These complements will be introduced in the next level.)

把 is also commonly used in imperative sentences, such as 把饭吃了！[Bǎ fàn chī le!] (Eat your meal!) or 把车开回来！[Bǎ chē kāi huílái!] (Drive the car back!).

>>Try it!   With a partner, practice using 把 to complete the following sentences.

1. 请 ___ 我的书带来。
   Qǐng ___ wǒde shū dàilái.

2. 妈妈说 ___ 感冒药吃了!
   Māma shuō ___ gǎnmàoyào chī le!

3. 哥哥要 ___ 爸爸的车开过来。
   Gēge yào ___ bàbade chē kāi guòlái.

4. 谁 ___ 他的蛋糕吃了?
   Shéi ___ tāde dàngāo chī le?

IV. 把 Sentences and the Directional Complement

In sentences with a directional complement, if the action has a definite object, the 把 [bǎ] structure is preferred. For example, look at the following sentence:

我带来我的室友了。   I've brought my roommate over.
Wǒ dàilái wǒde shìyǒu le.

The sentence simply describes an event. However, since there is a definite object (我的室友) for the action (带来), the 把 construction is more commonly used:

我把我室友带来了。   I've brought my roommate over.
Wǒ bǎ wǒ shìyǒu dàilái le.

The use of 把 implies that the location of the object has changed due to the subject, emphasizing that the subject is the cause of the change.

>>Try it!   Work with a partner. Change the sentences below into 把 sentences with directional complements.

1. 小方带来了这盘炒面。   _____
   Xiǎo Fāng dàilái le zhèpán chǎomiàn.

2. 他带去了他的中文作业。   _____
   Tā dàiqù le tāde Zhōngwén zuòyè.

3. 我室友搬来了他的电脑[1]。   _____
   Wǒ shìyǒu bānlái le tāde diànnǎo.

4. 她搬去了那张桌子。   _____
   Tā bānqù le nàzhāng zhuōzi.

Note:
1. 电脑(電腦) [diànnǎo]: computer

V. When to Use Sentences with 把

The 把 [bǎ] construction is also called a "disposal" construction. That is, the 把 [bǎ] sentence usually indicates that the object is disposed of, dealt with, or affected by the subject. The following guidelines can help in determining when to use a 把 [bǎ] construction or a non-把 construction.

Situations in which the 把 construction is usually **preferred** are:

- when the speaker wants to emphasize that an action has caused the object to change position or change from one state to another.

> 我把那包药吃了。 I took the medicine.
> Wǒ bǎ nàbāo yào chī le.
> (emphasizes that the medicine has been taken by the subject and is gone.)

- when there is a long or complicated direct object.

> 我把我妈妈昨天带回来的那包药吃了。
> Wǒ bǎ wǒ māma zuótiān dài huílái de nàbāo yào chī le.
> (I took the medicine that my mother brought back yesterday.)

- when using imperative sentences (commands).

> 把那包药吃了! Take the medicine!
> Bǎ nàbāo yào chī le!

Situations in which the 把 construction **must** be used (as there are no corresponding non-把 constructions) are:

- with sentences that have a plural object with the adverb 都.

> 我把我们的书都卖了。 I sold all our books.
> Wǒ bǎ wǒmende shū dōu mài le.

- with some resultative complements (words added to the verb to show a result). (Note: constructions with resultative complements will be introduced in the next level.)

Situations in which the 把 construction **cannot** be used are with verbs that do not allow a "disposal" explanation. The following is a sample list of verbs that are incompatible with the 把 construction:

- Intransitive verbs: 来 (to come), 去 (to go), 跑 (to run), 走 (to walk), 旅行 (to travel), 毕业 ([bìyè]: to graduate), 工作 (to work), 站 ([zhàn]: to stand), 坐 (to sit)

- Existence verbs: 是 (to be), 在 (to be at), 有 (to have)
- Emotion verbs: 喜欢 (to like), 爱 (to love), 怕 ([pà]: to fear)
- Sensory perception verbs: 会 (to be able to), 知道 (to know), 认识 (to recognize), 觉得 (to think, to feel), 希望 ([xīwàng]: to hope), 看见 ([kànjiàn]: to see), 听见 ([tīngjiàn]: to hear)
- Others: 欢迎 (to welcome), 赞成 ([zànchéng]: to approve)

🔊 补充课文 SUPPLEMENTARY PRACTICE

Read the following passage. Then listen and repeat.

四月二十日　　　　星期三

今天常天开车把我带去他住的地方。他和夏中明一起住在校外的一个公寓[1]楼里。前几天他们楼上有一个人搬出去了，常天把这个消息[2]告诉[3]了我，要我过去看看，如果[4]那儿不错，我就想搬过去。我不想住在宿舍里了。宿舍太小，又[5]不能做饭。我喜欢自己[6]做饭，我做饭也做得很好。

中明告诉我他们那儿有厨房，常天把我带上去看了一下，我觉得还不错，不大也不小，也很干净。中明还告诉我他们那儿不能养[7]宠物[8]。不过[9]这对我来说[10]没关系。以前我养狗，但是我妹妹有过敏[11]，所以为了她我就把我的狗给我女朋友了，也让我女朋友非常高兴[12]。

常天还说他们必须每个月的第一天付房租，这也没问题。我想明天给房东[13]打电话，希望[14]我能早一点儿搬过去。

Notes:
1. 公寓 [gōngyù]: apartment
2. 消息 [xiāoxi]: news
3. 告诉(告訴) [gàosu]: to tell
4. 如果……就 [rúguǒ . . . jiù]: if . . . then
5. 又 [yòu]: also
6. 自己 [zìjǐ]: self, by oneself
7. 养(養) [yǎng]: to raise
8. 宠物(寵物) [chǒngwù]: pet
9. 不过(不過) [búguò]: however, but
10. 对我来说(對我來說) [duì wǒ lái shuō]: to me
11. 过敏(過敏) [guòmǐn]: allergy
12. 高兴(高興) [gāoxìng]: happy
13. 房东(房東) [fángdōng]: landlord
14. 希望(希望) [xīwàng]: to hope

Pinyin version:

Sìyuè Èrshí Rì   Xīngqī Sān

Jīntiān Cháng Tiān kāichē bǎ wǒ dàiqù tā zhùde dìfang. Tā hé Xià Zhōngmíng yìqǐ zhù zài xiàowài de yíge gōngyùlóu lǐ. Qiánjǐtiān tāmen lóushàng yǒu yígerén bān chūqù le, Cháng Tiān bǎ zhège xiāoxi gàosu le wǒ, yào wǒ guòqù kànkan, rúguǒ nàr búcuò, wǒ jiù xiǎng bān guòqù. Wǒ bù xiǎng zhù zài sùshè lǐ le. Sùshè tài xiǎo, yòu bùnéng zuòfàn. Wǒ xǐhuān zìjǐ zuòfàn, wǒ zuòfàn yě zuòde hěnhǎo.

Zhōngmíng gàosu wǒ tāmen nàr yǒu chúfáng, Cháng Tiān bǎ wǒ dài shàngqu kànle yíxià, wǒ juéde hái búcuò, bú dà yě bù xiǎo, yě hěn gānjìng. Zhōngmíng hái gàosu wǒ tāmen nàr bùnéng yǎng chǒngwù. Búguò zhè duì wǒ lái shuō méiguānxi. Yǐqián wǒ yǎng gǒu, dànshì wǒ mèimei yǒu guòmǐn, suǒyǐ wèile tā wǒ jiù bǎ wǒde gǒu gěi wǒ nǚpéngyou le, yě ràng wǒ nǚpéngyou fēicháng gāoxìng.

Cháng Tiān háishuō tāmen bìxū měige yuè de dìyītiān fù fángzū, zhè yě méiwèntí. Wǒ xiǎng míngtiān gěi fángdōng dǎ diànhuà, xīwàng wǒ néng zǎo yìdiǎr bān guòqù.

Read the following statements and choose whether they are true or false.

1. The writer went to 常天's apartment today.   True   False

2. The writer is good at cooking and cooks at his dorm frequently.   True   False

3. The apartment building does not allow pets.   True   False

4. The rent has to be paid on the 5th of every month.   True   False

5. The writer will call the landlord tomorrow.   True   False

练习 ACTIVITIES

 I.   Listening Exercises

20-1   Listen and complete the sentences with the correct Pinyin. Then check your answers with a partner or the class.

1. _____ miàn _____ yǔ le, wǒmen jìn _____ ba!

2. Wǒ _____ lái le, wǒ yě _____ wǎnfàn _____ huílái le.

3. Wǒ _____ zài _____ fàn ne, hěn hǎo _____ , nǐmen _____ lái _____ ba!

4. Wǒmen _____ zài _____ gè _____ de _____ yìtiān _____ fáng _____ .

20-2 Work in groups of three or four. Take turns reading the lines of the following poem, paying special attention to the tones and rhythm.

Huí Xiāng Ǒu Shū
(Hè Zhīzhāng)

Shào xiǎo lí jiā lǎo dà huí,

Xiāngyīn wú gǎi bìnmáo shuāi.

Értóng xiāngjiàn bù xiāngshí,

Xiào wèn kè cóng hé chù lái.

回乡偶书
(贺知章)

少小离家老大回，

乡音无改鬓毛衰。

儿童相见不相识，

笑问客从何处来。

Returning Home
(He, Zhizhang)

I left home young, returned old,
My accent changed not, although my hair grew thin.
The youngsters see me, but don't know me,
With smiles they ask where I come from.

II. Character Exercises

20-3 Choose the correct meaning for the following words. Then check your answers with a partner.

1. 带来
   dàilái
   a. to come over   b. to come in   c. to bring over

2. 马上
   mǎshàng
   a. upstairs   b. immediately   c. downstairs

3. 必须
   bìxū
   a. should   b. but   c. must

4. 搬
   bān
   a. to move   b. to enter   c. to pay

5. 付
   fù
   a. to move   b. to enter   c. to pay

20-4 Write the radical for each of the following characters. Check your answers with a partner and discuss other words you have learned with the same radicals.

1. 把 ____   2. 进 ____   3. 搬 ____   4. 来 ____   5. 过 ____

III. Grammar Exercises

20-5 Look at the following example. With a partner, take turns extending the words below into phrases and then sentences. See how long you can keep extending the sentences.

Example: A: 带   dài

B: 带来   dài lái

A: 带回来   dài huílái

B: 把朋友带回来   bǎ péngyou dài huílái

A: 把朋友带回来了   bǎ péngyou dài huílái le

B: 我把我朋友从学校带回来了。
Wǒ bǎ wǒ péngyou cóng xuéxiào dài huílái le.

1. 但   2. 付   3. 必   4. 进   5. 楼   6. 帮   7. 马   8. 搬
 dàn   fù   bì   jìn   lóu   bāng   mǎ   bān

20-6 With a partner, take turns using words from the boxes to complete and practice the dialogues. Look carefully at the sentences to see which words fit most appropriately.

Example: A: 你买了什么回来?   Nǐ mǎile shénme huílái?

B: 我买了一瓶可乐回来。   Wǒ mǎile yìpíng kělè huílái.

1. A: 你 ___ 了什么 _____?
   Nǐ ___ le shénme _____ ?

B: 我 ___ 了 _____。
   Wǒ ___ le _____ .

借 jiè	两本书 liǎngběn shū	回来 huílái
搬 bān	一张桌子 yìzhāng zhuōzi	进来 jìnlái
拿 ná	一条裙子 yìtiáo qúnzi	上去 shàngqu
送 sòng	一张电影票 yìzhāng diànyǐngpiào	出去 chūqù

2. A: 你要他做什么？
　　　Nǐ yào tā zuò shénme?

　　B: 我要他把 ＿＿＿＿＿＿。
　　　Wǒ yào tā bǎ ＿＿＿＿＿＿ .

那辆车 nàliàng chē	买回来 mǎi huílái
这个月的房租 zhège yuè de fángzū	付出去 fù chūqù
那张桌子 nàzhāng zhuōzi	搬过去 bān guòqù
这碗汤 zhèwǎn tāng	喝下去 hē xiàqù

20-7　With a partner, complete the dialogues with either 来 or 去.

1. 小花：　　明明，这就是我的宿舍，外面有点儿冷，
　　　　　　Míngming, zhè jiùshì wǒde sùshè, wàimiàn yǒudiǎr lěng,

　　　　　　我们进 ＿＿＿ 吧！
　　　　　　wǒmen jìn ＿＿＿ ba!

　　　　　　小雪，我回 ＿＿＿ 了，我也把明明带 ＿＿＿ 了。
　　　　　　Xiǎoxuě, wǒ huí ＿＿＿ le, wǒ yě bǎ Míngming dài ＿＿＿ le.

2. 小雪：　　我在楼上，我正在看电影呢，
　　　　　　Wǒ zài lóushàng, wǒ zhèngzài kàn diànyǐng ne,

　　　　　　你们一起上 ＿＿＿ 看看吧！
　　　　　　Nǐmen yìqǐ shàng ＿＿＿ kànkan ba!

3. 明明：　　我们等一下再上 ＿＿＿ 。
　　　　　　Wǒmen děngyíxià zài shàng ＿＿＿ .

　　　　　　对了，小花，我把你要的书也带 ＿＿＿ 了。
　　　　　　Duì le, Xiǎohuā, wǒ bǎ nǐ yào de shū yě dài ＿＿＿ le.

4. 小花：　　太好了，谢谢。
　　　　　　Tài hǎo le, xièxie.

　　　　　　小雪，我们都在楼下，请你下 ＿＿＿ ，好吗？
　　　　　　Xiǎoxuě, wǒmen dōu zài lóuxià, qǐng nǐ xià ＿＿＿ , hǎo ma?

5. 小雪：　　好，我马上下 ＿＿＿ ！
　　　　　　Hǎo, wǒ mǎshàng xià ＿＿＿ !

20-8　With a partner, complete the sentences with 把, directional complements, and the prompts in parentheses.

1. 昨天我的好朋友要从纽约 ＿＿ ＿＿ 看我，(come over)
   Zuótiān wǒde hǎo péngyou yào cóng Niǔyuē ＿＿ ＿＿ kàn wǒ,

   昨天下课以后，我从教室走 ＿＿ ＿＿ 以后，(go out)
   zuótiān xiàkè yǐhòu, wǒ cóng jiàoshì zǒu ＿＿ ＿＿ yǐhòu,

   就 ＿＿ 宿舍 ＿＿ 了。(return)
   jiù ＿＿ sùshè ＿＿ le.

2. 我要开门 ＿＿ ＿＿ 的时候，我的钥匙¹不见了，(enter)
   Wǒ yào kāimén ＿＿ ＿＿ de shíhòu, wǒde yàoshi bú jiàn le,

   所以我 ＿＿ ＿＿ 教室 ＿＿ 。(run and return)
   suǒyǐ wǒ ＿＿ ＿＿ jiàoshì ＿＿ .

3. 我 ＿＿ ＿＿ ＿＿ 以后，(run and enter)
   Wǒ ＿＿ ＿＿ ＿＿ yǐhòu,

   ＿＿ 桌子搬 ＿＿ ＿＿，搬 ＿＿ ＿＿ 。(move the table back and forth)
   ＿＿ zhuōzi bān ＿＿ ＿＿ , bān ＿＿ ＿＿ .

4. 我也 ＿＿ 书 ＿＿ ＿＿ ＿＿ 看看，(pick up the books)
   Wǒ yě ＿＿ shū ＿＿ ＿＿ ＿＿ kànkan,

   还是没找到²。
   háishì méizhǎodào.

5. 我累³地 ＿＿ ＿＿ ＿＿，就发现⁴了钥匙在椅子⁵上！(sat down)
   Wǒ lèide ＿＿ ＿＿ ＿＿ , jiù fāxiàn le yàoshi zài yǐzi shàng!

Notes:
1. 钥匙(鑰匙) [yàoshi]: key
2. 没找到(沒找到) [méizhǎodào]: cannot find it
3. 累 [lèi]: tired
4. 发现(發現) [fāxiàn]: discover
5. 椅子 [yǐzi]: chair

IV. Communicative Activities

20-9   With a group of three or four, play 教练说 (The coach says . . .). Take turns being the coach of a basketball team. Give commands to the team to complete several actions, such as going back and forth and lifting things up. Use directional complements and 把 sentences in your commands.

Example: 把那个电视搬过来......
　　　　　　　bǎ nàge diànshì bānguòlái . . .

Words and phrases to use:

桌子　　　　椅子 (chair)
zhuōzi　　　yǐzi

三十本书　　篮球
sānshíběn shū   lánqiú

跑 (to run) 上去(下来)
pǎo shàngqu [xiàlái]

跳 (to jump) 过去(过来)
tiào guòqù [guòlái]

拿 (to take) 上去(下来)
ná shàngqu [xiàlái]

20-10   In pairs, role-play the following situation.

Situation: It is moving day at the dorm. There are a lot of students moving in and out around campus. You and a friend are chatting in the dorm. (Use the following prompts to form your dialogue.)

A: 明天我那儿有一个人要搬进来。
　　　Míngtiān wǒ nàr yǒu yíge rén yào bān jìnlái.

B: 他要从哪儿搬过来?
　　　Tā yào cóng nǎr bān guòlái?

A: 他要从纽约搬过来。
　　　Tā yào cóng Niǔyuē bān guòlái.

B: 我的宿舍要搬走[1]一个人。
　　　Wǒde sùshè yào bānzǒu yíge rén.

A: 他要搬到²哪儿去......?
Tā yào bāndào nǎr qù . . . ?

B: _____

从哪儿搬来: 芝加哥 (Chicago); 学校宿舍
cóng nǎr bānlái: Zhījiāgē; xuéxiào sùshè

从哪儿搬走: 学校宿舍; 洛杉矶 (Los Angeles)
cóng nǎr bānzǒu: xuéxiào sùshè; Luòshānjī

搬到哪儿去: 旧金山/三藩市 (San Francisco); 费城 (Philadelphia)
bāndào nǎr qù: Jiùjīnshān/Sānfánshì; Fèichéng

Notes:
1. 搬走 [bānzǒu]: move away
2. 搬到 [bāndào]: move to

20-11 In pairs, role-play the following situation.

Situation: You and your friend are chatting about a potluck party you went to at Professor Wang's house. Every teacher brought a few dishes. Your friend asks a lot of questions about what dishes the teachers brought, if they brought anyone with them, and how they travelled to the party. Try to use 把 sentences and directional complements in your questions and answers.

Example:

A: 田老师带了什么去?
Tián lǎoshī dàile shénme qù?

B: 田老师带了蛋糕去。
Tián lǎoshī dàile dàngāo qù.

A: 田老师把谁带去了?
Tián lǎoshī bǎ shéi dàiqù le?

B: 她把她先生带去了。
Tā bǎ tā xiānsheng dàiqù le.

A: 田老师是怎么过去的呢?
Tián lǎoshī shì zěnme guòqù de ne?

B: 她是开车过去的。
Tā shì kāichē guòqù de.

Teachers	Dishes	Companion	Transportation
田老师 [Tián lǎoshī]	蛋糕，绿茶 [dàngāo, lǜchá] (cake, green tea)	先生 [xiānsheng] (husband)	开车 [kāichē]
黄老师 [Huáng lǎoshī]	春卷 [chūnjuǎn] (spring roll)	孩子 [háizi] (child)	坐公车 [zuò gōngchē]
吴老师 [Wú lǎoshī]	酸辣汤 [suānlàtāng] (hot and sour soup)	没有带人 [méiyǒu dàirén] (didn't bring anyone)	走路 [zǒulù]
李老师 [Lǐ lǎoshī]	饺子 [jiǎozi] (dumpling)	男朋友 [nánpéngyou] (boyfriend)	骑自行车 [qí zìxíngchē]
张老师 [Zhāng lǎoshī]	炒饭 [chǎofàn] (fried rice)	太太 [tàitai] (wife)	走路 [zǒulù]
方老师 [Fāng lǎoshī]	不知道 [bùzhīdào] (don't know)	孩子 [háizi] (child)	骑自行车 [qí zìxíngchē]

文化知识 Culture Link

文化点滴 CULTURE NOTES

中国的住房 Houses in China

Though most people in Chinese cities today live in more modern apartments, housing in China has a varied history with many diverse styles unique to different regions and ethnic groups. In many rural communities, some of these houses can still be found.

Early homes were built using materials such as pounded earth and wood and usually faced south, if possible, to help provide protection from the wind and inclement weather. 风水 [fēngshuǐ] (Feng shui: geomancy) was important in the building process, with manuals for carpenters often providing construction suggestions to help promote the well-being of the house's residents. Many of the traditional houses provided a space for several generations to live together, sometimes even many families of the same clan.

In the north, the 四合院 [sìhéyuàn] (Si He Yuan), or courtyard houses, were common, especially in Beijing. Si He Yuan is a rectangular compound with traditional one-story buildings on four sides. They are connected by corridors, with a yard in the center. Entry to the enclosed compound is by a gate, which is usually located at the southeast corner. In 福建 [Fújiàn] (Fujian) in the south, 土楼 [tǔlóu] (earthen round

Do you know...

- what some traditional housing styles in China are?
- which direction early houses usually faced?
- if many people still live in traditional-style houses?

Read and find out!

houses) were a popular style for the Hakka people. The houses had a main entrance and a courtyard in the middle with rooms on several floors. The different floors provided storage and meeting areas, as well as rooms for many generations of a clan. Other housing styles are seen in the houses built along canals in 苏州 [Sūzhōu] (Suzhou), and the special roof scaffolding style that functions as fire-proofing in houses in 安徽 [Ānhuī] (Anhui) (often called 马头檐 [Mǎtóuyán] ("horse-head" roofs).

While most housing in China has moved away from traditional architectural styles to more modern styles, some traditional houses, for example, Si He Yuan, have been converted to housing complexes. In cities with large populations such as Beijing, these complexes can house many families. To address issues of overcrowding and a desire for modern amenities, however, many of these traditional houses have been torn down and replaced by high-rise apartments with modern electricity and plumbing. To preserve the tradition and the culture of these older homes, the Chinese government has now formulated laws to protect them so that future generations will still be able to see how their ancestors lived.

193

The Forbidden City in Beijing shows an example of Si He Yuan architecture. What are some other traditional housing styles in China?

The exterior of a 土楼 in Fujian Province. What do you think are the benefits of living in housing such as this?

Discuss the following with a group or your class.

1. What do you think are the most obvious differences between Western-style houses and traditional Chinese houses such as the Si He Yuan?

2. How do you think traditional Chinese housing affected daily life? Do you think there was a different sense of community in walled housing? What changes do you think might occur as housing becomes more modernized?

趣味中文 FUN WITH CHINESE

秀才不出门，能知天下事。

Even without going out the door, a learned person can still know everything.

xiùcai	bù	chū	mén,	néng	zhī	tiānxià	shì
秀才	不	出	门，	能	知	天下	事
learned person	not	out	door,	can	know	world	matter

Work in small groups or with your class.

1. Practice reading the saying aloud, paying attention to the pronunciation and rhythm.
2. Do you agree with the saying? Why or why not? Have you heard of any similar sayings in English or other languages?

行动吧! LET'S GO!

租屋广告 Apartment Rental Ad

谢中天 is studying abroad in Taipei. He is looking for an apartment and found an ad for a roommate with apartment information. Read the following ad.

地址： 台北市和平东路102号3楼
[dìzhǐ]

房租：月租6000元(不包括[1]网路、瓦斯[2]、水、电)

一厅二房公寓，在3楼，有公用的洗澡间、厨房、冰箱[3]和洗衣机[4]

附近[5]：有学校、超市[6]和公园

不能养宠物

我在找个室友搬进来跟我一起住。可以马上搬过来。学生、上班族[7]都可以！想过来看看吗？电话：22313448 小文

Notes:
1. 包括 [bāokuò]: to include
2. 瓦斯 [wǎsī]: gas. Gas is called 煤气(煤氣) [méiqì] in Mainland China.
3. 冰箱 [bīngxiāng]: refrigerator
4. 洗衣机(洗衣機) [xǐyījī]: washing machine
5. 附近 [fùjìn]: nearby
6. 超市 [chāoshì]: supermarket
7. 上班族 [shàngbān zú]: office worker, 9–5 employee

Answer the following questions with a partner or your group.

1. 房间是在几楼？从一楼到房间，是要上去还是下去？
   Fángjiān shì zài jǐlóu? Cóng yīlóu dào fángjiān, shìyào shàngqu háishì xiàqu?

2. 什么时候可以搬进去？
   Shénme shíhòu kěyǐ bān jìnqù?

3. 每个月的房租是多少？还有什么是应该付的？
   Měige yuè de fángzū shì duōshǎo? Háiyǒu shénme shì yīnggāi fùde?

4. 住这个房间的人能不能把狗带回家？
   Zhù zhège fángjiān de rén néngbunéng bǎ gǒu dàihuíjiā?

5. 附近有什么？
   Fùjìn yǒu shénme?

未来计画
Future Plans

Students of 清华大学 *[Qīnghuá dàxué] (Tsinghua University), one of the most prestigious universities in China, at their graduation ceremony.*

教学目标 OBJECTIVES

- Talk about future plans
- Express blessings and wishes

CONNECTIONS AND COMMUNITIES PREVIEW

Discuss the following questions with a partner or your class. What similarities and differences do you think there might be between Chinese culture and your own culture?

1. What do most students do after graduation in your culture?

2. Have you ever thought about studying abroad in China? What places in China would you like to visit and why?

生词 VOCABULARY

核心词 Core Vocabulary

	SIMPLIFIED	TRADITIONAL	PINYIN		
1.	暑假	暑假	shǔjià	N.	summer vacation
2.	毕业	畢業	bìyè	V.	to graduate
3.	决定	決定	juédìng	V.	to decide
4.	可能	可能	kěnéng	Adv.	perhaps, maybe, possibly
5.	申请	申請	shēnqǐng	V.	to apply
6.	研究生院	研究生院	yánjiūshēngyuàn	N.	graduate school
	研究	研究	yánjiū	V.	to research, to study/examine
7.	国外	國外	guówài	N.	overseas, abroad
8.	留学	留學	liúxué	V.O.	to study abroad
9.	找	找	zhǎo	V.	to seek, to look for
10.	打工	打工	dǎgōng	V.O.	to work for others, to be employed
11.	家	家	jiā	M.W.	(measure word for companies, enterprises, stores, etc.)
12.	公司	公司	gōngsī	N.	company
13.	实习	實習	shíxí	N.	internship
				V.	to practice, to intern
14.	电脑	電腦	diànnǎo	N.	computer
15.	暑期	暑期	shǔqī	N.	summer vacation
16.	班	班	bān	N.	class
17.	一面	一面	yímiàn	Adv.	at the same time
18.	有意思	有意思	yǒuyìsi	Adj.	interesting, enjoyable

	SIMPLIFIED	TRADITIONAL	PINYIN		
19.	愉快	愉快	yúkuài	Adj.	happy
20.	一路平安 平安	一路平安 平安	yílùpíng'ān píng'ān	Adj.	have a pleasant journey peaceful, safe
21.	好运	好運	hǎoyùn	N.	good luck

专名 Proper Nouns

	SIMPLIFIED	TRADITIONAL	PINYIN		
1.	程海华	程海華	Chéng Hǎihuá	N.	(name) Haihua Cheng
2.	白秋雨	白秋雨	Bái Qiūyǔ	N.	(name) Qiuyu Bai
3.	加州	加州	Jiāzhōu	N.	California

补充词 Supplementary Vocabulary

	SIMPLIFIED	TRADITIONAL	PINYIN		
1.	大学生	大學生	dàxuéshēng	N.	college student
2.	研究生	研究生	yánjiūshēng	N.	graduate student
3.	博士生	博士生	bóshìshēng	N.	doctoral student
4.	学位	學位	xuéwèi	N.	degree
5.	学士	學士	xuéshì	N.	(a person with a) bachelor's degree
6.	硕士	碩士	shuòshì	N.	(a person with a) master's degree
7.	博士	博士	bóshì	N.	(a person with a) doctoral degree
8.	简历 (履历表)	簡歷 (履歷表)	jiǎnlì (lǚlìbiǎo)	N.	resumé

语文知识 LANGUAGE LINK

Read and listen to the following sentence patterns. These patterns use vocabulary, expressions, and grammar that you will study in more detail in this lesson. After reading the sentence patterns, read and listen to the Language in Use section that follows.

句型 Sentence Patterns

A: 毕业以后你想做什么？
Bìyè yǐhòu nǐ xiǎng zuò shénme?

B: 我想申请研究生院。
Wǒ xiǎng shēnqǐng yánjiūshēngyuàn.

A: 今年暑假你要做什么？
Jīnnián shǔjià nǐ yào zuò shénme?

B: 我要去一家公司做暑期实习。
Wǒ yào qù yìjiā gōngsī zuò shǔqī shíxí.

A: 你去中国做什么？
Nǐ qù Zhōngguó zuò shénme?

B: 我想在那儿一面旅行，一面学中文。
Wǒ xiǎng zài nàr yímiàn lǚxíng, yímiàn xué Zhōngwén.

A: 祝你工作愉快！
Zhù nǐ gōngzuò yúkuài!

B: 祝你一路平安！祝你好运！
Zhù nǐ yílùpíng'ān! Zhù nǐ hǎoyùn!

🔊 **课文 Language in Use: 暑假你要做什么?**

程海华: 秋雨，我问你，你明年就要毕业了，
Qiūyǔ, wǒ wèn nǐ, nǐ míngnián jiùyào bìyè le,

毕业以后你想做什么?
bìyè yǐhòu nǐ xiǎng zuò shénme?

白秋雨: 我还没有决定呢。可是我很喜欢学习，
Wǒ hái méiyǒu juédìng ne. Kěshì wǒ hěn xǐhuān xuéxí,

我可能会申请研究生院，
wǒ kěnéng huì shēnqǐng yánjiūshēngyuàn,

或者去国外留学。你呢?
huòzhě qù guówài liúxué. Nǐ ne?

你什么时候毕业?
Nǐ shénme shíhou bìyè?

> **研究生院 [yánjiūshēngyuàn]**
>
> 研究生 means "graduate students." To refer to "graduate school," 研究生院 is used in Mainland China, while 研究所 [yánjiūsuǒ] is used in Taiwan.

程海华: 我还有两年才毕业呢。毕业以后我想去
Wǒ háiyǒu liǎngnián cái bìyè ne. Bìyè yǐhòu wǒ xiǎng qù

找工作。
zhǎo gōngzuò.

白秋雨: 我们就要放暑假了，今年暑假你要
Wǒmen jiùyào fàng shǔjià le, jīnnián shǔjià nǐ yào

做什么?
zuò shénme?

程海华: 我要去打工。我要去一家
Wǒ yào qù dǎgōng. Wǒ yào qù yìjiā

公司实习。
gōngsī shíxí.

> **打工 [dǎgōng], 工读 [gōngdú], and 实习 [shíxí]**
>
> 打工 is used to refer to work, or part-time work. 工读 is another common term, meaning "work-study." 实习 means "intern" or "internship."
> 暑期实习 means "summer internship."

白秋雨: 在哪儿? 是什么工作?
Zài nǎr? Shì shénme gōngzuò?

程海华： 在加州，是一家电脑公司。你呢？
Zài Jiāzhou, shì yìjiā diànnǎo gōngsī. Nǐ ne?

暑假你要做什么？
Shǔjià nǐ yào zuò shénme?

白秋雨： 我要去中国，我申请了去上海的暑期班学习，
Wǒ yào qù Zhōngguó, wǒ shēnqǐng le qù Shànghǎi de shǔqībān xuéxí,

我想一面学中文，一面在中国旅行。
wǒ xiǎng yímiàn xué Zhōngwén, yímiàn zài Zhōngguó lǚxíng.

程海华： 那一定很有意思！你什么时候去？
Nà yídìng hěn yǒuyìsi! Nǐ shénme shíhou qù?

白秋雨： 下个星期。
Xiàge xīngqī.

程海华： 这么快！你到中国以后
Zhème kuài! Nǐ dào Zhōngguó yǐhòu

要常常给我写电子邮件。
yào chángcháng gěi wǒ xiě diànzǐ yóujiàn.

这么快 [Zhème kuài]
这么快 means "so fast!" 这么/那么 + Adj. is used to indicate a sense of surprise.
这么多 "so many!"
那么小 "so small!"
这么贵 "so expensive!"

白秋雨： 没问题。我祝你工作愉快！
Méi wèntí. Wǒ zhù nǐ gōngzuò yúkuài!

程海华： 我也祝你一路平安！祝你好运！
Wǒ yě zhù nǐ yílùpíng'ān! Zhù nǐ hǎoyùn!

语法 GRAMMAR

1. 一面......一面......

一面......一面...... [yímiàn . . . yímiàn . . .] is a conjunction used to show two actions being done at the same time.

他一面看电视，一面做功课。
Tā yímiàn kàn diànshì, yímiàn zuò gōngkè.
(He's watching TV and doing homework at the same time.)

我想一面学中文，一面在中国旅行。
Wǒ xiǎng yímiàn xué Zhōngwén, yímiàn zài Zhōngguó lǚxíng.
(I'd like to study Chinese and travel at the same time.)

Similarly, 一边......一边...... [yìbiān . . . yìbiān . . .] is also a conjunction that is used to show simultaneous actions.

他一边听音乐[1]，一边看书。
Tā yìbiān tīng yīnyuè, yìbiān kànshū.
(He's listening to music and reading a book.)

我喜欢一边看书一边吃东西。
Wǒ xǐhuān yìbiān kànshū yìbiān chī dōngxi.
(I like to read and eat at the same time.)

Note:
1. 音乐(音樂) [yīnyuè]: music

Note that the "一" in 一边 can be omitted, as in 边......边...... while the "一" in 一面 must be present.

他常常边吃饭，边看电脑。
Tā chángcháng biān chīfàn, biān kàn diànnǎo.
(He often eats while looking at the computer.)

>>**Try it!**   With a partner, combine the actions given into one sentence with 一面……
一面…… (or 一边……一边……).

1. 看风景/走路
   kàn fēngjǐng/zǒulù

2. 骑自行车/唱歌[1]
   qí zìxíngchē/chànggē

3. 上网/听音乐
   shàngwǎng/tīng yīnyuè

4. 吃饭/看电视
   chīfàn/kàn diànshì

5. 看球赛/喝茶
   kàn qiúsài/hēchá

Notes:
1. 唱歌 [chànggē]: to sing

II.   Summary of Verbal Aspects

Chinese does not change word endings to reflect verb tense. Instead, time words are used to reflect when an action occurs and certain particles are used to show states of verbs (verbal aspects), such as progressive action, completed action, or continuous action, among others.

So far we have learned the following patterns to express different types of verbal aspects:

• The progressive aspect of an action 在 [zài]/正在 [zhèngzài] indicating that someone is currently in the process of doing something.

A: 你在看电视吗?
   Nǐ zài kàn diànshì ma?
   (Are you watching TV?)

B: 我没有在看电视。我正在学习呢。
   Wǒ méiyǒu zài kàn diànshì. Wǒ zhèngzài xuéxí ne.
   (I'm not watching TV. I'm studying right now.)

- Imminent action expressed by 就要 [jiùyào]/快要 [kuàiyào] . . . 了 [le]

我就要毕业了。
Wǒ jiùyào bìyè le.
(I'm graduating soon.)

我快要去中国了。
Wǒ kuàiyào qù Zhōngguó le.
(I'm going to China soon.)

- Completion of an action expressed with 了 [le]

	Pattern	Example
Question	• V. . . . 了吗	你去中国了吗？ Nǐ qù Zhōngguó le ma? (Did you go to China?)
	• V. . . . 了没有	你去中国了没有？ Nǐ qù Zhōngguó le méiyǒu? (Did you go to China?)
Positive answer	• V. . . . 了	我去了中国。 Wǒ qù le Zhōngguó. (I went to China.)
	• Sentence ends in 了	我去中国了。 Wǒ qù Zhōngguó le. (I went to China.)
Negative answer (了 is not used)	• 没有 + V.	我没有去中国。 Wǒ méiyǒu qù Zhōngguó. (I didn't go to China.)
	• 还没有……呢	我还没有去中国呢。 Wǒ hái méiyǒu qù Zhōngguó ne. (I haven't gone to China yet.)

🔊 补充课文 SUPPLEMENTARY PRACTICE

Read the following passage. Then listen and repeat.

秋雨明年就要毕业了。她还没有决定毕业以后要做什么。因为¹她很喜欢学习，所以²毕业以后她可能会申请研究生院，或者去国外留学。她的朋友海华两年后才毕业，毕业以后他想找一份³工作。

今年暑假海华要去加州的一家电脑公司实习。秋雨会去上海参加暑期班的学习。她想一面学中文，一面在中国旅行。她下个星期离开⁴这里⁵去中国。

秋雨和海华觉得暑假的时候应该常常给对方⁶写电子邮件。最后⁷他们祝对方愉快、平安和好运。

Notes:

1. 因为(因為) [yīnwèi]: because
2. 所以 [suǒyǐ]: therefore
3. 份 [fèn]: measure word for job
4. 离开(離開) [líkāi]: to depart
5. 这里(這裡) [zhèlǐ]: here
6. 对方(對方) [duìfāng]: opposite side, the other party
7. 最后(最後) [zuìhòu]: finally

Pinyin version:

Qiūyǔ míngnián jiùyào bìyè le. Tā hái méiyǒu juédìng bìyè yǐhòu yào zuòshénme. Yīnwèi tā hěn xǐhuān xuéxí, suǒyǐ bìyè yǐhòu tā kěnéng huì shēnqǐng yánjiūshēngyuàn, huòzhě qù guówài liúxué. Tāde péngyou Hǎihuá liǎngnián hòu cái bìyè, bìyè yǐhòu tā xiǎng zhǎo yífèn gōngzuò.

Jīnnián shǔjià Hǎihuá yàoqù Jiāzhōu de yìjiā diànnǎo gōngsī shíxí. Qiūyǔ huì qù Shànghǎi cānjiā shǔqībān de xuéxí. Tā xiǎng yímiàn xué Zhōngwén, yímiàn zài Zhōngguó lǚxíng. Tā xiàge xīngqī líkāi zhèlǐ qù Zhōngguó.

Qiūyǔ hé Hǎihuá juéde shǔjià de shíhòu yīnggāi chángcháng gěi duìfāng xiě diànzǐ yóujiàn. Zuìhòu tāmen zhù duìfāng yúkuài, píng'ān hé hǎoyùn.

Choose the correct answer for the following questions.

1. 秋雨毕业以后想做什么？
   Qiūyǔ bìyè yǐhòu xiǎng zuò shénme?

   a. 她想去找工作。
      Tā xiǎng qù zhǎo gōngzuò.

   b. 她要去公司实习。
      Tā yào qù gōngsī shíxí.

   c. 她可能会申请研究生院。
      Tā kěnéng huì shēnqǐng yánjiūshēngyuàn.

   d. 她会去参加暑期班学习。
      Tā huì qù cānjiā shǔqībān xuéxí.

2. 海华什么时候毕业？
   Hǎihuá shénme shíhòu bìyè?

   a. 明年　　　b. 今年　　c. 一年以后　　d. 两年以后
   míngnián　　jīnnián　　yìnián yǐhòu　　liǎngnián yǐhòu

3. 海华毕业以后想做什么？
   Hǎihuá bìyè yǐhòu xiǎng zuò shénme?

   a. 找工作　　b. 去电脑公司实习　　c. 去上海　　d. 学中文
   zhǎo gōngzuò　qù diànnǎo gōngsī shíxí　qù Shànghǎi　xué Zhōngwén

4. 秋雨今年暑假要做什么？
   Qiūyǔ jīnnián shǔjià yào zuò shénme?

   a. 去北京　　b. 参加暑期班　　c. 找工作　　d. 多学一点儿法文
   qù Běijīng　　cānjiā shǔqībān　　zhǎo gōngzuò　　duō xué yìdiǎr Fǎwén

5. 秋雨什么时候去中国？
   Qiūyǔ shénme shíhòu qù Zhōngguó?

   a. 明年　　b. 两年后　　c. 两天后　　d. 下个星期
   míngnián　liǎngnián hòu　liǎngtiān hòu　xiàge xīngqī

练习 ACTIVITIES

I.　Listening Exercises

21-1 Listen and write the Pinyin for the words you hear.

1. Bì _____ yǐhòu nǐ xiǎng _____ shénme?

2. Wǒ yàoqù dǎ _____ . Shì yì _____ diàn _____ gōngsī.

3. Wǒ_____ yǒu liǎngnián _____ bìyè ne.

4. Nǐ yào _____ gěi wǒ _____ diànzǐ yóu _____ .

21-2 Work in groups of three or four. Take turns reading the lines of the following poem, paying special attention to the tones and rhythm.

Dēng Yōuzhōutái Gē
(Chén Zǐ'áng)

Qián bú jiàn gǔrén,

Hòu bú jiàn láizhě.

Niàn tiāndì zhī yōuyōu,

Dú chuàngrán ér tì xià.

登幽州台歌
(陈子昂)

前不见古人，

后不见来者。

念天地之悠悠，

独怆然而涕下。

Ballad on Ascending Youzhou Tower
(Chen, Zi'āng)

Ahead, there is no sight of ancients,
Behind, those to come are unseen.
Pondering over the enormity of heaven and earth,
Alone and in sadness, tears fall.

II. Character Exercises

21-3 Choose the correct meaning for the following words. Then check your answers with a partner.

____ 1. 暑期   a. summer   b. summer vacation   c. to study abroad
       shǔqī

____ 2. 暑假   a. summer intern   b. summer vacation   c. to study abroad
       shǔjià

____ 3. 实习   a. to study abroad   b. internship   c. company
       shíxí

____ 4. 毕业   a. internship   b. to decide   c. to graduate
       bìyè

____ 5. 留学   a. overseas   b. to study abroad   c. to apply
       liúxué

____ 6. 申请   a. to apply   b. to study abroad   c. to decide
       shēnqǐng

21-4 Write the radical for each of the following characters. Check your answers with a partner and discuss how the radical relates to the meaning of the word and any other characters you have learned with the same radical.

1. 暑 _____

2. 找 _____

3. 意 _____

4. 愉 _____

5. 电 _____

6. 研 _____

III. Grammar Exercises

21-5 Look at the following example. With a partner, take turns extending the words below into phrases and then sentences. See how long you can keep extending the sentences.

Example:

A: 一面   yímiàn

B: 一面学中文   yímiàn xué Zhōngwén

A: 我想一面学中文   wǒ xiǎng yímiàn xué Zhōngwén

B: 我想一面学中文，一面旅行。
   Wǒ xiǎng yímiàn xué Zhōngwén, yímiàn lǚxíng.

A: 我想一面学中文，一面在中国旅行。
   Wǒ xiǎng yímiàn xué Zhōngwén, yímiàn zài Zhōngguó lǚxíng.

1. 毕   2. 决   3. 申   4. 司   5. 脑   6. 意   7. 愉   8. 运
  bì   jué   shēn   sī   nǎo   yì   yú   yùn

21-6 With a partner, take turns using words from the boxes to complete and practice the dialogues. Look carefully at the sentences to see which words fit most appropriately.

Example:

A: 我喜欢一面<u>看球赛</u>一面<u>喝可乐</u>。你呢？
   Wǒ xǐhuān yímiàn <u>kàn qiúsài</u> yímiàn <u>hē kělè</u>. Nǐ ne?

B: 我不喜欢一面<u>看球赛</u>一面<u>喝可乐</u>。
   Wǒ bù xǐhuān yímiàn <u>kàn qiúsài</u> yímiàn <u>hē kělè</u>.

1. A: 我喜欢一面 ＿＿ 一面 ＿＿。
       Wǒ xǐhuān yímiàn ＿＿＿ yímiàn ＿＿＿ .

    你呢?
    Nǐ ne?

    B: 我也喜欢一面 ＿＿ 一面 ＿＿。
       Wǒ yě xǐhuān yímiàn ＿＿＿ yímiàn ＿＿＿ .

    (or B: 我不喜欢一面 ＿＿ 一面 ＿＿。)
       Wǒ bù xǐhuān yímiàn ＿＿＿ yímiàn ＿＿＿ .

看书 kànshū	听音乐 tīng yīnyuè
看电影 kàn diànyǐng	吃东西 chī dōngxi
洗澡 xǐzǎo	唱歌 chànggē
打手机 dǎ shǒujī	上网 shàngwǎng
开车 kāichē	看风景 kàn fēngjǐng

2. A: 毕业以后，你想做什么?
       Bìyè yǐhòu, nǐ xiǎng zuò shénme?

    B: ＿＿＿＿＿＿＿＿＿＿ 。

还没决定呢 hái méi juédìng ne
想去国外旅行 xiǎng qù guówài lǚxíng
申请研究生院 shēnqǐng yánjiūshēngyuàn
去中国留学 qù Zhōngguó liúxué
去纽约工作 qù Niǔyuē gōngzuò

21-7 With a partner, take turns asking and answering the following questions.

1. 你常一面 ＿＿ 一面 ＿＿，是不是?
   Nǐ cháng yímiàn ＿＿＿ yímiàn ＿＿＿ , shìbushì?

2. 昨天下午三点的时候，你正在做什么?
   Zuótiān xiàwǔ sāndiǎn de shíhòu, nǐ zhèngzài zuò shénme?

3. 你今年就要 ＿＿ 岁了，是吗?
   Nǐ jīnnián jiùyào ＿＿＿ suì le, shì ma?

4. 第二十课的作业，你做了吗？
   Dì èrshí kè de zuòyè, nǐ zuò le ma?

5. 你以前常常＿＿＿，现在不＿＿了，是不是？
   Nǐ yǐqián chángcháng ＿＿＿ , xiànzài bù ＿＿ le, shìbushì?

IV. Communicative Activities

21-8 In groups of three or four, role-play the following situation.

Situation: A famous Chinese painting was reported stolen from a museum between 8:00 P.M. and 12:00 A.M. last night. A police officer cross-examines some suspects.

Words and phrases to use:

中国画
Zhōngguó huà (Chinese painting)

有人偷了
yǒurén tōu le (someone stole)

博物馆
bówùguǎn (museum)

一面……一面
yímiàn . . . yímiàn

正在　　　了　　就要/快要……了
zhèngzài　　le　　jiùyào/kuàiyà . . . le

Example:

Police officer:　昨天晚上八点的时候，你正在做什么？
　　　　　　　　Zuótiān wǎnshang bādiǎn de shíhòu, nǐ zhèngzài zuò shénme?

Suspect:　　　　我正在一面看电视，一面打电话。
　　　　　　　　Wǒ zhèngzài yímiàn kàn diànshì, yímiàn dǎ diànhuà.

Police officer:　九点半呢？
　　　　　　　　jiǔdiǎn bàn ne?

21-9 In pairs, role-play the following situation.

Situation: Last year you and your friend made some New Year's resolutions. Some of them were successful and others were not. Talk about the resolutions you made and the changes you have made in your daily routine and habits. Ask each other for advice on the resolutions you were not successful in keeping. Remember to provide some blessings or wishes to encourage him/her.

Words and expressions to use:

一面……一面	了	不……了	就要……了	正在……
yímiàn . . . yímiàn	le	bù . . . le	jiùyào . . . le	zhèngzà . . .

得	想	要	会	应该	然后
děi	xiǎng	yào	huì	yīnggāi	ránhòu

觉得	以前	以后	祝你……
juéde	yǐqián	yǐhòu	zhùnǐ . . .

文化知识 Culture Link

文化点滴 CULTURE NOTES

暑假在中国 Summer Study in China

In China, summer vacation usually starts in late June or early July and ends in late August or early September. While many Western students might take this time to take a break from studying, many Chinese students regard summer as an opportunity for more practice and revision rather than a time to take a break.

Many high school students participate in summer classes to help prepare for future college exams and to build their academic competitiveness. College students take classes not only to help prepare academically, but also to learn life-skills such as sewing, cooking, or driving, as well as music, art, and foreign languages. Many college students also look for part-time work or internships. Other students may take time to volunteer to help rural communities.

Summer is also a good time to study abroad. Just as Chinese students go abroad to study English or other languages and skills, students from overseas come to China to study. The number of students who are interested in studying abroad in Mainland China and Taiwan is increasing every year. Study in 暑期班 [shǔqī bān] (summer programs) is most popular and often combines language study with travel

Do you know...

- what students in China usually do during summer vacation?
- what kinds of classes you can take when studying abroad in China?

Read and find out!

and exploration of the culture and society.

In addition to language and culture classes, there are classes to study Chinese medicine, Chinese martial arts, Chinese calligraphy, and Chinese traditional arts and music.

Most programs have special dorms for international students. These dorms provide all kinds of services, including cafeterias, restaurants, laundry, foreign-currency exchange, and internet connections.

Some programs also provide home-stay opportunities so that students are able to get even closer to the daily life of the Chinese. Even though there are many different dialects of Chinese spoken in different areas of China, all the Chinese study programs offer Mandarin courses and Mandarin is spoken and understood throughout China. Overseas students may also have the opportunity to learn another Chinese dialect in addition to Mandarin.

Studying in China can be a novel experience for international students. Many aspects of their life and study may be different in China, from the style of teaching, to how to handle a washing machine. Some of these differences can be really fascinating, while others may be challenging. One may be able to learn many idiomatic colloquial expressions from a vendor selling wonton soup on the corner of a small street and also have a chance to visit scenic and historic places. Whether focusing on study or travel, one is sure to have an unforgettable summer!

Some students participate in life-skills classes, such as cooking, during the summer. What other things might Chinese students do during summer break?

Children in China are usually required to sit straight during classes. Does this common classroom setting differ from the way classrooms look in your country?

Discuss the following with a group or your class.

1. Have you ever been to China or do you have any plans to study abroad in China? If so, share your experiences or plans with your classmates.
2. What do you think might be the biggest challenges for overseas students in China? Do you think international students studying in your country face the same challenges?

趣味中文 FUN WITH CHINESE

> 活到老，学到老。
>
> One is never too old to learn.

huó	dào	lǎo,	xué	dào	lǎo.
活	到	老,	学	到	老。
live	to	old,	learn	to	old.

Work in small groups or with your class.

1. Practice reading the saying aloud, paying attention to the pronunciation and rhythm.
2. Have you ever encountered or can you imagine a situation where one might say 活到老，学到老? Describe the situation.
3. Have you heard a similar saying in any other languages? If so, what was the saying?

🔊 行动吧！ LET'S GO!

入学申请表 Overseas Student Application Form

文中 is applying to a summer overseas student program in China. Read his application form.

中文暑期班入学[1]申请表[2]				
英文姓名	姓：	*Lee*		
	名：	*John*		
中文姓名	李文中			
国籍[3]	法国			
出生日期	*1990* **年**	*7* **月**	*22* **日**	
性别[4]	☑ 男	☐ 女		
最高学历[5]	大学生，还没毕业			
现在就读学校[6]	纽约州立[7]文化大学			
专业[8]	工程			
通讯地址[9]	美国纽约州纽约市 *3720-A* 春天街 *10020*			
电子邮件地址	*johnlee@nyscu.edu*			
电话 *201-555-7876*		**传真**[10]	*323-555-3321*	
希望住在学生宿舍还是跟中国家庭[11]**住？**　　☐ 学生宿舍　　☑ 跟中国家庭住。				
想参加的活动[12]**？**　　☑ 太极拳[13]　　☐ 书法　　☐ 中国舞　　☐ 中国烹饪[14]				

Notes:

1. 入学(入學) [rùxué]: admission
2. 申请表(申請表) [shēnqǐngbiǎo]: application form
3. 国籍(國籍) [guójí]: nationality
4. 性别 [xìngbié]: gender
5. 学历(學歷) [xuélì]: academic degree
6. 现在就读学校(現在就讀學校) [xiànzài jiùdú xuéxiào]: current school
7. 州立 [zhōulì]: state (e.g. school), belonging to the state
8. 专业(專業) [zhuānyè]: major
9. 通讯地址(通訊地址) [tōngxùn dìzhǐ]: mailing address
10. 传真(傳真) [chuánzhēn]: fax
11. 家庭 [jiātíng]: family
12. 活动(活動) [huódòng]: activity
13. 太极拳(太極拳) [tàijíquán]: tai chi
14. 烹饪(烹飪) [pēngrèn]: cooking, cuisine

Answer the following questions with your partner or group.

1. 文中是哪国人？
   Wénzhōng shì nǎguórén?

2. 他大学毕业了吗？
   Tā dàxué bìyè le ma?

3. 他的专业是什么？你觉得他毕业以后会想做什么？
   Tāde zhuānyè shì shénme? Nǐ juéde tā bìyè yǐhòu huì xiǎng zuòshénme?

4. 你觉得他想一面学中文，一面做什么？
   Nǐ juéde tā xiǎng yímiàn xué Zhōngwén, yímiàn zuò shénme?

22

艺术和文化
Arts and Culture

Dancers in Shanghai practice the fan dance, one of China's traditional dances.

CONNECTIONS AND COMMUNITIES PREVIEW

Discuss the following questions with a partner or your class. What similarities and differences do you think there might be between Chinese culture and your own culture?

1. What are the most representative arts and cultural practices in your culture or community?

2. Have you studied any traditional cultural art of your own or other cultures? What did you study?

教学目标 OBJECTIVES

- Give examples
- Describe cause and effect
- Describe your current situation

生词 VOCABULARY

核心词 Core Vocabulary

	SIMPLIFIED	TRADITIONAL	PINYIN		
1.	因为	因為	yīnwèi	Conj.	because
2.	不过	不過	búguò	Conj.	but, however
3.	认真	認真	rènzhēn	Adj.	conscientious, serious
4.	已经	已經	yǐjīng	Adv.	already
5.	美丽	美麗	měilì	Adj.	beautiful
6.	城市	城市	chéngshì	N.	city
7.	到处	到處	dàochù	N.	everywhere
8.	新	新	xīn	Adj.	new
9.	大楼	大樓	dàlóu	N.	tall building
10.	一些	一些	yìxiē	N.	some
11.	地方	地方	dìfang	N.	place
12.	活动	活動	huódòng	N.	activity
13.	比如	比如	bǐrú	Conj.	for example
14.	京剧	京劇	jīngjù	N.	Peking Opera
15.	书法	書法	shūfǎ	N.	calligraphy
16.	等等	等等	děngděng	Part.	et cetera
17.	东西	東西	dōngxi	N.	thing
18.	小笼包	小籠包	xiǎolóngbāo	N.	little steamed buns with stuffing

	SIMPLIFIED	TRADITIONAL	PINYIN		
19.	机会	機會	jīhuì	N.	opportunity
20.	尝尝	嚐嚐	chángchang	V.	to have a taste
21.	开始	開始	kāishǐ	V.	to start, to begin
22.	高兴	高興	gāoxìng	Adj.	happy
23.	收到	收到	shōudào	V.C.	to receive
24.	看来	看來	kànlái	Conj.	it seems
25.	开心	開心	kāixīn	Adj.	happy
26.	同事	同事	tóngshì	N.	colleague, co-worker
27.	热心	熱心	rèxīn	Adj.	warm-hearted
28.	老板	老闆	lǎobǎn	N.	boss
29.	学到	學到	xuédào	V.C.	to learn, to master
30.	来信	來信	láixìn	V.O.	to write a letter (to the speaker)
31.	保重	保重	bǎozhòng	V.	take care

补充词 Supplementary Vocabulary

	SIMPLIFIED	TRADITIONAL	PINYIN		
1.	心想事成	心想事成	xīnxiǎngshìchéng		Every wish comes true.
2.	健康	健康	jiànkāng	Adj.	healthy
3.	顺利	順利	shùnlì	Adj.	smooth

语文知识 LANGUAGE LINK

Read and listen to the following sentence patterns. These patterns use vocabulary, expressions, and grammar that you will study in more detail in this lesson. After reading the sentence patterns, read and listen to the Language in Use section that follows.

句型 Sentence Patterns

A: 上海怎么样?
Shànghǎi zěnmeyàng?

B: 上海是一个非常美丽的
Shànghǎi shì yíge fēicháng měilìde

城市，到处都是新的大楼。
chéngshì, dàochù dōu shì xīnde dàlóu.

A: 你们在那儿做了什么?
Nǐmen zài nàr zuò le shénme?

B: 我们参加了一些活动，比如:
Wǒmen cānjiā le yìxiē huódòng, bǐrú:

看京剧、写书法等等。
kàn jīngjù, xiě shūfǎ děngděng.

A: 你的实习生活怎么样?
Nǐde shíxí shēnghuó zěnmeyàng?

B: 因为我的同事都很好，
Yīnwèi wǒde tóngshì dōu hěnhǎo,

所以我过得很开心。
suǒyǐ wǒ guòde hěn kāixīn.

课文 Language in Use: 我到上海了

海华:
Hǎihuá:

你好! 今天是六月十五号，我一个星期以前就到上海了。
Nǐhǎo! Jīntiān shì liùyuè shíwǔhào, wǒ yíge xīngqī yǐqián jiù dào Shànghǎi le.

对不起，因为太忙了，所以今天才给你写电子邮件。
Duìbuqǐ, yīnwèi tài máng le, suǒyǐ jīntiān cái gěi nǐ xiě diànzǐ yóujiàn.

我们每天都有很多课，功课也不少。不过老师教得很好，
Wǒmen měitiān dōu yǒu hěnduō kè, gōngkè yě bùshǎo. Búguò lǎoshī jiāode hěnhǎo,

也很认真。我们每天都说中文。我的中文进步得很快，
yě hěn rènzhēn. Wǒmen měitiān dōu shuō Zhōngwén. Wǒde Zhōngwén jìnbù de hěnkuài.

现在我已经能说很多中文了。
Xiànzài wǒ yǐjīng néng shuō hěnduō Zhōngwén le.

上海是一个非常美丽的城市，到处都是新的大楼。
Shànghǎi shì yíge fēicháng měilìde chéngshì, dàochù dōu shì xīnde dàlóu.

我们参观了一些地方，也参加了一些活动，
Wǒmen cānguān le yìxiē dìfang, yě cānjiā le yìxiē huódòng,

比如：看京剧、写书法等等，都很有意思。
bǐrú: kàn jīngjù, xiě shūfǎ děngděng, dōu hěn yǒuyìsi.

等等 [děngděng]
等等 means "et cetera," and is usually used after a list of people or things. Sometimes one character 等 is used instead of two.

还有，上海有很多好吃的东西，
Háiyǒu, Shànghǎi yǒu hěnduō hǎochī de dōngxi,

其中我最喜欢吃的是小笼包。
qízhōng wǒ zuì xǐhuān chī de shì xiǎolóngbāo.

还有 [háiyǒu]
还有 means "furthermore," "also," "in addition." It is used to introduce additional information.

你有机会应该尝尝。
Nǐ yǒu jīhuì yīnggāi chángchang.

你开始实习了吗? 忙不忙? 有空请给我写电子邮件。
Nǐ kāishǐ shíxí le ma? Mángbumáng? Yǒukòng qǐng gěi wǒ xiě diànzǐ yóujiàn.

祝　好!
Zhù　Hǎo!

秋雨
Qiūyǔ

二〇一〇年六月十五日
èr líng yī líng nián liù yuè shíwǔ rì

秋雨：
Qiūyǔ:

你好！很高兴收到你的电子邮件。看来你在
Nǐhǎo! Hěn gāoxìng shōudào nǐde diànzǐ yóujiàn. Kànlái nǐ zài

上海过得很开心。
Shànghǎi guòde hěn kāixīn.

我现在在洛杉矶，已经开始实习了。这儿的同事都很好，
Wǒ xiànzài zài Luòshānjī, yǐjīng kāishǐ shíxí le. Zhèr de tóngshì dōu hěnhǎo,

也很热心，常常教我很多东西，老板也不错。我的
yě hěn rèxīn, chángcháng jiāo wǒ hěnduō dōngxi, lǎobǎn yě búcuò. Wǒde

工作有时候忙，有时候不太忙，我想我得认真地工作，
gōngzuò yǒushíhou máng, yǒushíhou bútàimáng. Wǒ xiǎng wǒ děi rènzhēn de gōngzuò,

才能学到一些东西。
cái néng xué dào yìxiē dōngxi.

好了，不多写了。有空请多来信。
Hǎo le, bù duō xiě le. Yǒukòng qǐng duō láixìn.

多保重。
Duō bǎozhòng.

祝　好！
Zhù　Hǎo!

来信 [láixìn]
来信 is a V.O. that means "a letter coming from . . .". 来 is used here to indicate that this is said from the speaker's point of view, which means the letter is coming to the speaker.

海华
Hǎihuá

二〇一〇年六月十七日
èr líng yī líng nián liù yuè shíqī rì

语法 GRAMMAR

I. 比如

比如 [bǐrú] is an expression equivalent to "for example," "for instance," or "such as" in English. It is used to introduce specific examples.

我们的晚会有很多活动，比如：唱歌、跳舞、写书法等等。
Wǒmende wǎnhuì yǒu hěnduō huódòng, bǐrú: chànggē, tiàowǔ, xiě shūfǎ děngděng.
(Our party had many activities, such as singing, dancing, and calligraphy.)

他会说很多语言，比如：英文、中文、法文、西班牙文。
Tā huì shuō hěnduō yǔyán, bǐrú: Yīngwén, Zhōngwén, Fǎwén, Xībānyáwén.
(He knows many languages, such as English, Chinese, French, and Spanish.)

>> **Try it!** With a partner, practice using 比如 with examples.

1. A: 你喜欢吃中国菜吗?
      Nǐ xǐhuān chī Zhōngguócài ma?

   B: 我很喜欢吃中国菜，_____ : _____ 。
      Wǒ hěn xǐhuān chī Zhōngguócài, _____ : _____ .

2. A: 你想不想去国外旅行?
      Nǐ xiǎngbuxiǎng qù guówài lǚxíng?

   B: 我很想去国外旅行，_____ : _____ 。
      Wǒ hěn xiǎng qù guówài lǚxíng, _____ : _____ .

3. A: 你常锻炼吗?
      Nǐ cháng duànliàn ma?

   B: 我常锻炼，_____ : _____ 。
      Wǒ cháng duànliàn, _____ : _____ .

II. 因为......所以......

As we previously learned, 所以 [suǒyǐ] is used to indicate causality, meaning "so" or "therefore." 所以 [suǒyǐ] is often used with 因为 [yīnwèi] as a pair of conjunctions. Note that while in English *because* and *so* are not used together, in Chinese 因为 [yīnwèi] and 所以 [suǒyǐ] are often used together in one sentence. Sometimes 因为 [yīnwèi] can be omitted if the cause-effect relationship between the first and the second clauses is clear.

Note also that though one usually doesn't start a sentence with *because* in English, in Chinese 因为 comes at the beginning of the sentence.

(因为)冬天太冷，所以我不喜欢冬天。
(Yīnwèi) dōngtiān tài lěng, suǒyǐ wǒ bù xǐhuān dōngtiān.
(I don't like winter because it is too cold.)

(因为)她常常锻炼，所以她的身体[1]很好。
(Yīnwèi) tā chángcháng duàn liàn, suǒyǐ tāde shēntǐ hěn hǎo.
(She is in good shape because she exercises often.)

Note:
1. 身体(身體) [shēntǐ]: body, health

>>Try it! With a partner, complete the sentences with 因为......所以...... and your own ideas.

1. ＿＿＿ 今天是我妈妈的生日，＿＿＿ 我会 ＿＿＿＿＿＿。
   ＿＿＿ jīntiān shì wǒ māma de shēngrì, ＿＿＿ wǒ huì ＿＿＿＿＿＿ .

2. ＿＿＿ 明天我朋友会来我家，＿＿＿ 我应该 ＿＿＿＿＿＿。
   ＿＿＿ míngtiān wǒ péngyou huì lái wǒ jiā, ＿＿＿ wǒ yīnggāi ＿＿＿＿＿＿ .

3. ＿＿＿ 他不要跟很多人一起住，＿＿＿ 他 ＿＿＿＿＿＿。
   ＿＿＿ tā búyào gēn hěnduō rén yìqǐ zhù, ＿＿＿ tā ＿＿＿＿＿＿ .

4. ＿＿＿ 她要参加球赛，＿＿＿ 她 ＿＿＿＿＿＿。
   ＿＿＿ tā yào cānjiā qiúsài, ＿＿＿ tā ＿＿＿＿＿＿ .

🔊 补充课文 **SUPPLEMENTARY PRACTICE**

Read the following dialogue. Then listen and repeat.

(打电话)
秋雨：喂，你好！请问海华在吗？
海华：我就是。你是秋雨吧？
秋雨：对，是我。
海华：你在哪儿？
秋雨：我在上海。我一个星期以前就到了。对不起，因为太忙了，所以到现在才给你打电话。
海华：没关系。你在那儿好吗？

秋雨：　很好，可是太忙了。我们每天都有很多课，功课也不少。

海华：　你们的老师怎么样？

秋雨：　老师很不错，教得很认真。

海华：　你现在中文一定进步得很快吧？

秋雨：　还不错，我们每天都说中文。我现在已经可以说很多了。

海华：　太好了。你觉得上海怎么样？

秋雨：　我很喜欢上海。上海非常漂亮[1]。我们去了很多地方玩儿，还看了京剧，写了书法，参加了很多活动，很有意思。对了，这儿有很多好吃的东西。

海华：　真的[2]？那[3]你最喜欢吃什么？

秋雨：　我最喜欢吃小笼包。真的很好吃。有机会你一定要尝尝。

海华：　好的。看来你在上海过得很开心。

秋雨：　你呢？你在洛杉矶还好吗？

海华：　还可以。我已经开始实习了，老板还不错，同事们都很好，也很热心，还教了我不少东西。

秋雨：　工作忙不忙？

海华：　有时候忙，有时候不太忙。我想多学一些东西，所以得认真地工作。

秋雨：　有志者事竟成[4]。祝你成功[5]！

海华：　谢谢。好，就这样[6]。请多保重。

秋雨：　我也要挂[7]电话了。再见！

海华：　再见！

Notes:

1. 漂亮 [piàoliang]: pretty, beautiful
2. 真的 [zhēnde]: really
3. 那 [nà]: (in this context, it has the meaning of "so . . .")
4. 有志者事竟成 [Yǒuzhìzhě shì jìng chéng]: expression meaning "Where there is a will, there is a way."
5. 成功 [chénggōng]: success
6. 就这样(就這樣) [jiùzhèyàng]: that's it, that's all
7. 挂(掛) [guà]: to hang up (the phone)

Pinyin version:

(dǎ diànhuà)

Qiūyǔ:　Wéi, nǐhǎo! Qǐngwèn Hǎihuá zài ma?

Hǎihuá:　Wǒ jiùshì. Nǐ shì Qiūyǔ ba?

Qiūyǔ:　Duì, shì wǒ.

Hǎihuá:　Nǐ zài nǎr?

Qiūyǔ:　Wǒ zài Shànghǎi. Wǒ yíge xīngqī yǐqián jiù dào le. Duìbuqǐ, yīnwèi tài máng le, suǒyǐ dào xiànzài cái gěi nǐ dǎ diànhuà.

Hǎihuá: Méiguānxi. Nǐ zài nàr hǎo ma?

Qiūyǔ: Hěn hǎo, kěshì tài máng le. Wǒmen měitiān dōu yǒu hěnduō kè, gōngkè yě bùshǎo.

Hǎihuá: Nǐmende lǎoshī zěnmeyàng?

Qiūyǔ: Lǎoshī hěn búcuò, jiāode hěn rènzhēn.

Hǎihuá: Nǐ xiànzài Zhōngwén yídìng jìnbù de hěnkuài ba?

Qiūyǔ: Hái búcuò, wǒmen měitiān dōu shuō Zhōngwén. Wǒ xiànzài yǐjīng kěyǐ shuō hěnduō le.

Hǎihuá: Tài hǎo le. Nǐ juéde Shànghǎi zěnmeyàng?

Qiūyǔ: Wǒ hěn xǐhuān Shànghǎi. Shànghǎi fēicháng piàoliang. Wǒmen qùle hěnduō dìfang wár, hái kànle Jīngjù, xiěle shūfǎ, cānjiā le hěnduō huódòng, hěn yǒuyìsi. Duì le, zhèr yǒu hěnduō hǎochī de dōngxi.

Hǎihuá: Zhēnde? Nà nǐ zuì xǐhuān chī shénme?

Qiūyǔ: Wǒ zuì xǐhuān chī xiǎolóngbāo. Zhēnde hěn hǎochī. Yǒu jīhuì nǐ yídìng yào chángchang.

Hǎihuá: Hǎode. Kànlái nǐ zài Shànghǎi guòde hěn kāixīn.

Qiūyǔ: Nǐ ne? Nǐ zài Luòshānjī háihǎo ma?

Hǎihuá: Hái kěyǐ. Wǒ yǐjīng kāishǐ shíxí le, lǎobǎn hái búcuò, tóngshìmen dōu hěnhǎo, yě hěn rèxīn, hái jiāole wǒ bùshǎo dōngxi.

Qiūyǔ: Gōngzuò mángbumáng?

Hǎihuá: Yǒushíhòu máng, yǒushíhòu bú tài máng. Wǒ xiǎng duō xué yìxiē dōngxi, suǒyǐ děi rènzhēn de gōngzuò.

Qiūyǔ: Yǒu zhì zhě shì jìng chéng. Zhù nǐ chénggōng!

Hǎihuá: Xièxie. Hǎo, jiù zhèyàng. Qǐng duō bǎozhòng.

Qiūyǔ: Wǒ yě yào guà diànhuà le. Zàijiàn!

Hǎihuá: Zàijiàn!

Write the answers to the following questions in Chinese.

1. 秋雨在上海怎么样?   _____
   Qiūyǔ zài Shànghǎi zěnmeyàng?

2. 秋雨的老师怎么样?   _____
   Qiūyǔ de lǎoshī zěnmeyàng?

3. 秋雨觉得上海怎么样?   _____
   Qiūyǔ juéde Shànghǎi zěnmeyàng?

4. 在上海秋雨最喜欢吃什么? _____
   Zài Shànghǎi Qiūyǔ zuì xǐhuān chī shénme?

5. 海华的同事们怎么样?   _____
   Hǎihuá de tóngshìmen zěnmeyàng?

练习 ACTIVITIES

I. Listening Exercises

22-1 Listen and write down the short dialogues you hear in Pinyin.

1. _____

    _____

2. _____

    _____

3. _____

    _____

4. _____

    _____

22-2 Work in groups of three or four. Take turns reading the lines of the following poem, paying special attention to the tones and rhythm.

Gǔyuán Cǎo **(Bái Jūyì)**	**古原草** **(白居易)**

Lílí yuán shàng cǎo,   离离原上草，

Yí suì yì kū róng.   一岁一枯荣。

Yěhuǒ shāo bú jìn,   野火烧不尽，

Chūnfēng chuī yòu shēng.   春风吹又生。

Grass on the Old Grassland
(Bai, Juyi)

The grass is growing in full bloom on the grassland,
Every year it withers and grows again.
Wild fire will not burn it dead,
It grows again with the coming of spring wind.

II.   Character Exercises

22-3 Match each Chinese word with its English meaning. Then check your answers with a partner.

_____ 1. 热心   a. to start
rèxīn

_____ 2. 开心   b. thing
kāixīn

_____ 3. 认真   c. already
rènzhēn

_____ 4. 开始   d. Peking Opera
kāishǐ

_____ 5. 活动   e. warm-hearted
huódòng

_____ 6. 东西   f. happy
dōngxi

_____ 7. 京剧   g. activity
jīngjù

_____ 8. 已经   h. conscientious
yǐjīng

22-4 Write the radical for each of the following characters. Then write another character with the same radical for each. Check your answers with a partner.

1. 认   _____

2. 城   _____

3. 热   _____

4. 尝   _____

5. 板   _____

6. 活   _____

III. Grammar Exercises

22-5 Look at the following example. With a partner, take turns extending the words below into phrases and then sentences. See how long you can keep extending the sentences.

Example:

A: 城市   chéngshì

B: 大城市   dà chéngshì

A: 是一个大城市   shì yíge dà chéngshì

B: 上海是一个大城市。   Shànghǎi shì yíge dà chéngshì.

A: 上海是一个美丽的大城市。   Shànghǎi shì yíge měilìde dà chéngshì.

1. 处   2. 新   3. 方   4. 京   5. 东   6. 始   7. 收   8. 保

   chù   xīn   fāng   jīng   dōng   shǐ   shōu   bǎo

22-6 Connect the following sentences with 因为……所以…… [yīnwèi . . . suǒyǐ . . .]. Then check your answers with a partner or the class.

1. 上海很美。我很想去上海看看。

   Shànghǎi hěnměi. Wǒ hěnxiǎng qù Shànghǎi kànkan.

   _____

2. 现在已经是六月了。天气不冷。

   Xiànzài yǐjīng shì liùyuè le. Tiānqì bùlěng.

   _____

3. 我要上北京的暑期班。我要去北京。

   Wǒ yào shàng Běijīng de shǔqībān. Wǒ yào qù Běijīng.

   _____

4. 我今天十一点才起床。我还没有吃早饭。

   Wǒ jīntiān shíyīdiǎn cái qǐchuáng. Wǒ hái méiyǒu chī zǎofàn.

   _____

22-7 Complete the following sentences with 比如 [bǐrú], 等等, and your own examples. Then share your answers with a partner.

Example: 我们参加了很多活动……

              Wǒmen cānjiā le hěnduō huódòng . . .

   我们参加了很多活动，比如：看京剧，写书法等等。

1. 我喜欢吃中国菜......
   Wǒ xǐhuān chī Zhōngguócài . . .

   _____

2. 我很想去中国看看，想去很多地方......
   Wǒ hěnxiǎng qù Zhōngguó kànkan, xiǎng qù hěnduō dìfang . . .

   _____

3. 我朋友会说很多语言......
   Wǒ péngyou huì shuō hěnduō yǔyán . . .

   _____

IV. Communicative Activities

22-8 In pairs, role-play the following situation.

Situation: You and a friend are talking on the phone. Your friend is now studying Chinese in Beijing, China, and you are doing an internship at a company in New York. This is your second week at work.

Ask your friend about their life and studies in Beijing. Your friend tells you about their classes, teachers, and homework. Your friend also talks about their daily activities. Your friend asks about your internship. Tell your friend how you feel about your work at the company. Share some arts and culture experiences you have had in Beijing and New York. Finally, you encourage each other to do a good job in both studies and work and promise that you will email each other as often as possible.

Words and expressions to use:

对不起	因为......所以	一个星期
duìbuqǐ	yīnwèi . . . suǒyǐ	yíge xīngqī
还是	每天	机会
háishì	měitiān	jīhuì
参观	比如	
cānguān	bǐrú	
一面......一面......		
yímiàn . . . yímiàn . . .		

22-9 With a partner, ask and answer "why" questions. Start by asking a question with "为什么......?" [wèishénme] (Why . . . ?). The partner answers using 因为......所以...... and then asks a new "why" question.

Example:

A: 他为什么要吃三盘炒饭？
　　Tā wèishénme yào chī sānpán chǎofàn?

B: 因为他今天到现在都还没有吃饭，他很饿，
　　Yīnwèi tā jīntiān dào xiànzài dōu hái méiyǒu chīfàn, tā hěn è,

　　所以他要吃三盘炒饭！
　　suǒyǐ tā yào chī sānpán chǎofàn!

文化知识 Culture Link

文化点滴 CULTURE NOTES

京剧和书法 Peking Opera and Chinese Calligraphy

Of the different examples of Chinese arts, Peking Opera and Chinese calligraphy are perhaps the most famous. Peking Opera, also known as 京剧 (Beijing Opera) originated in the 安徽 [Ānhuī] (Anhui) and 湖北 [Húběi] (Hubei) Provinces of China in the 18th century and is now known as China's national opera. In fact, in Taiwan it is referred to as 国剧 [guójù] (national opera). There are two types of 京剧: 文戏 [wénxì] (civil pieces), which contain mostly singing, and 武戏 [wǔxì] (martial pieces), which feature acrobatics and stunts. Some operas are a combination of both.

The repertoire of 京剧 includes historical subjects, comedic performances, and tragedies. Two groups of musicians (a string section and a percussion section) accompany the singing and action on traditional Chinese instruments. The operatic dialogues and monologues are recited in the Beijing dialect, with some words pronounced in ways unique to Peking Opera. Special movements are used by the performers to portray emotions, such as smoothing a beard, raising a foot, jerking a sleeve, or adjusting a hat. Costuming is based on Ming Dynasty dress and is extravagant and colorful.

Do you know...

- what the two types of Peking opera are?
- what the personality is of a character with a red-painted face?
- what the expression "the four treasures of the study room" refers to?

Read and find out!

In 京剧, there are usually four roles: 生 [shēng] (male), 旦 [dàn] (female), 净 [jìng] (painted face), and 丑 [chǒu] (the clown). These roles are further classified by age and profession. The personalities of the characters are often revealed by the way the character sings and moves as well as the color of their face makeup. The clown role is marked by white on the ridge of his nose and can have a number of personalities, from a light-hearted and humorous character, to an evil and crafty one. The painted-face characters have different personalities depending on the main color of their face. Red indicates uprightness and loyalty; white represents craftiness and cunning; blue represents vigor and courage; yellow represents intelligence; black represents honesty; and brown represents stubbornness.

While Peking Opera is one of the best-known performing arts, 书法 is considered the highest form of art in China. Together with painting, it is the best embodiment of Chinese philosophy around the world. The Daoist theory of yin-yang is integrated to create balance and harmony not only in the calligraphy produced but also in the actual writing process. Many calligraphers are both scholars and artists who often incorporate poems in their calligraphic art as well. For calligraphers, the tools used are often referred to as the 文房四宝 [wénfángsìbǎo] (the four treasures of the study room), an expression that refers to paper, writing brush, ink slab, and ink stick.

Both Peking Opera and calligraphy are popular today. There are a number of schools in China and Taiwan dedicated to training children to be future performers in Peking Opera and there are many classes for learning calligraphy for students of any age. Today, you might even see people practicing their calligraphy on the ground, using a large brush with water as ink, and the ground as the paper!

Colorful makeup of a Peking Opera performer. How can you tell which role the performer is playing?

Calligraphy practice in the park, using water to write on the ground. Which of the "four treasures of the study room" do the ground and the water take the place of?

Discuss the following with a group or your class.

1. What are some of the similarities and differences between Peking Opera and Western opera?
2. Are there any special performing arts in your culture? What are they? Are they popular in your culture?
3. Are there any special styles of writing or painting in your culture? What are they? Do many people study them?

趣味中文 FUN WITH CHINESE

心想事成

May your heart's desire come true.

xīn	xiǎng	shì	chéng
心	想	事	成
mind/heart	think	matter	accomplish

Work in small groups or with your class.

1. Practice reading the idiom aloud, paying attention to the pronunciation and rhythm.
2. Do you believe in 心想事成? Why or why not?

行动吧! LET'S GO!

书画展 Calligraphy and Painting Exhibition

After the summer program in Shangai, 秋雨 went to visit her friends in Taipei. Knowing that 秋雨 is fond of Chinese calligraphy and painting, her friends took her to see a calligraphy exhibition. Read the following information about the exhibition.

国立故宫博物院¹书画展²

展览³地点⁴：二楼，201，202展览室⁵
展览日期⁶：六月一日到八月三十一日
票价⁷：40元

Notes:

1. 国立故宫博物院(國立故宮博物院) [Guólì Gùgōng Bówùyuàn]: National Palace Museum
2. 书画展(書畫展) [shūhuà zhǎn]: calligraphy and painting exhibition
3. 展览(展覽) [zhǎnlǎn]: exhibition, show
4. 地点(地點) [dìdiǎn]: location
5. 展览室(展覽室) [zhǎnlǎn shì]: gallery, exhibition room
6. 日期 [rìqī]: date
7. 价(價) [jià]: price

Answer the following questions with a partner or your group.

1. 书画展在哪儿? 展览室在几楼?
   Shūhuàzhǎn zài nǎr? Zhǎnlǎnshì zài jǐlóu?

2. 展览是从几月几日到几月几日?
   Zhǎnlǎn shì cóng jǐyuè jǐrì dào jǐyuè jǐrì?

3. 书画展的票多少钱?
   Shūhuàzhǎn de piào duōshǎoqián?

4. 你觉得秋雨看书画展会不会很开心? 为什么?
   Nǐ juéde Qiūyǔ kàn shūhuàzhǎn huìbuhuì hěn kāixīn? Wèishénme?

复习 Review

LESSON 19 TO LESSON 22

I. Conversation Review

1. With a partner, take turns asking and answering questions to find out the following information about each other.

- 生病的时候，应该做什么？
  shēngbìngde shíhòu, yīnggāi zuò shénme?

- 上次感冒，有什么症状？(上次 [shàngcì]: last time; 症状 [zhèngzhuàng]: symptoms)
  shàngcì gǎnmào, yǒu shénme zhèngzhuàng?

- 会听医生说的话吗？会把药吃了吗？
  huì tīng yīshēng shuōde huà ma? huì bǎ yào chīle ma?

- 上次怎么生病了？
  shàngcì zěnme shēngbìng le?

- 因为生病所以不能做什么？
  yīnwèi shēngbìng suǒyǐ bùnéng zuò shénme?

- 搬家的时候，一定要带什么去？
  bānjiā de shíhòu, yídìng yào dài shénme qù?

- 今天有没有空要不要过来一起 _____ ?
  jīntiān yǒuméiyǒu kòng yàobuyào guòlái yìqǐ _____ ?

- 得付房租吗？什么时候付房租？
  děi fù fángzū ma? shénme shíhòu fù fángzū?

- 今年暑假你想做什么？
  jīnnián shǔjià nǐ xiǎng zuò shénme?

- 想不想实习？想在什么公司实习？
  xiǎngbuxiǎng shíxí? xiǎng zài shénme gōngsī shíxí?

- 有没有打工？你的老板怎么样？同事呢？
  yǒuméiyǒu dǎgōng? Nǐde lǎobǎn zěnmeyàng? tóngshì ne?

- 什么让你很高兴?
  shénme ràng nǐ hěn gāoxìng?

- 学习得怎么样?
  xuéxí de zěnmeyàng?

2. With a partner, talk about a previous summer vacation experience. Then talk about your plans for after your graduation.

Words and expressions to use:

实习　　申请　　决定　　比如
shíxí　　shēnqǐng　　juédìng　　bǐrú

因为……所以……　　不过/可是/但是……　　还是　　或者
yīnwèi . . . suǒyǐ . . .　　búguò/kěshì/dànshì . . .　　háishì　　huòzhě

先……再……然后……　　一面……一面……
xiān . . . zài . . . ránhòu . . .　　yímiàn . . . yímiàn . . .

暑期班　　活动　　最　　参观　　忙　　城市
shǔqībān　　huódòng　　zuì　　cānguān　　máng　　chéngshì

II. Writing and Character Review

1. Radical practice game. Form groups of three or four. Write the following radicals on separate squares of paper.

广　　心(忄)　　人(亻)　　手(扌)　　口　　火(灬)

Turn all the squares over so that the blank sides face up. As you take turns, flip over one of the paper squares and say a character you have learned that has the same radical in it. Write the character on a piece of paper so the group can keep track of which characters have already been said. (Once a character has been said, it cannot be used again.)

Keep playing until you have come up with as many characters as you can think of. Then compare your group's list with other groups. Did you find all the same characters for the radicals?

2. Race to write! Divide into two teams. Spend a few minutes looking over the characters you have learned in Lessons 19–22. Then your teacher will call out a word, and a member from each team will race to write the character on the board. The first person who writes the word correctly will gain a point for their team. See which team can get 10 points first!

3. Fill in the Overseas Student Application Form below with your own information. (Refer to the form in the *Let's Go!* section of Lesson 21 on page 215 for help.)

<table>
<tr><td colspan="4" align="center">中文暑期班入学申请表</td></tr>
<tr><td rowspan="2">英文姓名
[Yīngwén xìngmíng]</td><td>姓：</td><td></td><td></td></tr>
<tr><td>名：</td><td></td><td></td></tr>
<tr><td>中文姓名
[Zhōngwén xìngmíng]</td><td colspan="3"></td></tr>
<tr><td>国籍
[guójí]</td><td colspan="3"></td></tr>
<tr><td>出生日期 [chūshēng rìqī]</td><td>年</td><td>月</td><td>日</td></tr>
<tr><td>性别 [xìngbié]</td><td colspan="3">□ 男   □ 女</td></tr>
<tr><td>最高学历
[zuìgāo xuélì]</td><td colspan="3"></td></tr>
<tr><td>现在就读学校
[xiànzài jiùdú xuéxiào]</td><td colspan="3"></td></tr>
<tr><td>专业
[zhuānyè]</td><td colspan="3"></td></tr>
<tr><td>通讯地址
[tōngxùn dìzhǐ]</td><td colspan="3"></td></tr>
<tr><td>电子邮件地址
[diànzǐ yóujiàn dìzhǐ]</td><td colspan="3"></td></tr>
<tr><td>电话 [diànhuà]</td><td colspan="3"></td></tr>
</table>

希望住在学生宿舍还是跟中国家庭住？

[xīwàng zhùzài xuéshēng sùshè háishì gēn Zhōngguó jiātíng zhù?]

□ 学生宿舍   □ 跟中国家庭住

想参加的活动？ [xiǎng cānjiā de huódòng]

□ 太极拳   □ 书法   □ 中国舞   □ 中国烹饪
   [tàijíquán]   [shūfǎ]   [Zhōngguó wǔ]   [Zhōngguó pēngrèn]

III. Comprehensive Review

1. Work with a partner or in small groups. Last Saturday, 海华, 志信, 秋雨, and 欧阳明 were all planning to attend a graduation party and bring a dish. One person couldn't make it. At the party they all talked about what they will do in the summer. Discuss the following clues and use the chart below to figure out how each person came to the party, what item they brought, and what they will do this summer.

Clues:

1. 欧阳明有一点不舒服，他发烧头疼，这几天他都没出去。

   Ōuyáng Míng yǒu yìdiǎn bù shūfu, tā fāshāo tóuténg, zhèjǐtiān tā dōu méi chūqù.

2. 志信把他的车借给妹妹了。

   Zhìxìn bǎ tāde chē jiègěi mèimei le.

3. 在夏天的时候，欧阳明决定要学日文。他应该认真地在
   学校学习。

   Zài xiàtiān de shíhòu, Ōuyáng Míng juédìng yào xué Rìwén. Tā yīnggāi rènzhēnde zài xuéxiào xuéxí.

4. 海华做饭做得很好吃，比如：炒饭、汤、蛋糕。她要在一家蛋糕店
   实习。

   Hǎihuá zuòfàn zuòde hěn hǎochī, bǐrú: chǎofàn, tāng, dàngāo. Tā yàozài yìjiā dàngāodiàn shíxí.

5. 秋雨把昨天买的飞机票带来给大家看。她想一面去法国旅行
   一面学法文。

   Qiūyǔ bǎ zuótiān mǎide fēijīpiào dàilái gěi dàjiā kàn. Tā xiǎng yímiàn qù Fǎguó lǚxíng yímiàn xué Fǎwén.

6. 因为秋雨的家离晚会很近，所以她会走过来。

   Yīnwèi Qiūyǔde jiā lí wǎnhuì hěnjìn, suǒyǐ tā huì zǒu guòlái.

7. 志信很爱吃中国菜。他一定会带中国菜去晚会。

   Zhìxìn hěn ài chī Zhōngguó cài. Tā yídìng huì dài Zhōngguó cài qù wǎnhuì.

8. 秋雨带了三瓶可乐去晚会。

   Qiūyǔ dàile sānpíng kělè qù wǎnhuì.

	开车	走路	坐公共汽车	没来	可乐	蛋糕	小笼包	没带东西	实习	暑期班	去国外	还没决定
海华												
志信												
秋雨												
欧阳明												

With your partner or group, answer the following questions, using the information above.

1. 暑假的时候，大家会做什么？
   Shǔjià de shíhòu, dàjiā huì zuò shénme?

2. 大家是怎么过来的？大家都带了什么？
   Dàjiā shì zěnme guòlái de? Dàjiā dōu dàile shénme?

3. 你觉得欧阳明怎么了？
   Nǐ juéde Ōuyáng Míng zěnme le?

4. 为什么志信没开车去？
   Wèishénme Zhìxìn méi kāichē qù?

5. 蛋糕好吃极了！大家一定会把蛋糕怎么了？
   Dàngāo hǎochī jí le! Dàjiā yídìng huì bǎ dàngāo zěnme le?

6. 在晚会上，大家都做什么了？
   Zài wǎnhuì shàng, dàjiā dōu zuò shénme le?

7. 志信为什么带小笼包来了？
   Zhìxìn wèishénme dài xiǎolóngbāo lái le?

8. 秋雨为什么要去法国？
   Qiūyǔ wèishénme yào qù Fǎguó?

语法小结 GRAMMAR SUMMARY

I. Optative Verbs

OPTATIVE VERB	MEANING	EXAMPLE	NEGATION
要 [yào]	1. want, will, to be going to	我要去机场。 Wǒ yào qù jīchǎng. (I'm going to go to the airport.)	不想 (irregular negation)
	2. have to, should	你要多练习中文。 Nǐ yào duō liànxí Zhōngwén. (You should practice Chinese more.)	不用 (irregular negation)
想 [xiǎng]	want, intend, would like to	我想吃饺子。 Wǒ xiǎng chī jiǎozi. (I would like to eat dumplings.)	不想
应该 [yīnggāi]	should, ought to, to be supposed to	你应该在宿舍学习。 Nǐ yīnggāi zài sùshè xuéxí. (You should study at the dorm.)	不应该
得 [děi]	have to, to be required to	我得去机场接人。 Wǒ děi qù jīchǎng jiē rén. (I have to pick someone up from the airport.)	不用 (irregular negation)
能 [néng]	1. have the ability to, can	我能开手排挡的车。 Wǒ néng kāi shǒupáidǎng de chē. (I'm able to drive a car with manual transmission.)	不会 (irregular negation)
	2. can (depending on circumstances)	他明天能来上课。 Tā míngtiān néng lái shàngkè. (He can come to class tomorrow.)	不能
	3. permission — may	我能借他的车。 Wǒ néng jiè tāde chē. (We may borrow his car.)	不能

OPTATIVE VERB	MEANING	EXAMPLE	NEGATION
可以 [kěyǐ]	1. permission — may	我可以借他的车。 Wǒ kěyǐ jiè tāde chē. (I may borrow his car.)	不可以 不能 (irregular negation)
	2. can (depending on circumstances)	他明天可以来。 Tā míngtiān kěyǐ lái. (He can come tomorrow.)	不能 (irregular negation)
会 [huì]	1. know how to, have the ability to	我会开车。 Wǒ huì kāichē. (I know how to drive.)	不会
	2. be likely to, will	他明天会来。 Tā míngtiān huì lái. (He will come tomorrow.)	不会

II. 从……去/到……

From one place to another:

从 Place 1 + Means + 去/到 Place 2

他从上海坐飞机去洛杉矶玩。
Tā cóng Shànghǎi zuò fēijī qù Luòshānjī wán.
(He flew from Shanghai to LA for fun.)

From one point in time to another:

从 Time 1 + 到 Time 2

这个学期是从一月到五月。
Zhège xuéqī shì cóng yīyuè dào wǔyuè.
(This semester runs from January to May.)

III. 多/少 + V./V.P.

多/少 + V./V.P. is used to indicate doing more/less of an action.

你要多学习。
Nǐ yào duō xuéxí.

You need to study more.

他应该少喝咖啡。
Tā yīnggāi shǎo hē kāfēi.

He should drink less coffee.

我要多睡一点儿。
Wǒ yào duō shuì yìdiǎr.

I want to sleep a little more.

IV. Duplication of Verbs

Duplicated verbs indicate a quick action, doing a little bit of something, or doing something in a relaxed way. Only verbs that express active actions or behaviors can be duplicated.

single-syllable verbs	试试 [shìshi] (to try)
	穿穿 [chuānchuan] (to try on)
	说说 [shuōshuo] (to say a little)
	看看 [kànkan] (to have a look)
	写写 [xiěxie] (to write a little)
	想想 [xiǎngxiang] (to think a little)
two-syllable verbs	介绍介绍 [jièshao jièshao] (to give a little introduction)
	学习学习 [xuéxi xuéxi] (to study a little)

V. Days of the Week; Referring to Days, Weeks, Months, and Years

MONDAY	TUESDAY	WEDNESDAY	THURSDAY	FRIDAY	SATURDAY	SUNDAY
星期一 礼拜一 周一	星期二 礼拜二 周二	星期三 礼拜三 周三	星期四 礼拜四 周四	星期五 礼拜五 周五	星期六 礼拜六 周六	星期日/天 礼拜日/天 周日
					周末	

前天 [qiántiān] *the day before yesterday*	昨天 [zuótiān] *yesterday*	今天 [jīntiān] *today*	明天 [míngtiān] *tomorrow*	后天 [hòutiān] *the day after tomorrow*
前年 [qiánnián] *the year before last year*	去年 [qùnián] *last year*	今年 [jīnnián] *this year*	明年 [míngnián] *next year*	后年 [hòunián] *the year after next year*

上上个星期 [shàngshàngge xīngqī] *the week before last week*	上个星期 [shàngge xīngqī] *last week*	这个星期 [zhège xīngqī] *this week*	下个星期 [xiàge xīngqī] *next week*	下下个星期 [xiàxiàge xīngqī] *the week after next week*
上上个月 [shàngshàngge yuè] *the month before last month*	上个月 [shàngge yuè] *last month*	这个月 [zhège yuè] *this month*	下个月 [xiàge yuè] *next month*	下下个月 [xiàxiàgge yuè] *the month after next month*

VI. The Preposition 为

The preposition 为 [wèi] is used with an object and a verb phrase (V.P.) to indicate doing something for someone.

Subj.	P.P. (为 + Obj.)	V.P.	
他	为我	开一个晚会。	He is having a party for me.
Tā	wèi wǒ	kāi yíge wǎnhuì.	
(He)	(for me)	(holds a party)	

VII. Position Words

POSITION WORDS	ENGLISH	POSITION WORDS	ENGLISH
前边/前面 qiánbiān/qiánmiàn	front	后边/后面 hòubiān/hòumiàn	back
上边/上面 shàngbiān/shàngmiàn	top	下边/下面 xiàbiān/xiàmiàn	under, beneath
里边/里面 lǐbiān/lǐmiàn	inside	外边/外面 wàibiān/wàimiàn	outside
左边 zuǒbiān	left	右边 yòubiān	right
旁边 pángbiān	beside	对面 duìmiàn	opposite
中间 zhōngjiān	middle		

VIII. Expressing Location and Existence with 在, 有, and 是

PATTERN	FOCUS	EXAMPLE
N. (definite)[1] + 在 + Place	location	图书馆在宿舍(的)前边。 Túshūguǎn zài sùshè (de) qiánbiān. (The library is in front of the dorm.)
Place + 有 + N. (indefinite)[2]	existence	宿舍(的)前边有一个图书馆。 Sùshè (de) qiánbiān yǒu yíge túshūguǎn. (There is a library in front of the dorm.)
Place + 是 + N. (definite or indefinite)	identification	宿舍(的)前边是图书馆。 Sùshè (de) qiánbiān shì túshūguǎn. (In front of the dorm is the library.)

Notes:
1. A definite noun is a specific noun (e.g., "the library").
2. An indefinite noun is a general noun (e.g., "a library").

IX. Degree of Complement Sentences

Single verb: Subject + V. + 得 + Adv. + Adj.

| 你游得怎么样? | How well do you swim? |
| Nǐ yóude zěnmeyàng? | |

我游得很快。 I swim very fast.
Wǒ yóude hěnkuài.

Verb Object (V.O.): Subject + V.O. + V. + 得 + Adv. + Adj.

他打篮球打得好不好? Does he play basketball well?
Tā dǎ lánqiú dǎde hǎobuhǎo?

他打篮球打得不太好。 He doesn't play basketball very well.
Tā dǎ lánqiú dǎde bútài hǎo.

X. Expressing Superlatives with 最

最 + V./Adj. is used to express the superlative form (-est, most, best).

我最喜欢秋天。 I like autumn the most.
Wǒ zuì xǐhuān qiūtiān.

他游泳游得最快。 He is the fastest swimmer.
Tā yóuyǒng yóude zuì kuài.

XI. Showing Imminent Action with 就要/快要.....了

我就要毕业了。 Wǒ jiùyào bìyè le.	I'm graduating soon.
我快要去中国了。 Wǒ kuàiyào qù Zhōngguó le.	I'm going to China soon.

XII. Adjective + 极了

极了 is an intensifier. It occurs after an adjective to indicate a very high degree of the adjective.

热极了! Rè jí le!	It is extremely hot!
我忙极了! Wǒ máng jí le!	I am extremely busy!

XIII. 离

To express how near or far a location is, use the pattern: **A + 离 + B + Adjective Phrase**

宿舍离学校很近。 Sùshè lí xuéxiào hěnjìn.	The dorm is very close to the school.
中国离美国很远。 Zhōngguó lí Měiguó hěnyuǎn.	China is very far from the U.S.

XIV. 坐, 骑, and 开

VERB	VEHICLE USED WITH	TRANSLATION
坐 (to take, to ride in)	汽车 [qìchē] 出租汽车 [chūzūqìchē] 公共汽车 [gōnggòngqìchē] 火车 [huǒchē] 飞机 [fēijī] 船 [chuán]	to go by car to take (ride in) a taxi/cab to take (ride in) a (public) bus to take (ride in) a train to take (fly in) an airplane to go by boat
骑 (to ride)	自行车 [zìxíngchē] 马 [mǎ]	to ride a bike to ride a horse
开 (to drive)	车 [chē]	to drive a car

XV. Expressing a Change of State/New Situation with 了

Completed Action:

USE	PATTERN	EXAMPLE
Question	• V. . . . 了吗	你看医生了吗? Nǐ kàn yīshēng le ma? (Did you go to see a doctor?)
	• V. . . . 了没有	你看医生了没有? Nǐ kàn yīshēng le méiyǒu? (Did you go to see a doctor?)
Positive answer	• V. . . . 了	我看了医生。 Wǒ kàn le yīshēng. (I saw the doctor.)
	• Sentence ends in 了	我看医生了。 Wǒ kàn yīshēng le. (I saw the doctor.)
Negative answer (了 is not used)	• 没有 + V.	我没有去看医生。 Wǒ méiyǒu qù kàn yīshēng. (I didn't see the doctor.)
	• 还没有……呢	我还没有去看医生呢。 Wǒ hái méiyǒu qù kàn yīshēng ne. (I haven't seen the doctor yet.)

Change of State:

PATTERN	EXAMPLE	
Sentence ends with 了	你会开车了吗? Nǐ huì kāichē le ma?	Do you know how to drive now?
	我会开车了。 Wǒ huì kāichē le.	I can drive now.
不 . . . V. 了 (not doing V. any more)	他不喝咖啡了。 Tā bùhē kāfēi le.	He does not drink coffee any more.

XVI. 的, 得, and 地

PATTERN	FEATURES	EXAMPLES
的 + N.	Used with a noun to show possessive case.	我的车 [wǒde chē] (my car)
	Used as a structural particle to describe the noun that follows.	这是上课的笔记。 Zhèshì shàngkè de bǐjì. (These are the notes taken in class.)
V. + 得 + Adv. + Adj.	Used in degree of complement sentences to show how an action is performed.	他说中文说得很快。 Tā shuō Zhōngwén shuō de hěn kuài. (He speaks Chinese very fast.)
Adj. + 地 + V.	Used in combination with an adjective, all preceding a verb to indicate the attitude or manner of an action; similar to *-ly* in English.	他慢慢地吃饭。 Tā mànmàn de chīfàn. (He eats slowly.)

XVII. Simple Directional Complements (Simple DC)

Motion verb + 来/去 to describe the direction of a motion:

(Motion verb)	上 upward	下 downward	进 enter	出 outward	回 return	过 cross	起 up	搬 move	带 take with
+ 来 (coming toward)	上来	下来	进来	出来	回来	过来	起来	搬来	带来
+ 去 (going away)	上去	下去	进去	出去	回去	过去	(NA)[1]	搬去	带去

Note:

1. 起 can only be combined with 来.

When the verb has an object, use the pattern: **Verb + Object + 来/去**

他回宿舍去了。   He went back to the dorm.
Tā huí sùshè qù le.   (The speaker is not at the dorm.)

你们都进客厅来吧!   Everyone come into the living room!
Nǐmen dōu jìn kètīng lái ba! (The speaker is in the living room.)

XVIII. Compound Directional Complements (Compound DC)

Action V. + simple DC to indicate the direction of movement.

Common action verbs: 走 [zǒu] to walk; 跑 [pǎo] to run; 跳 [tiào] to jump; 坐 [zuò] to sit; 站 [zhàn] to stand; 搬 [bān] to move; 带 [dài] to bring; 拿 [ná] to take

Compound DCs:

上来/上去：	坐上来	坐下去	跑上来	跑下去
下来/下去：	走下来	走下去	跳下来	跳下去
进来/进去：	走进来	走进去	拿进来	拿进去
出来/出去：	搬出来	搬出去	带进来	带出去
回来/回去：	跑回来	跑回去	拿回来	拿回去
过来/过去：	带过来	带过去	搬过来	搬过去
起来：	站起来	跳起来	拿起来	

When the verb has an object, use the pattern: **Verb + Object + simple DC**

他要<u>搬</u>桌子<u>过来</u>。   他<u>带</u>一瓶水<u>回来</u>了。
Tā yào <u>bān</u> zhuōzi <u>guòlái</u>.   Tā <u>dài</u> yìpíng shuǐ <u>huílái</u> le.
(He wants to move the table over here.)   (He returned with a bottle of water.)

起来 is an expression with idiomatic usage and has the following patterns:

他<u>拿起来</u>一本书。   他<u>拿起</u>书<u>来</u>。
Tā <u>ná qǐlái</u> yìběn shū.   Tā <u>ná qǐ</u> shū <u>lái</u>.
(He takes a book with him.)   (He takes a book with him.)

XIX. 把 Sentences

Subject + 把 + Object + Verb + complement

- Commonly occurs in imperative sentences 把饭吃了! [Bǎ fàn chī le!] (Eat your meal!)
- Used most often with action verbs.
- The object of the verb must be definite and the verb must incorporate a complement. Some common complements used with 把 are:

  a. degree of complement
     他把这个字写得很好。   He wrote this character very well.
     Tā bǎ zhège zì xiě de hěnhǎo.

  b. 了, used as a complement showing completed action.
     我把汤喝了。   I drank the soup.
     Wǒ bǎ tāng hē le.

  c. directional complement
     我要把那张桌子搬过去。   I want to move that table out.
     Wǒ yào bǎ nàzhāng zhuōzi bān guòqù.

XX. When to Use Sentences with 把

Situations in which the 把 construction is usually **preferred**	Situations in which the 把 construction **must** be used	Situations in which the 把 construction **cannot** be used (with verbs that do not allow a "disposal" explanation)
• to emphasize that an action has caused the object to change position or to change state: 我把那包药吃了。 Wǒ bǎ nàbāo yào chī le. (I took the medicine.) • when there is a long or complicated direct object: 我把我妈妈昨天带回来的那包药吃了。 Wǒ bǎ wǒ māma zuótiān dài huílái de nàbāo yào chī le. (I took the medicine that my mother brought back yesterday.) • when using imperative sentences (commands): 把那包药吃了！ Bǎ nàbāo yào chī le! (Take that medicine!)	• with sentences that have a plural object with the adverb 都. 我把我们的书都卖了。 Wǒ bǎ wǒmen de shū dōu mài le. (I sold all our books.) • with some resultative complements (words added to the verb to show a result). (Resultative complements will be introduced in the next level)	• Intransitive verbs: 来, 去, 跑 (to run), 走, 旅行, 毕业, 工作, 站 (to stand), 坐 • Existence verbs: 是, 在, 有 • Emotion verbs: 喜欢, 爱, 怕 [pà] (to fear) • Sensory perception verbs: 会, 知道, 认识, 觉得, 希望 [xīwàng] (to hope), 看见 [kànjiàn] (to see), 听见 [tīngjiàn] (to hear) • Others: 欢迎 (to welcome), 赞成 [zànchéng] (to approve)

XXI. 比如

比如 is used to introduce specific examples:

我们的晚会有很多活动，比如：唱歌、跳舞、写毛笔字等等。
Wǒmen de wǎnhuì yǒu hěn duō huódòng, bǐrú: chànggē, tiàowǔ, xiě máobǐzì děngdeng.
(Our party will have many activities, such as singing, dancing, and calligraphy.)

XXII. Summary of Measure Words in Chinese

MEASURE WORD	FEATURE	EXAMPLE
个	the most commonly used measure word for people and things in general	那个电话 [nàge diànhuà] (that phone) 六十个学生 [liùshí ge xuésheng] (60 students)
位	used only with people (polite)	几位客人？两位，请进。 [Jǐwèi kèrén? Liǎngwèi, qǐng jìn.] (How many guests? The two of you, please come in.)
本	used for bound items (book-like things)	两本中文书 [liǎngběn Zhōngwén shū] (2 Chinese books)
张	used for sheet-like things with a flat surface	三张电影票 [sānzhāng diànyǐngpiào] (3 movie tickets) 那张桌子 [nàzhāng zhuōzi] (that table)
只	used for animals in general	六只猫 [liùzhī māo] (6 cats)
门	used for subjects and courses	这门课 [zhèmén kè] (this class)
辆	used for vehicles	那辆公共汽车 [nàliàng gōnggòngqìchē] (that bus)
家	used for a facility such as a company, a hospital, a factory, a store, etc.	一家书店 [yìjiā shūdiàn] (a bookstore/one bookstore)
点, 分, 刻, 秒	used for time	十二点三十分十六秒 [shí'èr diǎn sānshí fēn shíliù miǎo] (12:30:16)

MEASURE WORD	FEATURE	EXAMPLE
元/块, 角/毛	used for money	九块四毛六分 [jiǔkuài sìmáo liùfēn] (¥9.46)
件	used for clothing in general	一件衬衫 [yíjiàn chènshān] (a shirt)
条	used for things with a long and slim shape	三条裙子 [sāntiáo qúnzi] (three skirts)
双, 副, 对	used for things in pairs	一双筷子 [yìshuāng kuàizi] (a pair of chopsticks) 一副手套 [yífù shǒutào] (a pair of gloves) 一对姐妹 [yíduì jiěmèi] (two sisters)
碗, 盘, 杯	refers to containers, used for food or drinks	一碗汤 [yìwǎn tāng] (a bowl of soup) 两盘炒面 [liǎngpán chǎomiàn] (two plates of fried noodles) 三杯水 [sānbēi shuǐ] (three glasses of water)

XXIII. Referring to Indefinite Amounts with 一点儿, 一下, and 一些

一点儿	means a little, used to indicate quantity (used before a noun)	我会说一点儿中文。 Wǒ huì shuō yìdiǎr Zhōngwén.
一下儿	means a little, used to indicate a brief action (used after a verb)	你来一下儿，好吗？ Nǐ lái yíxiàr, hǎo ma?
一些	used to refer to "a few," things in plural	我们参观了一些城市。 Wǒmen cānguān le yìxiē chéngshì.

XXIV. Summary of Conjunctions in Chinese

CONJUNCTION	USAGE	EXAMPLE
和	– usually used to connect nouns, pronouns, and noun phrases – cannot be used to connect two sentences/clauses	我们点一盘饺子和一碗汤吧。 Wǒmen diǎn yìpán jiǎozi hé yìwǎn tāng ba.
可是, 但是, 不过	– used to indicate transition, similar to "but," "however," "nevertheless" – can be used interchangeably – usually used to introduce a clause that bears a meaning contrary to what might have been expected based on the previous clause	中国文学不太难，可是功课不少。 Zhōngguó wénxué bú tài nán, kěshì gōngkè bù shǎo. 我打球打得不太好，但是我很喜欢打球。 Wǒ dǎqiú dǎ de bú tài hǎo, dànshì wǒ hěn xǐhuān dǎqiú. 今天气温 (temperature) 不太高，不过很舒服。 Jīntiān qìwēn bú tài gāo, búguò hěn shūfu.
所以	– used to indicate causality, meaning "so" or "therefore" in English – often used together with 因为 as a pair of conjunctions in one sentence (sometimes 因为 can be omitted if the cause–effect relationship between the first and the second clauses is clear)	(因为)冬天太冷，所以我不喜欢冬天。 (Yīnwèi) dōngtiān tài lěng, suǒyǐ wǒ bù xǐhuān dōngtiān.

CONJUNCTION	USAGE	EXAMPLE
还是, 或者	– used to indicate alternatives – can be translated as "or" in English – 还是 is used in questions while 或者 is used in statements	你去体育馆还是健身房？ Nǐ qù tǐyùguǎn háishì jiànshēnfáng? 我想明天或者后天搬过来。 Wǒ xiǎng míngtiān huòzhě hòutiān bān guòlái.
然后	– used to indicate succession and order of things – often used together with 先 and 再 – When using 先, 再, and 然后, 先 always comes first, but 再, and 然后 can be reversed	我想先回家，再去洛杉矶看朋友，然后去公司实习。 Wǒ xiǎng xiān huíjiā, zài qù Luòshānjī kàn péngyou, ránhòu qù gōngsī shíxí.
一面…… 一面…… (一边…… 一边……)	– usually connects two verbs or verb phrases to indicate that two actions are happening at the same time	他常一面吃饭一面看电视。 Tā cháng yímiàn chīfàn yímiàn kàn diànshì.

常见部首表 LIST OF COMMON RADICALS

1 stroke

一 [yī] one

丿 [piě] left slanted stroke

2 strokes

二 [èr] two

八 [bā] eight

刀/刂 [dāo] knife

人/亻 [rén] person

冫 [bīng] ice

厶 [sī] private

儿 [ér] walking man

力 [lì] strength

又 [yòu] right hand

入 [rù] enter

冂 [jiōng] borders

十 [shí] ten

3 strokes

彳 [chì] step

巾 [jīn] napkin

大 [dà] big

小 [xiǎo] small

口 [kǒu] mouth

女 [nǚ] female

囗 [wéi] enclosure

宀 [mián] roof

山 [shān] mountain

土 [tǔ] earth

夕 [xī] night

广 [yǎn] shelter

子 [zǐ] child

寸 [cùn] inch

幺 [yāo] small

4 strokes

水/氵 [shuǐ] water

犬/犭 [quǎn] dog

心/忄 [xīn] heart

火/灬 [huǒ] fire

户 [hù] door

气 [qì] air

木 [mù] wood

日 [rì] sun, day

月 [yuè] moon

手/扌 [shǒu] hand

父 [fù] father

曰 [yuē] say

爪/爫 [zhǎo] claw

止 [zhǐ] stop

欠 [qiàn] owe

5 strokes

石 [shí] stone

疒 [chuáng] sick

田 [tián] land

禾 [hé] grain

玉/王 [yù] jade

母 [mǔ] mother

示/礻 [shì] reveal

目 [mù] eye

生 [shēng] produce

皿 [mǐn] vessel

6 strokes

舟 [zhōu] boat

肉/月 [ròu] meat

米 [mǐ] rice

艸/艹 [cǎo] grass

耳 [ěr] ear

竹/⺮ [zhú] bamboo

衣/衤 [yī] clothing

糸/纟 [mì] silk

老/耂 [lǎo] old

7 strokes

車/车 [chē] vehicle

言/讠 [yán] words, speech

貝/贝 [bèi] shell

足/⻊ [zú] foot

邑/阝 [yì] city

見 [jiàn] see

辵/辶 [chuò] motion

8 strokes

門/门 [mén] door

隹 [zhuī] short-tailed birds

金/钅 [jīn] metal

雨 [yǔ] rain

9 strokes

食/饣 [shí] food/eat

10 strokes

馬/马 [mǎ] horse

11 strokes

魚 [yú] fish

麥/麦 [mài] wheat

麻 [má] hemp

12 strokes

黑 [hēi] black

简繁体字对照表
SIMPLIFIED/TRADITIONAL CHARACTER TABLE

简体字： [jiǎn tǐ zì]   simplified character
繁體字： [fán tǐ zì]   traditional character (complex character)

第十二课   Lesson 12

简：	场	飞	挡	开	应	该	题	练	习	进
繁：	場	飛	擋	開	應	該	題	練	習	進

第十三课   Lesson 13

简：	买	衬	条	裤	黄	错	较	试	帮	让	钱	块	张
繁：	買	襯	條	褲	黃	錯	較	試	幫	讓	錢	塊	張

第十四课   Lesson 14

简：	岁	过	为	参	气
繁：	歲	過	為	參	氣

第十五课   Lesson 15

简：	边	观	里	厨	厅	卧	园
繁：	邊	觀	裡	廚	廳	臥	園

第十六课   Lesson 16

简：	篮	俩	体	锻	炼	现	赛	业
繁：	籃	倆	體	鍛	煉	現	賽	業

第十七课   Lesson 17

简：	热	华	极	风
繁：	熱	華	極	風

第十八课   Lesson 18

简：	离	远	钟	骑	听
繁：	離	遠	鐘	騎	聽

第十九课　Lesson 19

简：	饿	头	发	烧	复	医	药	准	备	笔	记
繁：	餓	頭	發	燒	復	醫	藥	準	備	筆	記

第二十课　Lesson 20

简：	带	关	系	须	楼	马
繁：	帶	關	係	須	樓	馬

第二十一课　Lesson 21

简：	毕	决	实	脑	运
繁：	畢	決	實	腦	運

第二十二课　Lesson 22

简：	经	丽	处	动	剧	东	笼	尝	兴	板
繁：	經	麗	處	動	劇	東	籠	嚐	興	闆

课文 (繁体字) (第十二课至第二十二课)
LANGUAGE IN USE (TRADITIONAL CHARACTERS)
(LESSON 12 TO LESSON 22)

第十二課　我可以借你的車嗎?

于影：　　本樂，明天下午你用不用車?

王本樂：我不用。你有什麼事兒嗎?

于影：　　我得去機場接人，可以借你的車嗎?

王本樂：可以。你要去接誰?

于影：　　我妹妹和她男朋友。他們從上海坐飛機去洛杉磯玩兒，明天會到我這兒來。

王本樂：我的車是手排擋的，你會不會開?

于影：　　應該沒問題。我爸爸的車也是手排擋的，我常開他的車。

王本樂：我的車是白色的，車號是BD5730，停在五號停車場。

于影：　　知道了。謝謝!

王本樂：不謝。你妹妹他們會說英文嗎?

于影：　　會一點兒，這次他們想多學習一點兒英文。

王本樂：太好了，我得跟他們多練習一點兒中文。這樣，我的中文就能進步了。

第十三課　我想買一件襯衫

店員：　　兩位小姐想買什麼?

毛愛紅：我想買一件襯衫。

方子英：我想買一條裙子或者褲子。

店員：　　這件黃襯衫怎麼樣?

毛愛紅：還不錯。可是我比較喜歡穿黑色的，有沒有黑色的?

店員：　　有，在這兒，你試試!

方子英：愛紅，來，你幫我看看，我穿裙子好看還是穿褲子好看?

毛愛紅：你穿穿，讓我看看。我覺得你穿這條裙子好看。

方子英：請問，這條裙子多少錢?

店員：　　十五塊。

方子英：好，我買了。

毛愛紅：我要買這件黑襯衫。

店員：　　對了，小姐，這張電影票是你的嗎?

方子英：是的，這張電影票是我的。謝謝! 我們等一下要去看電影。

第十四課　我今年二十歲

方子英：愛紅，二月十八日你有沒有空？
毛愛紅：二月十八日那天是星期幾？
方子英：星期六。
毛愛紅：我有空。有什麼事兒嗎？
方子英：那天我過生日，我男朋友要為我開一個生日舞會，我想請你參加。
毛愛紅：謝謝你，我一定去。還有誰會去？
方子英：我們想請我們的同學和朋友都參加。
毛愛紅：我會做蛋糕。我送你一個生日蛋糕，怎麼樣？
方子英：太棒了！謝謝你！
毛愛紅：不客氣。你今年多大？
方子英：我今年二十歲。你呢？你的生日是幾月幾號？
毛愛紅：我的生日是十月三號，我今年二十二歲。你的舞會在哪兒開？
方子英：在我男朋友的家，這是他的地址。你知道怎麼去嗎？
毛愛紅：沒問題！我有地圖。星期六下午五點見！
方子英：再見！

第十五課　圖書館在宿舍前邊

Situation: 今天是宿舍參觀日，在學生宿舍。

田進：　你們好！歡迎你們來看我的宿舍。請跟我來。
梁園生：田進，你的宿舍裡邊有沒有廚房？
田進：　有廚房，是公用的。
包志中：你的房間在哪兒？
田進：　我的房間在旁邊，從這兒走。來，請進。這是客廳，客廳的對面是一個餐廳。
梁園生：洗澡間呢？
田進：　洗澡間在客廳和臥室的中間。你看，這是我的臥室。
包志中：桌子上邊的中文書都是你的嗎？
田進：　有的是我的，有的是我朋友的。
包志中：你常在宿舍學習嗎？
田進：　不，我不常在宿舍學習，我常去圖書館學習。
梁園生：圖書館在哪兒？
田進：　圖書館在宿舍前邊。圖書館的後邊還有一個公園。我常去那兒打球。
梁園生，包志中：你們的宿舍真不錯！

第十六課　她打籃球打得很好

張正然：你們倆要去哪兒？
孫信美，楊歡：　我們去打籃球。
張正然：你們籃球打得怎麼樣？
孫信美：楊歡籃球打得很好。我還不太會打籃球，她是我的教練，她教得很好。

楊歡：　　不行，我還打得不太好。
張正然：我不常打籃球，我常常和我室友去游泳，他游泳游得非常快。
楊歡：　　你們常去哪兒游泳？
張正然：我們常去體育館裡邊的游泳池游泳，我們也常去健身房鍛煉。
孫信美：你現在要不要跟我們去打籃球？
張正然：現在不行。我昨天看球賽看得太晚了，今天起得很晚，現在得去做
　　　　　作業。
楊歡：　　昨天我們那兒包餃子、做中國菜。你晚上到我們那兒吃餃子吧。
張正然：太好了！我很喜歡吃餃子。你們包餃子包得快不快？
孫信美：我們包得很慢。
楊歡：　　信美很會做飯。她做飯做得很好。

第十七課　　春天就要來了

小玲：

　　好久不見！

　　你現在怎麼樣？時間過得真快，春天就要來了，我們也快要放春假了。

　　我們這兒的氣候春夏秋冬都有。其中我最喜歡春天，很暖和，可是很
短。夏天有時候很熱，最熱的時候，會到華氏一百度，熱極了。秋天有時候
會颱風、下雨。這兒的冬天非常冷，常常下雪。

　　放春假的時候我想去你那兒玩玩，我們很快就要見面了！

　　祝　好！

大中

二〇一〇年三月十日

第十八課　　我們要坐火車去旅行

季長風：秋影，你住在校外嗎？離學校遠不遠？
白秋影：不太遠，開車只要五分鐘。
季長風：你每天怎麼來學校？
白秋影：我常騎自行車，下雨下雪的時候就坐公共汽車，有時候我也走路，
　　　　　可以鍛煉鍛煉。你呢？
季長風：我住在宿舍，離學校很近，我每天走路來學校。
白秋影：對了，這個春假你要做什麼？
季長風：我要跟我的室友一起去西部旅行。
白秋影：你們怎麼去？
季長風：我們想先坐火車去，路上可以看看風景。然後坐船去加拿大，再從
　　　　　加拿大坐飛機回來。你呢？
白秋影：我很想我爸爸、媽媽和妹妹，我要先回家。然後再跟朋友開車去玩
　　　　　兒。
季長風：你們要去哪兒玩兒？
白秋影：我們想去南部玩兒。聽說那兒的海邊景色很美。
季長風：你們有幾個人去？
白秋影：我們一共有五個人去，我們想租一輛車。

第十九課　我感冒了

唐志信：歐陽迎，你吃飯了嗎？
歐陽迎：還沒有呢。我不餓。
唐志信：你怎麼了？好像不舒服。
歐陽迎：我感冒了。我頭疼發燒，還有一點兒咳嗽。
唐志信：你怎麼生病了呢？
歐陽迎：這幾天我有很多考試，每天都在復習，睡覺睡得太少，所以就病
　　　　了。
唐志信：你看醫生了沒有？
歐陽迎：看了。我也吃藥了。可是還沒有好呢。
唐志信：你應該在家好好地休息。不應該來上課。
歐陽迎：你說得很對。可是我有很多考試。我得好好地準備。
唐志信：這是我上課的筆記，借給你看看。
歐陽迎：非常感謝！好吧，我現在就回家休息。
唐志信：好，我開車送你回去。你得好好地睡覺。

第二十課　我把小謝帶來了……

常天：　中明，我回來了。我把車開回來了，還把小謝也帶來了。
夏中明：是小謝啊！快請他進來。
謝進學：我聽說你們這兒有一個人搬出去了，我想搬進來，所以過來看看。
常天：　你不想住宿舍了，是不是？
謝進學：是的。宿舍太小了，我想搬出來住。這兒可以不可以做飯？
夏中明：可以，我們有廚房。
謝進學：太好了！我很喜歡做飯。搬出來以後就可以常常做飯了。
常天：　你有狗嗎？我們這兒不能有狗。
謝進學：沒關係。以前我有一隻狗，但是宿舍不可以有狗，所以我把我的狗
　　　　給我女朋友了。現在沒有狗了。
夏中明：還有，我們必須在每個月的第一天付房租。
謝進學：沒問題！
常天：　喂，小謝，我在樓上，你要不要上來看看？中明，你把小謝帶上來
　　　　看看吧。
夏中明：常天，我們現在還不能上去。你得先下來幫我把這張桌子搬上去。
常天：　好的，我馬上下去。

第二十一課　暑假你要做什麼?

程海華: 秋雨,我問你,你明年就要畢業了,畢業以後你想做什麼?

白秋雨: 我還沒有決定呢。可是我很喜歡學習,我可能會申請研究生院,或者去國外留學。你呢? 你什麼時候畢業?

程海華: 我還有兩年才畢業呢。畢業以後我想去找工作。

白秋雨: 我們就要放暑假了,今年暑假你要做什麼?

程海華: 我要去打工。我要去一家公司實習。

白秋雨: 在哪兒? 是什麼工作?

程海華: 在加州,是一家電腦公司。你呢? 暑假你要做什麼?

白秋雨: 我要去中國,我申請了去上海的暑期班學習,我想一面學中文,一面在中國旅行。

程海華: 那一定很有意思! 你什麼時候去?

白秋雨: 下個星期。

程海華: 這麼快! 你到中國以後要常常給我寫電子郵件。

白秋雨: 沒問題。我祝你工作愉快!

程海華: 我也祝你一路平安! 祝你好運!

第二十二課　我到上海了

海華:

你好! 今天是六月十五號,我一個星期以前就到上海了。對不起,因為太忙了,所以今天才給你寫電子郵件。

我們每天都有很多課,功課也不少。不過老師教得很好,也很認真。我們每天都說中文,我的中文進步得很快,現在我已經能說很多中文了。

上海是一個非常美麗的城市,到處都是新的大樓。我們參觀了一些地方,也參加了一些活動,比如:看京劇、寫書法等等,都很有意思。還有,上海有很多好吃的東西,其中我最喜歡吃的是小籠包。你有機會應該嚐嚐。

你開始實習了嗎? 忙不忙? 有空請給我寫電子郵件。

祝　好!

秋雨

二〇一〇年六月十五日

秋雨:

你好! 很高興收到你的電子郵件。看來你在上海過得很開心。

我現在在洛杉磯,已經開始實習了。這兒的同事都很好,也很熱心,常常教我很多東西,老闆也不錯。我的工作有時候忙,有時候不太忙,我想我得認真地工作,才能學到一些東西。

好了,不多寫了。有空請多來信。

多保重。

祝　好!

海華

二〇一〇年六月十七日

课文英文翻译
ENGLISH TRANSLATIONS OF LANGUAGE IN USE

Lesson 12   May I Borrow Your Car?

Xin Yu:	Benle, will you be using your car tomorrow afternoon?
Benle Wang:	No. What's up?
Xin Yu:	I need to go to the airport to pick someone up. May I borrow your car?
Benle Wang:	Sure. Who are you picking up?
Xin Yu:	My younger sister and her boyfriend. They're flying to Los Angeles from Shanghai to do some sightseeing. They'll arrive tomorrow.
Benle Wang:	My car has a manual transmission. Do you know how to drive it?
Xin Yu:	It shouldn't be a problem. My dad's car also has a manual transmission; I often drove his car.
Benle Wang:	My car's white. The license plate number is BD5730, and it is parked at parking lot number 5.
Xin Yu:	Got it. Thanks!
Benle Wang:	You're welcome. Does your sister speak English?
Xin Yu:	A little bit. They want to learn some English this time.
Benle Wang:	Great! I should practice some Chinese with them. That way, my Chinese will improve.

Lesson 13   I'd Like to Buy a Shirt

Sales:	What would you like to buy?
Aihong Mao:	I would like to buy a shirt.
Ziying Fang:	I want to buy a skirt or pants.
Sales:	How about this yellow shirt?
Aihong Mao:	Not bad. But I like wearing black better. Do you have black ones?
Sales:	Yes, here. Try it on.
Ziying Fang:	Aihong, come and look. Would I look better in a skirt or in pants?
Aihong Mao:	Put them on and let me see. I think you look good in this skirt.
Ziying Fang:	How much is this skirt?
Sales:	Fifteen dollars.
Ziying Fang:	OK, I'll buy it.
Aihong Mao:	I'll take this shirt too.
Sales:	Oh! Miss, is this movie ticket yours?
Ziying Fang:	Yes, thank you! The ticket is mine. We're going to see a movie later.

Lesson 14 I'll Be 20 This Year

Ziying Fang:	Aihong, are you free on February 18?
Aihong Mao:	What day of the week is February 18?
Ziying Fang:	It's a Saturday.
Aihong Mao:	I'll be free. Is there something going on?
Ziying Fang:	It's my birthday. My boyfriend is having a party for me. I'd like to invite you.
Aihong Mao:	Thank you. I'll definitely come. Who else is coming?
Ziying Fang:	We want to invite all our classmates and friends.
Aihong Mao:	I know how to make cakes. I'll make a cake for you, how's that?
Ziying Fang:	Great! Thank you!
Aihong Mao:	You're welcome. How old will you be?
Ziying Fang:	I'll be twenty this year. How about you? When's your birthday?
Aihong Mao:	My birthday is October 3. I'm twenty-two. Where will the party be?
Ziying Fang:	At my boyfriend's place. This is his address. Do you know how to get there?
Aihong Mao:	No problem! I have a map. See you at 5:00 Saturday afternoon!
Ziying Fang:	See you!

Lesson 15 The Library Is in Front of the Dorm

Situation: At the students' dorm

Jin Tian:	Hello! Welcome to my dorm. Please come with me.
Yuansheng Liang:	Jin Tian, is there a kitchen in your dorm?
Jin Tian:	Yes, it's shared.
Zhizhong Bao:	Where's your room?
Jin Tian:	My room is on the side, along this way. Come, please come in! This is the living room. The dining room is across from it.
Yuansheng Liang:	Where's the bathroom?
Jin Tian:	The bathroom is between the living room and the bedroom. Look, this is my bedroom.
Zhizhong Bao:	Are all the Chinese books on the table yours?
Jin Tian:	No. Some are mine, some are my friends'.
Zhizhong Bao:	Do you usually study in the dorm?
Jin Tian:	No, I don't study in the dorm very often. I usually go to the library to study.
Yuansheng Liang:	Where's the library?
Jin Tian:	The library is in front of the dorm. Behind the library is a park. I often go there to play ball.
Yuansheng Liang and Zhizhong Bao:	Your dorm is very nice!

Lesson 16   She Plays Basketball Very Well

Zhengran Zhang:	Where are you going?
Xinmei Sun and Huan Yang:	We're going to play basketball.
Zhengran Zhang:	Are you good at it?
Xinmei Sun:	Huan Yang plays very well. I'm not very good at it. She's my coach. She coaches me very well.
Huan Yang:	No, I don't play very well.
Zhengran Zhang:	I don't play basketball very often. I usually go swimming with my roommate. He swims really fast!
Huan Yang:	Where do you usually go?
Zhengran Zhang:	The swimming pool in the gym. And we also go to the gym a lot to exercise.
Xinmei Sun:	Do you want to come play basketball with us?
Zhengran Zhang:	Not now. I stayed up too late watching the game last night, so I got up very late this morning. Now I have to do homework.
Huan Yang:	Yesterday we made dumplings and Chinese food. Why don't you come to our place and eat dumplings tonight?
Zhengran Zhang:	Great! I really like dumplings. Are you quick at making dumplings?
Xinme Sun:	No, we're very slow.
Huan Yang:	Xinmei is very good at cooking. She cooks very well.

Lesson 17   Spring Is Almost Here

Xiao Ling:

Long time no see! How are you? Time is going by so quickly. Spring is almost here and we will have our spring break soon.

We have all four seasons here. Of all the seasons, I like spring the most. It's warm, but very short. In the summer, sometimes it's very hot. On the hottest days, the temperature often reaches 100°F. So hot! In the fall, sometimes it's rainy and windy. Winter is very cold here, with lots of snow.

During spring break, I'm thinking about going over to your place, so we'll see each other soon!

Best wishes!

Dazhong
March 10, 2010

Lesson 18   We're Going to Take a Train Trip

Ji Changfeng:	Qiuying, do you live off campus? Is it far from school?
Bai Qiuying:	Not too far. Only a five-minute drive.
Ji Changfeng:	How do you go to school every day?
Bai Qiuying:	I usually ride a bike. When it's raining or snowing, I take the bus. Sometimes I walk, which gives me some exercise. How about you?
Ji Changfeng:	I live in the dorm, which is very close to school. I walk to school every day.
Bai Qiuying:	So, what will you do during the spring break?
Ji Changfeng:	I'll travel to the West with my roommates.
Bai Qiuying:	How will you be traveling?
Ji Changfeng:	We want to go by train. We'd like to do some sightseeing on the way. Then we'll go to Canada by boat. Finally, from Canada, we'll fly home. How about you?
Bai Qiuying:	I miss my parents and sister a lot. I'll go home first. Then I'll drive somewhere with my friends.
Ji Changfeng:	Where do you want to go?
Bai Qiuying:	We'd like to go to the South. I've heard that the coast is beautiful there.
Ji Changfeng:	How many people will go with you?
Bai Qiuying:	There are five of us going. We want to rent a car.

Lesson 19   I Have a Cold

Zhixin Tang:	Ouyang Ying, have you eaten yet?
Ouyang Ying:	Not yet. I'm not hungry.
Zhixin Tang:	What's wrong? You don't look well.
Ouyang Ying:	I have a cold. I have a headache, a fever, and a bit of a cough.
Zhixin Tang:	How did you get sick?
Ouyang Ying:	I've had lots of exams these past few days. I was reviewing every day and didn't get enough sleep. So I'm sick.
Zhixin Tang:	Did you see the doctor?
Ouyang Ying:	Yes. I also took medicine. But I'm not better yet.
Zhixin Tang:	You should stay home and get some rest. You shouldn't come to class.
Ouyang Ying:	You're right. But I have lots of exams. I have to be well prepared.
Zhixin Tang:	These are my class notes. You can borrow them.
Ouyang Ying:	Thank you so much! Well, I guess I'll go home and rest.
Zhixin Tang:	OK, I'll drive you home. You should try to get some sleep.

Lesson 20   I Brought Xiao Xie Over

Tian Chang:	Zhongming, I'm back. I drove the car back, and I also brought Xiao Xie over.
Zhongming Xia:	Oh, it's Xiao Xie! Ask him to come in.
Jinxue Xie:	I heard that one of your roommates moved out. I'd like to move in. So I came over to look around.
Tian Chang:	You don't want to live in the dorm any more, right?
Jinxue Xie:	Right. The dorm is too small. I want to move out. Can you cook here?
Zhongming Xia:	Yes. We have a kitchen.
Jinxue Xie:	Great. I like to cook. After moving out of the dorm, I'd be able to cook often.
Tian Chang:	Do you have a dog? Dogs aren't allowed here.
Jinxue Xie:	That's OK. I used to have a dog, but dogs are prohibited in the dorm, so I gave it to my girlfriend. Now I don't have a dog.
Zhongming Xia:	And, we have to pay the rent on the first of each month.
Jinxue Xie:	No problem.
Tian Chang:	Hey, Xiao Xie, I'm upstairs. Don't you want to come up to look around? Zhongming, bring Xiao Xie up here.
Zhongming Xia:	Chang Tian, we can't come up now. You'd better come down to help me move the table up first.
Tian Chang:	OK. I'll be right down.

Lesson 21   What Will You Do during Summer Vacation?

Haihua Cheng:	Qiuyu, let me ask you, you'll graduate next year. What will you do after graduation?
Qiuyu Bai:	I haven't decided yet. But I love to study. I'll probably apply for graduate school or go to study abroad. How about you? When will you graduate?
Haihua Cheng:	I still have two more years to go. After graduation, I want to find a job.
Qiuyu Bai:	We'll have summer vacation soon. What will you do this summer?
Haihua Cheng:	I'll work. I have a summer internship with a company.
Qiuyu Bai:	Where? What kind of job?
Haihua Cheng:	In California, a computer company. How about you? What will you do this summer?
Qiuyu Bai:	I'm going to China. I applied for a summer class in Shanghai. I want to learn some Chinese and at the same time do some traveling in China.
Haihua Cheng:	That will definitely be very interesting! When are you going?
Qiuyu Bai:	Next week.
Haihua Cheng:	So soon! After you get to China, be sure to send me lots of emails.
Qiuyu Bai:	No problem. I hope your work goes well!
Haihua Cheng:	Have a safe journey, and good luck!

Lesson 22   I Arrived in Shanghai

Haihua,

How are you? Today is June 15. I arrived in Shanghai a week ago. Sorry, I've been too busy to write you an email before today.

We have a lot of classes every day and lots of homework too. The instructor is good and very earnest. We speak Chinese every day. My Chinese has improved very quickly. Now I can speak lots of Chinese.

Shanghai is a beautiful city, with new buildings everywhere. We visited several places, and we also took part in some activities, such as watching Peking Opera, learning to write calligraphy, etc. All very interesting! And, there is a lot of good food here. Of all the food, I love the little steamed buns the best. If you get a chance, you should definitely try one.

Have you begun your internship yet? Are you busy? When you have time, please email me.

Best wishes,

Qiuyu
June 15, 2010

Qiuyu:

How are you? I was so glad to get your email. It sounds like you are very happy in Shanghai. I've begun my internship in Los Angeles. My co-workers here are all very nice and friendly. They're teaching me lots of things. The boss is nice too. I'm busy from time to time. I think if I take work seriously, I will learn a lot of things.

OK, I should stop here. Write to me more when you have time. Take care.

Best wishes,

Haihua
June 17, 2010

拼音索引 PINYIN GLOSSARY

Each entry lists the Pinyin, simplified character, traditional character, part of speech, English meaning, and lesson number.

Note: The letter *s* indicates vocabulary supplementary to that lesson.

A

a	啊	啊	*Int.*	(used at the end of a sentence to indicate surprise)	20
ài	爱	愛	*V.*	to love	6
áoyè	熬夜	熬夜	*V.O.*	to burn the midnight oil	10s

B

ba	吧	吧	*Part.*	(indicates assumption or suggestion)	9
bā	八/捌	八/捌	*Num.*	eight	7
bǎ	把	把	*Prep.*	(introduces the object of a verb)	20
bàba	爸爸	爸爸	*N.*	father	6
bái	白	白	*Adj.*	white	12
báifàn	白饭	白飯	*N.*	steamed rice	11s
bǎi	百	百	*Num.*	hundred	17
bān	搬	搬	*V.*	to move	20
bān	班	班	*N.*	class	21
bàn	半	半	*Adj.*	half	10
bāng	帮	幫	*V.*	to help	13
bàng	棒	棒	*Adj.*	wonderful	14
bàngqiú	棒球	棒球	*N.*	baseball	16s
bānjiā	搬家	搬家	*V.O.*	to move	20s
bāo	包	包	*V.*	to wrap	16
bǎozhòng	保重	保重		take care	22s
bēi	杯	杯	*M.W.*	cup	11
běi	北	北	*N.*	north	18s
běn	本	本	*M.W.*	(measure word for bound items such as books and magazines)	4
bǐjì	笔记	筆記	*N.*	notes	19
bǐjiào	比较	比較	*Adv.*	relatively, comparatively	13
bīng	冰	冰	*N.*	ice	11
			Adj.	iced, ice-cold, with ice	11
bìng	病	病	*N.*	disease, illness	19
bǐnggān	饼干	餅乾	*N.*	cracker, cookie	11s
bǐrú	比如	比如	*Conj.*	for example	22

bìxū	必须	必須	Aux.	must	20
bìyè	毕业	畢業	V.	to graduate	21
bóshì	博士	博士	N.	(a person with a) doctoral degree	21s
bóshìshēng	博士生	博士生	N.	doctoral students	21s
bù	不	不	Adv.	(used to form a negative) not, no	1
bù	步	步	N.	step	16s
búcuò	不错	不錯	Adv.	not bad, pretty good	13
búguò	不过	不過	Conj.	but, however	22
búkèqi	不客气	不客氣		(in reply to thank you) you're welcome, don't mention it	9s, 14
búxiè	不谢	不謝		(in reply to thank you) you're welcome	9s

C

cái	才	才	Adv.	not until, only then	10
cài	菜	菜	N.	dish (type of food), cuisine	8
càidān	菜单	菜單	N.	menu	11s
cānguān	参观	參觀	V.	to visit	15
cānjiā	参加	參加	V.	to participate, to join	14
cāntīng	餐厅	餐廳	N.	dining room	11s, 15
cèsuǒ	厕所	廁所	N.	bathroom, toilet	15s
chá	茶	茶	N.	tea	11
chà	差	差	V.	to lack, to be short of	10s
cháng	常	常	Adv.	often, frequently	5
cháng	长	長	Adj.	long	17s
chángchang	尝尝	嚐嚐	V.	to have a taste	22
chànggē	唱歌	唱歌	V.O.	to sing a song	14s
chǎo	炒	炒	V.	to stir fry	11
chē	车	車	N.	car	6
chéngsè (júsè)	橙色 (橘色)	橙色 (橘色)	Adj.	orange	13s
chéngshì	城市	城市	N.	city	22
chènshān	衬衫	襯衫	N.	shirt	13
chēzhàn	车站	車站	N.	stop, station	18s
chī	吃	吃	V.	to eat	8
chīfàn	吃饭	吃飯	V.O.	to eat, to have a meal	8
chīyào	吃药	吃藥	V.O.	to take medicine	19
chǒngwù	宠物	寵物	N.	pet	6s
chū	出	出	V.	to be out	20
chuān	穿	穿	V.	to wear (used with clothing in general)	13
chuán	船	船	N.	ship	18

chuáng	床	床	N.	bed	15s
chuānghu	窗户	窗戶	N.	window	15s
chúfáng	厨房	廚房	N.	kitchen	15
chuī	吹	吹	V.	to blow	14s
chūnjià	春假	春假	N.	spring break	17
chūntiān	春天	春天	N.	spring	17
chūqù	出去	出去	V.C.	to go out	20
chúshī	厨师	廚師	N.	chef	6s
chūzūqìchē (jìchéngchē)	出租汽车 (计程车)	出租汽車 (計程車)	N.	taxi	18s
cóng	从	從	Prep.	from	6

D

dǎ	打	打	V.	to call, to make, to hit	9
dà	大	大	Adj.	big, large	7, 13s
dǎ diànhuà	打电话	打電話	V.O.	to make a phone call	9
dǎcuòle	打错了	打錯了	V.	to dial a wrong number	9s
dǎgōng	打工	打工	V.O.	to work for others, to be employed	21
dài	戴	戴	V.	to wear, to put on (used with accessories)	13s
dàilái	带来	帶來	V.C.	to bring over	20
dàjiā	大家	大家	N.	all, everybody	6
dàlóu	大楼	大樓	N.	tall building	22
dānchē (jiǎotàchē)	单车 (脚踏车)	單車 (腳踏車)	N.	bicycle	18s
dàngāo	蛋糕	蛋糕	N.	cake	11s, 14
dànjì	淡季	淡季	N.	off-season	18s
dànshì	但是	但是	Conj.	but	20
dǎqiú	打球	打球	V.O.	to play basketball/badminton/ tennis/table tennis	10
dào	到	到	V.	to arrive	12
dàochù	到处	到處	Adv.	everywhere	22
dàxué	大学	大學	N.	college, university	10
dàxuéshēng	大学生	大學生	N.	college student(s)	4s, 21s
dǎzhēn	打针	打針	V.O.	to give or receive an injection	13s, 19s
de	的	的	Part.	(a structural particle used to show possession)	2
de	得	得	Part.	(used between a verb or an adjective and its complement to indicate a result, possibility, or degree)	16

de	地	地	*Part.*	(attached to an adjective to transform the whole unit into an adverb when preceding a verb; describes manner of the verb)	19
Déguó	德国	德國	N.	Germany	3s
děi	得	得	*Aux.*	must, have to	12
děng	等	等	V.	to wait	9
děng yíxiàr	等一下儿	等一下兒	V.	to wait for a moment, to hang on (on the phone)	9
děngděng	等等	等等	*Part.*	et cetera	22
dì	第	第		(prefix indicating an ordinal number)	20
diǎn	点	點	*M.W.*	o'clock (point on clock)	10
diǎn	点	點	V.	to order	11
diàn	电	電	N.	electric, electricity	7
diàn	店	店	N.	store	13
diǎncài	点菜	點菜	V.O.	to order food	11
diǎnzhōng	点钟	點鐘	*M.W.*	o'clock	10s
diànhuà	电话	電話	N.	phone	7
diànnǎo	电脑	電腦	N.	computer (used in Taiwan, also used in Mainland China)	4s, 21
diànshì	电视	電視	N.	television	9
diànyǐng	电影	電影	N.	movie	9s, 13
diànyuán	店员	店員	N.	salesman, saleswoman	13
diànzǐ yóujiàn	电子邮件	電子郵件	N.	email	10
dìdi	弟弟	弟弟	N.	younger brother	6s
dìfang	地方	地方	N.	place	22
dìtiě	地铁	地鐵	N.	subway	18s
dìtú	地图	地圖	N.	map	14
dìxiàdào	地下道	地下道	N.	underground walkway	18s
dìyītiān	第一天	第一天	N.	first day	20
dìzhǐ	地址	地址	N.	address	10
dōng	冬	冬	N.	winter	17
dōng	东	東	N.	east	18s
dōngxi	东西	東西	N.	thing	22
dōu	都	都	*Adv.*	all, both	5
dòufu	豆腐	豆腐	N.	bean curd	11s
dù	度	度	N.	degree	17
duǎn	短	短	*Adj.*	short	17
duǎnkù	短裤	短褲	N.	shorts	13s
duànliàn	锻炼	鍛煉	V.	to exercise	16
duì	对	對	*Adj.*	correct, right	9
duìbuqǐ	对不起	對不起		I'm sorry	9
duìle	对了	對了	N.	by the way (a phrase used to start a new topic)	3

duìmiàn	对面	對面	*N.*	opposite	15
duō	多	多	*Adj.*	many, much	4
duōdà	多大	多大		how old	14
duōshǎo	多少	多少	*Pron.*	how many, how much	7

E

è	饿	餓	*Adj.*	hungry	19
			V.	to starve	
ér	儿	兒		(retroflex ending)	3
èr	二/贰	二/貳	*Num.*	two	7
ěrhuán	耳环	耳環	*N.*	earring	13s

F

fā duǎnxìn	发短信	發短信	*V.O.*	to send a short (cell phone) message	9s
(sòng jiǎnxùn)	(送简讯)	(送簡訊)			
Fǎguó	法国	法國	*N.*	France	3
fàn	饭	飯	*N.*	cooked rice, meal	8
fàng	放	放	*V.*	to have, to start (a vacation)	17
fángdōng	房东	房東	*N.*	landlord	20s
fàngjià	放假	放假	*V.O.*	to have a holiday or vacation	17s
fángjiān	房间	房間	*N.*	room	7
fángkè	房客	房客	*N.*	tenant	20s
fànguǎn	饭馆	飯館	*N.*	restaurant	11s
fángzi	房子	房子	*N.*	house, room	7s
fángzū	房租	房租	*N.*	rent	20
fāshāo	发烧	發燒	*V.O.*	to have a fever	19
Fǎwén	法文	法文	*N.*	French (language)	3
fēicháng	非常	非常	*Adv.*	very	16
fēijī	飞机	飛機	*N.*	airplane	12
fēn	分	分	*N.*	minute	10
fēng	风	風	*N.*	wind	17
fēngjǐng	风景	風景	*N.*	scenery	18
fēnzhōng	分钟	分鐘	*N.*	minute	10s, 18
fù	付	付	*V.*	to pay	20
fúwùyuán	服务员	服務員	*N.*	waiter/waitress	11
fùxí	复习	復習	*V.*	to review	19
fǔxiū	辅修	輔修	*N.*	minor	4s

G

| Gǎngbì | 港币 | 港幣 | *N.* | currency of Hong Kong | 13s |
| gānjìng | 干净 | 乾淨 | *Adj.* | clean | 15s |

gǎnlǎnqiú	橄榄球	橄欖球	N.	football	16s
gǎnmào	感冒	感冒	N.	cold, flu	19
			V.	to catch a cold	
gǎnxiè	感谢	感謝	V.	to thank, to be grateful	19
gāoxìng	高兴	高興	Adj.	happy	22
gē	歌	歌	N.	song	14s
gè	个	個	M.W.	(the most commonly used measure word for people, characters, things in general)	5
gēge	哥哥	哥哥	N.	elder brother	6s
gěi	给	給	Prep.	for, to	9
			V.	to give	
gēn	跟	跟	Prep.	with	5
gōngchē (bāshì)	公车 (巴士)	公車 (巴士)	N.	bus	18s
gōngchéng	工程	工程	N.	engineering	4
gōngchéngshī	工程师	工程師	N.	engineer	6
gōnggòngqìchē	公共汽车	公共汽車	N.	bus	18
gōngkè	功课	功課	N.	homework, assignment	4
gōngsī	公司	公司	N.	company	21
gōngyòng	公用	公用	Adj.	for public use, communal	15
gōngyù	公寓	公寓	N.	apartment	7s
gōngyuán	公园	公園	N.	park	15
gōngzuò	工作	工作	N.	job	6
			V.	to work	6
gǒu	狗	狗	N.	dog	6
guāfēng	刮风	刮風	V.O.	to blow (wind)	17
guì	贵	貴	Adj.	noble, honored, expensive	2, 13s
guó	国	國	N.	country	3
guò	过	過	V.	to pass (time), to celebrate (birthday, holiday), to cross, to live	10s, 14, 17
guòlái	过来	過來	V.C.	to come over	20
guówài	国外	國外	N.	overseas, abroad	21
guǒzhī	果汁	果汁	N.	juice	11s

H

hái	还	還		still, also	11
hái hǎo	还好	還好		not bad, okay	4s
hǎibiān	海边	海邊	N.	seaside	18
háishì	还是	還是	Conj.	or	11
hǎitān	海滩	海灘	N.	seashore	18s
hǎixiān	海鲜	海鮮	N.	seafood	11s
háizi	孩子	孩子	N.	child	6s

Hánguó	韩国	韓國	N.	Korea	3s, 8
hánjià	寒假	寒假	N.	winter vacation	17s
hǎo	好	好	Adj.	good, well	1
hào	号	號	N.	number, size	7, 13s
hǎokàn	好看	好看	Adj.	good-looking	13
hàomǎ	号码	號碼	N.	number	7
hǎoxiàng	好像	好像	V.	to be like, to seem	19
hǎoyùn	好运	好運		good luck	21
hē	喝	喝	V.	to drink	11
hé/hàn	和	和	Conj.	and	3
hēi	黑	黑	Adj.	black	13
hěn	很	很	Adv.	very, quite	3
hóng	红	紅	Adj.	red	11
hòubiān	后边	後邊	N.	behind, at the back	15
hùshi	护士	護士	N.	nurse	6s, 19s
huáng	黄	黃	Adj.	yellow	13
huānyíng	欢迎	歡迎	V.	to welcome	15
huáshì	华氏	華氏	N.	Fahrenheit	17
huáxuě	滑雪	滑雪	V.O.	to ski	16s
huí	回	回	V.	to return	8
huì	会	會	Aux.	can, be able to, know how to	3
huílai	回来	回來	V.	to return	9
húntun	馄饨	餛飩	N.	wonton	11s
huǒchē	火车	火車	N.	train	18, 18s
huódòng	活动	活動	N.	activity	22
huòzhě	或者	或者	Conj.	or, either . . . or . . .	13

J

jī	机	機	N.	machine	7
jí	极	極	Adv.	extremely	17
jǐ	几	幾		how many	5
jǐ hào	几号	幾號	Pron.	what size	13s
jiā	家	家	N.	home, family	6
			M.W.	(measure word for companies, enterprises, stores, etc.)	21
jiān	间	間	M.W.	(measure word for rooms)	15s
jiàn	见	見	V.	to see	8
jiàn	件	件	M.W.	(measure word for clothes)	13
Jiānádà	加拿大	加拿大	N.	Canada	3s
jiànkāng	健康	健康	Adj.	healthy	22s
jiǎnlì (lǚlìbiǎo)	简历 (履历表)	簡歷 (履歷表)	N.	resumé	21s
jiànmiàn	见面	見面	V.O.	to meet each other	17
jiànshēnfáng	健身房	健身房	N.	gym (workout facility)	16

jiāo	教	教	V.	to teach, to coach	16
jiào	叫	叫	V.	to call, to be called	2
jiàoliàn	教练	教練	N.	coach, trainer	16
jiàoshòu	教授	教授	N.	professor	1s
jiǎozi	饺子	餃子	N.	dumpling (crescent-shaped)	11
jiàqī	假期	假期	N.	vacation	17s
jiātíng zhǔfù	家庭主妇	家庭主婦	N.	housewife	6s
Jiāzhōu	加州	加州	N.	California	21
jīchǎng	机场	機場	N.	airport	12
jiē	接	接	V.	to pick up	12
jiè	借	借	V.	to borrow	12
jiějie	姐姐	姐姐	N.	elder sister	6
jièshào	介绍	介紹	V.	to introduce	5
			N.	introduction	5
jiéyùn	捷运	捷運	N.	MRT (Mass Rapid Transportation) in Taiwan	18s
jīhuì	机会	機會	N.	opportunity	22
jìn	近	近	Adj.	near	18
jìn	进	進	V.	to enter	15
jìnbù	进步	進步	V.	to improve	12
jīngjù	京剧	京劇	N.	Peking Opera	22
jǐngsè	景色	景色	N.	scenery, view	18
jīnhuángsè	金黄色	金黄色	Adj.	gold	13s
jīntiān	今天	今天	N.	today	8
jīròu	鸡肉	雞肉	N.	chicken	11s
jìsuànjī	计算机	計算機	N.	computer (used in Mainland China only)	4s
jiǔ	九/玖	九/玖	Num.	nine	7
jiǔ	久	久	Adj.	for a long time	17
jiù	就	就	Adv.	as early as, precisely, then (connects two clauses, the first being the premise of the second)	10, 12
juéde	觉得	覺得	V.	to think, to feel	13
juédìng	决定	決定	V.	to decide	21
jùlèbù	俱乐部	俱樂部	N.	club	16s

K

kāfēi	咖啡	咖啡	N.	coffee	11s
kāi	开	開	V.	to drive, to turn on, to open	12
kāishǐ	开始	開始	V.	to start, to begin	22
kāixīn	开心	開心	Adj.	happy	22
kàn	看	看	V.	to look at, to see, to watch	9
kànlái	看来	看來		it seems	22

kǎoshì	考试	考試	N.	exam	4s, 19
kè	课	課	N.	class, lesson	8
kè	刻	刻	M.W.	a quarter (of an hour)	10
kělè	可乐	可樂	N.	cola	11
kěnéng	可能	可能		perhaps, maybe, possibly	21
kěshì	可是	可是	Conj.	but, yet, however	4
késòu	咳嗽	咳嗽	V.	to cough	19
kètīng	客厅	客廳	N.	living room	15
kěyǐ	可以	可以	Aux.	can, may	12
kuài	快	快	Adj.	fast	16
kuài	块	塊	N.	dollar	13
kuàizi	筷子	筷子	N.	chopstick	11
kùzi	裤子	褲子	N.	pants	13

L

lái	来	來	V.	to come (also used before a verb to indicate that one is about to do something)	5
láixìn	来信	來信	V.O.	to write a letter (to the speaker)	22
lánqiú	篮球	籃球	N.	basketball	16
lánsè	蓝色	藍色	Adj.	blue	13s
lǎobǎn	老板	老闆	N.	boss	22
lǎoshī	老师	老師	N.	teacher	1
làzhú	蜡烛	蠟燭	N.	candle	14s
lèi	累	累	Adj.	tired	4s
lěng	冷	冷	Adj.	cold	17
lí	离	離	V.	to be away from	18
lǐ	里	裡	N.	inside	15
liǎ	俩	倆		two people (colloquial)	16
liáng	凉	涼	Adj.	cool	17s
liǎng	两	兩	Num.	two	5
liàng	辆	輛	M.W.	(measure word for vehicles)	6
liànxí	练习	練習	V.	to practice	12
lǐbiān	里边	裡邊	N.	inside	15
lìhài	厉害	厲害	Adj.	severely, very much	19s
líng	零	零	Num.	zero	7s
liù	六/陆	六/陸	Num.	six	7
liúgǎn (liúxíngxìng gǎnmào)	流感 (流行性感冒)	流感 (流行性感冒)	N.	flu	19s
liúgǎn yìmiáo	流感疫苗	流感疫苗	N.	flu shot	19s
liúhuà	留话	留話	V.O.	to leave a message (used both in Mainland China and Taiwan)	9
liúxué	留学	留學	V.O.	to study abroad	21

liúyán	留言	留言	V.O.	to leave a message (used in Mainland China)	9
lǐwù	礼物	禮物	N.	gift	14s
lóushàng	楼上	樓上	N.	upstairs	20
lóuxià	楼下	樓下	N.	downstairs	20s
lù	路	路	N.	road	18
lǜ	绿	綠	Adj.	green	11
luàn	乱	亂	Adj.	messy	15s
lǜshī	律师	律師	N.	lawyer	6s
lǚxíng	旅行	旅行	V.	to travel	18

M

ma	吗	嗎	Part.	(used at the end of a declarative sentence to transform it into a question)	1
mǎi	买	買	V.	to buy	13
mài	卖	賣	V.	to sell	13s
mǎidān	买单	買單	V.O.	to pay the bill	11s
mǎlù	马路	馬路	N.	road, street	18s
māma	妈妈	媽媽	N.	mother	6
màn	慢	慢	Adj.	slow	16
máng	忙	忙	Adj.	busy	4s, 9
māo	猫	貓	N.	cat	6s
máoyī	毛衣	毛衣	N.	sweater	13s
màozi	帽子	帽子	N.	hat	13s
mǎshàng	马上	馬上	Adv.	immediately	20
mǎtóu	码头	碼頭	N.	wharf, dock, pier	18s
měi	每	每	Pron.	every, each	10
méiguānxi	没关系	沒關係		no problem	20
Měiguó	美国	美國	N.	United States	3
Měijīn	美金	美金	N.	U.S. dollar	13s
měilì	美丽	美麗	Adj.	beautiful	22
mèimei	妹妹	妹妹	N.	younger sister	6s, 12
měitiān	每天	每天	Adj.	every day	10
méiyǒu	没有	沒有	V.	to not have, to be without, there isn't/aren't	5s, 6
men	们	們		(suffix used after a personal pronoun to show plural number)	4
mén	门	門	M.W.	(measure word for school courses)	10
			N.	door	15s
miàn	面	麵	N.	noodle	11
miàn	面	面	N.	face	17
miànbāo	面包	麵包	N.	bread	11s

miǎo	秒	秒	M.W.	second	10s
míngpiàn	名片	名片	N.	name card, business card	8s
míngtiān	明天	明天	N.	tomorrow	12
míngzi	名字	名字	N.	name	2
mótuōchē (jīchē)	摩托车 (机车)	摩托車 (機車)	N.	scooter, motorcycle	18s
Mòxīgē	墨西哥	墨西哥	N.	Mexico	3s

N

nǎ /něi	哪	哪	Pron.	which	3
nà/nèi	那	那	Pron.	that	4
nǎinai	奶奶	奶奶	N.	paternal grandmother (father's mother)	6s
nán	难	難	Adj.	difficult	4
nán	男	男	N.	male	6
nánbù	南部	南部	N.	the South	18
nánpéngyou	男朋友	男朋友	N.	boyfriend	5s, 6
nǎr	哪儿	哪兒	Pron.	where	7
ne	呢	呢	Part.	(used at the end of an interrogative sentence)	1
nèi	内	內	N.	inside	7s
néng	能	能	Aux.	can, may, be able to	12
nǐ	你	你	Pron.	you	1
nián	年	年	N.	year	10
nín	您	您	Pron.	(polite) you	2
niúròu	牛肉	牛肉	N.	beef	11s
Niǔyuē	纽约	紐約	N.	New York	6
niúzǎikù	牛仔裤	牛仔褲	N.	jeans	13s
nuǎnhuo	暖和	暖和	Adj.	warm	17
nǚ	女	女	N.	female	6s
nǚpéngyou	女朋友	女朋友	N.	girlfriend	5s, 6s, 20

P

pán	盘	盤	M.W.	plate	11
pángbiān	旁边	旁邊	N.	beside, nearby	15
páshān	爬山	爬山	V.O.	to climb a mountain	16s
pǎo	跑	跑	V.	to run	16s
pǎobù	跑步	跑步	V.O.	to run	16s
péngyou	朋友	朋友	N.	friend	5
piányi	便宜	便宜	Adj.	inexpensive, cheap (pronounced as [piányí] in Taiwan)	13s
piào	票	票	N.	ticket	13

píng	瓶	瓶	*M.W.*	bottle	11
píng'ān	平安	平安	*Adj.*	peaceful, safe	21

Q

qī	七/柒	七/柒	*Num.*	seven	7
qí	骑	騎	*V.*	to ride	18
qí zìxíngchē	骑自行车	騎自行車	*V.O.*	to ride a bike	16s
qián	钱	錢	*N.*	money	13
qiánbiān	前边	前邊	*N.*	in front of	15
qiānyuē	签约	簽約	*V.O.*	to sign a contract	20s
qìchē	汽车	汽車	*N.*	car	18s
qǐchuáng	起床	起床	*V.*	to get up	10
qìhòu	气候	氣候	*N.*	climate	17
qíng	晴	晴	*Adj.*	clear, sunny	17s
qǐng	请	請		(polite) please	2
			V.	to invite	14
qǐng wèn	请问	請問		may I ask	2
qīngcài	青菜	青菜	*N.*	vegetable	11s
qìngshēng	庆生	慶生	*V.O.*	to celebrate a birthday	14s
qiū	秋	秋	*N.*	autumn	17
qiú	球	球	*N.*	ball	10
qiújì	球季	球季	*N.*	season (of a sport)	16s
qiúsài	球赛	球賽	*N.*	ball game, match	16
qìwēn	气温	氣溫	*N.*	temperature	17s
qízhōng	其中	其中		among (whom, which)	17
qù	去	去	*V.*	to go	8
qúnzi	裙子	裙子	*N.*	skirt	13

R

ránhòu	然后	然後	*Adv.*	then, after that, afterwards	10
ràng	让	讓	*V.*	to let, to allow	13
rè	热	熱	*Adj.*	hot	17
rén	人	人	*N.*	person	3
Rénmínbì	人民币	人民幣	*N.*	currency of the People's Republic of China	13s
rènshi	认识	認識	*V.*	to know, to recognize, to be acquainted with/familiar with	5s, 8
rènzhēn	认真	認真	*Adj.*	conscientious, serious	22
rèxīn	热心	熱心	*Adj.*	warm-hearted	22
rì	日	日	*N.*	day	10
Rìběn	日本	日本	*N.*	Japan	3s, 8
rìlì	日历	日曆	*N.*	calendar	14s

| róngyì | 容易 | 容易 | *Adj.* | easy | 4s |
| ròu | 肉 | 肉 | *N.* | meat, flesh | 11s |

S

sān	三/叁	三/叁	*Num.*	three	7
sè	色	色	*N.*	color	12
shālā	沙拉	沙拉	*N.*	salad	11s
shāngrén	商人	商人	*N.*	businessman	6s
shǎo	少	少	*Adj.*	few, little	4
shàngbiān	上边	上邊	*N.*	on top of, above, over	15
shàngkè	上课	上課	*V.O.*	to attend class	8
shàngwǎng	上网	上網	*V.O.*	to be online	9
shàngwǔ	上午	上午	*N.*	morning (roughly after 9 A.M.)	10s
shéi/shuí	谁	誰	*Pron.*	who, whom	2
shēngbìng	生病	生病	*V.O.*	to fall ill, to get sick	19
shēnghuó	生活	生活	*N.*	life	10
shēngrì	生日	生日	*N.*	birthday	14
shénme	什么	什麼	*Pron.*	what	2
shénme shíhou	什么时候	什麼時候		when, at what time	9
shēnqǐng	申请	申請	*V.*	to apply	21
shèr	事儿	事兒	*N.*	matter, thing, business	8
shèshì	摄氏	攝氏	*N.*	Celsius, Centigrade	17s
shètuán	社团	社團	*N.*	organization	16s
shí	十/拾	十/拾	*Num.*	ten	7s, 11
shì	是	是	*V.*	to be, (affirmative answer) yes	1
shíhou	时候	時候	*N.*	(the duration of) time, (a point in) time	9
shíjiān	时间	時間	*N.*	time	17
shìshi	试试	試試	*V.*	to try	13
shíxí	实习	實習	*N.*	internship	21
			V.	to practice, to intern	
shìyǒu	室友	室友	*N.*	roommate	5
shǒu	手	手	*N.*	hand	7, 12
shǒubiǎo	手表	手錶	*N.*	watch	13s
shōudào	收到	收到	*V.C.*	to receive	22
shǒujī	手机	手機	*N.*	cell phone	7
shǒupáidǎng	手排挡	手排擋	*N.*	manual transmission (手排 in Taiwan)	12
shū	书	書	*N.*	book	4
shuāng	双	雙	*M.W.*	pair	11
shūfǎ	书法	書法	*N.*	calligraphy	22
shūfu	舒服	舒服	*Adj.*	comfortable, well	19
shuǐ	水	水	*N.*	water	11
shuǐguǒ	水果	水果	*N.*	fruit	11s

shuìjiào	睡觉	睡覺	V.O.	to go to bed, to sleep	9s, 10
shǔjià	暑假	暑假	N.	summer vacation	17s, 21
shùnlì	顺利	順利	Adj.	smooth	22s
shuō	说	說	V.	to speak	3
shuòshì	硕士	碩士	N.	(a person with a) master's degree	21s
shǔqī	暑期	暑期	N.	summer vacation	21
shùxué	数学	數學	N.	mathematics	4s
shūzhuō	书桌	書桌	N.	desk	15s
sījī	司机	司機	N.	driver	18s
sìjì	四季	四季	N.	four seasons	17s
sì	四/肆	四/肆	Num.	four	6
sòng	送	送	V.	to give (as a present), to send	14
			V.	to deliver, to escort, to see off	19
suì	岁	歲	N.	age, years	14
suìdào	隧道	隧道	N.	tunnel	18s
suǒyǐ	所以	所以	Conj.	therefore, consequently	19
sùshè	宿舍	宿舍	N.	dorm	7

T

tā	他	他	Pron.	he, him	1
tā	她	她	Pron.	she, her	1s, 2
tài	太	太	Adv.	too	4
tāng	汤	湯	N.	soup	11
téng	疼	疼	V.	to ache	19
tiān	天	天	N.	day	10
tiándiǎn	甜点	甜點	N.	dessert	11s
tiānqì	天气	天氣	N.	weather	17s
tiáo	条	條	M.W.	(measure word for skirts/pants)	13
tiào	跳	跳	V.	to jump	14s
tiàowǔ	跳舞	跳舞	V.O.	to dance	14s
tīng	听	聽	V.	to listen	14s
			V.	to hear	18
tíng	停	停	V.	to park	12
tíngchēchǎng	停车场	停車場	N.	parking lot	12
tīngshuō	听说	聽說	V.	to hear of, it is said that . . .	18
tǐwēn	体温	體溫	N.	body temperature	19s
tīxùshān	T-恤衫	T-恤衫	N.	T-shirt	13s
tǐyùguǎn	体育馆	體育館	N.	gymnasium	16
tōng	通	通	M.W.	(measure word for telephone calls)	9s
tóng	同	同		same, similar	2
tóngshì	同事	同事	N.	colleague, co-worker	22
tóngxué	同学	同學	N.	classmate	2
tóu	头	頭	N.	head	19

tóuténg	头疼	頭疼	V.	to have a headache	19
tuō	脱	脱	V.	to take off (used with clothing in general)	13s
túshūguǎn	图书馆	圖書館	N.	library	10

W

wài	外	外	N.	outside	7
wàigōng	外公	外公	N.	maternal grandfather (mother's father)	6s
wàipó	外婆	外婆	N.	maternal grandmother (mother's mother)	6s
wàitào	外套	外套	N.	coat	13s
wán	玩	玩	V.	to play, to have fun	12
wǎn	晚	晚	Adj.	late	10
wǎn	碗	碗	M.W.	bowl	11
wǎnfàn	晚饭	晚飯	N.	dinner	8s
wǎngluò (wǎnglù)	网络 (网路)	網絡 (網路)	N.	Internet	9s
wàngjì	旺季	旺季	N.	busy season	18s
wǎngqiú	网球	網球	N.	tennis	16s
wǎngzhàn	网站	網站	N.	Web site	9s
wǎnhuì	晚会	晚會	N.	party (evening party)	14s
wǎnshang	晚上	晚上	N.	evening, night	9, 10s
wàzi	袜子	襪子	N.	socks	13s
(wéi)	喂	喂	Int.	(used in greeting or to attract attention) hello, hey	9
wèi	位	位	M.W.	(polite measure word for people)	9
wèi	为	為	Prep.	for (to do something for someone; used before the object of one's act of service)	14
wèn	问	問	V.	to ask	2
wèntí	问题	問題	N.	problem, question	12
wénxué	文学	文學	N.	literature	4
wǒ	我	我	Pron.	I, me	1
wǒ jiù shì	我就是	我就是		(on the phone) this is he/she speaking	9
wǒmen	我们	我們	Pron.	we, us	4
wòshì	卧室	臥室	N.	bedroom	15
wǔ	五/伍	五/伍	Num.	five	7
wǔ	舞	舞	N.	dance	14
wǔfàn (zhōngfàn)	午饭 (中饭)	午飯 (中飯)	N.	lunch	8s
wǔhuì	舞会	舞會	N.	dance party	14

X

xì	系	系	N.	major, college department	4s
xià	夏	夏	N.	summer	17
xiàbiān	下边	下邊	N.	under	15
xiàcì	下次	下次		next time	8
xiàkè	下课	下課	V.O.	to end class, class dismissed	8
xiān	先	先	Adv.	first	11, 18
xiǎng	想	想	V.	to want, to think, to miss	8
xiānsheng	先生	先生	N.	mister	11
xiànzài	现在	現在	N.	now	10s
			Adv.	now	16
xiǎo	小	小	Adj.	small	7, 13s
xiào	校	校	N.	school	7
xiǎofèi	小费	小費	N.	tip	11s
xiǎojiě	小姐	小姐	N.	miss	11
xiǎolóngbāo	小笼包	小籠包	N.	little steamed buns with stuffing	22
xiàonèi	校内	校內	N.	on campus	7s
xiǎoshí	小时	小時	N.	hour	10s
xiàowài	校外	校外	N.	off campus	7
xiāoyè	宵夜	宵夜	N.	midnight snack	8s
xiàwǔ	下午	下午	N.	afternoon	10s
xiàxuě	下雪	下雪	V.O.	to snow	17
xiàyǔ	下雨	下雨	V.O.	to rain	17
Xībānyá	西班牙	西班牙	N.	Spain	3s
xībù	西部	西部	N.	the West	18
xiě	写	寫	V.	to write	10
xièxie	谢谢	謝謝		thanks	9
xiézi	鞋子	鞋子	N.	shoes	13s
xǐhuān	喜欢	喜歡	V.	to like	10
xīn	新	新	Adj.	new	22
xìn	信	信	N.	letter	10
xíng	行	行	V.	to be all right, to be okay	8
xìng	姓	姓	N.	surname, family name	2
			V.	have as a surname	2
xīngqī	星期	星期	N.	week	14
xīngqīliù	星期六	星期六	N.	Saturday	14
Xīntáibì	新台币	新台幣	N.	currency of Taiwan (New Taiwan dollars)	13s
xīnxiǎngshìchéng	心想事成	心想事成		Every wish comes true.	22s
xiōngdìjiěmèi	兄弟姐妹	兄弟姐妹	N.	siblings	6s
xiūxi	休息	休息	V.	to rest	8s, 19
xǐzǎojiān	洗澡间	洗澡間	N.	bathroom, restroom	15
xué	学	學	V.	to study, to learn	1
xuě	雪	雪	N.	snow	17

xuédào	学到	學到	*V.C.*	to learn, to master	22
xuéqī	学期	學期	*N.*	semester	10
xuésheng	学生	學生	*N.*	student	1
xuéshì	学士	學士	*N.*	(a person with a) bachelor's degree	21s
xuéwèi	学位	學位	*N.*	degree	21s
xuéxí	学习	學習	*V.*	to study, to learn	15
xuéxiào	学校	學校	*N.*	school	18

Y

yǎnjìng	眼镜	眼鏡	*N.*	glasses	13s
yánjiū	研究	研究	*N.*	to research, to study/examine	21
yánjiūshēng	研究生	研究生	*N.*	graduate student	21s
yánjiūshēngyuàn	研究生院	研究生院	*N.*	graduate school	21
yánsè	颜色	顏色	*N.*	color	13s
yánzhòng	严重	嚴重	*Adj.*	severe	19s
yào	要	要	*V.*	to want, to desire	9
yào	药	藥	*N.*	medicine	19
yě	也	也	*Adv.*	also	1
yéye	爷爷	爺爺	*N.*	paternal grandfather (father's father)	6s
yī	一/壹	一/壹	*Num.*	one	6
yīchú	衣橱	衣櫥	*N.*	wardrobe	15s
yìdiǎr	一点儿	一點兒		a little	3
yídìng	一定	一定	*Aux.*	certainly, surely	14
yīfu	衣服	衣服	*N.*	clothes	13s
yígòng	一共	一共	*Adv.*	altogether, in all	18
yǐhòu	以后	以後	*Adv.*	after, afterwards, later	8
yǐjīng	已经	已經	*Adv.*	already	22
yílùpíng'ān	一路平安	一路平安		have a pleasant journey	21
yímiàn	一面	一面	*Adv.*	at the same time	21
yīn	阴	陰	*Adj.*	cloudy, overcast	17s
yīnggāi	应该	應該	*Aux.*	should	12
Yīngguó	英国	英國	*N.*	Britain	3
Yīngwén	英文	英文	*N.*	English (language)	2
yínhuīsè	银灰色	銀灰色	*Adj.*	silver	13s
yǐnliào	饮料	飲料	*N.*	drink	11s
yīnwèi	因为	因為	*Conj.*	because	22
yīnyuè	音乐	音樂	*N.*	music	14s
yìqǐ	一起	一起	*Adv.*	together	8
yǐqián	以前	以前	*N.*	before, previously	20
yīshēng	医生	醫生	*N.*	doctor	6s, 19
yīwùshì (yīhùshì)	医务室 (医护室)	醫務室 (醫護室)	*N.*	medical exam room	19s

yíxià	一下	一下		(used after a verb to indicate a brief action)	5
yìxiē	一些	一些	*Adj.*	some	22
yīyuàn	医院	醫院	*N.*	hospital	19s
yǐzi	椅子	椅子	*N.*	chair	15s
yòng	用	用	*V.*	to use	12
yǒu	有	有	*V.*	to have, there is/are	5
yòubiān	右边	右邊	*N.*	on the right	15s
yǒudiǎr	有点儿	有點兒	*Adv.*	a little	4s
yǒukòng	有空	有空	*V.O.*	to have free time	14
yǒushíhou	有时候	有時候	*Adv.*	sometimes	17
yǒuyìsi	有意思	有意思	*Adj.*	interesting, enjoyable	21
yóuyǒng	游泳	游泳	*V.O.*	to swim, swimming	16
yóuyǒngchí	游泳池	游泳池	*N.*	swimming pool	16
yú	鱼	魚	*N.*	fish	11s
yǔ	雨	雨	*N.*	rain	17
yuǎn	远	遠	*Adj.*	far	18
yuǎnzú	远足	遠足	*N.*	a hike, hiking	16s
yuè	月	月	*N.*	month	10
yuèlì	月历	月曆	*N.*	monthly calendar	14s
yùfángzhēn	预防针	預防針	*N.*	immunization shot	19s
yúkuài	愉快	愉快	*Adj.*	happy	21
yùndòng	运动	運動	*V.*	to exercise	16s
			N.	sports	
yǔyán	语言	語言	*N.*	language	3s

Z

zài	在	在	*V.*	to be at, to be in	6
			Prep.	at, in	
zài	再	再	*Adv.*	again	8
zàijiàn	再见	再見		see you again, goodbye	8
zāng	脏	髒	*Adj.*	dirty	15s
zǎo	早	早	*Adj.*	early	10s
zǎofàn	早饭	早飯	*N.*	breakfast	8s
zǎoshang	早上	早上	*N.*	morning (around 7–9 A.M.)	10s
zázhì	杂志	雜志	*N.*	magazine	15s
zěnmele	怎么了	怎麼了		what happened, what's wrong	19
zěnmeyàng	怎么样	怎麼樣	*Pron.*	how is it, how about it	8
zhāi	摘	摘	*V.*	to take off (used with accessories)	13s
zhāng	张	張	*M.W.*	(measure word for piece of paper)	13
zhànxiàn	占线	佔線	*V.O.*	to occupy a (phone) line, the line is busy	9s

zhǎo	找	找	*V.*	to seek, to look for	21
zhè/zhèi	这	這	*Pron.*	this	4
zhècì	这次	這次	*Pron.*	this time	12
zhēn	真	真	*Adv.*	really	15
zhěngqí	整齐	整齊	*Adj.*	tidy	15s
zhèngzài	正在	正在	*Adv.*	(to indicate an action in progress) in the process of, in the course of	9
zhěnsuǒ	诊所	診所	*N.*	clinic	19s
zhèyàng	这样	這樣	*Pron.*	thus, in this way, like this	12
zhī	只	隻	*M.W.*	(measure word for certain animals, or for one of a pair)	6
zhīdào	知道	知道	*V.*	to know, to be aware of, to realize	9
zhīdào le	知道了	知道了		"Got it."	9
zhǐyào	只要	只要	*Adv.*	only	18
zhōng	中	中	*Adj.*	medium	13s
Zhōngguó	中国	中國	*N.*	China	3
zhōngjiān	中间	中間	*N.*	middle	15
zhōngtóu	钟头	鐘頭	*N.*	hour	10s
Zhōngwén	中文	中文	*N.*	Chinese (language)	1s, 2
zhōngwǔ	中午	中午	*N.*	noon	10s
zhù	住	住	*V.*	to live	7
zhù	祝	祝	*V.*	to wish	10
Zhù nǐ shēngrì kuàilè.	祝你生日快乐	祝你生日快樂		Happy birthday to you.	14s
zhuānyè	专业	專業	*N.*	major (used in Mainland China)	4s
zhǔnbèi	准备	準備	*V.*	to prepare	19
zhuōzi	桌子	桌子	*N.*	table	15
zhūròu	猪肉	豬肉	*N.*	pork	11s
zhǔxiū	主修	主修	*N.*	major (used in Taiwan)	4s
zìdòngpáidǎng	自动排挡	自動排擋	*Adj.*	automatic transmission (自排 in Taiwan)	12s
zǐsè	紫色	紫色	*Adj.*	purple	13s
zìxíngchē	自行车	自行車	*N.*	bicycle	18
zōngsè (kāfēisè)	棕色 (咖啡色)	棕色 (咖啡色)	*Adj.*	brown	13s
zǒu	走	走	*V.*	to walk	15
zǒulù	走路	走路	*V.O.*	to walk	18
zū	租	租	*V.*	to rent, to hire, to lease	18
zuì	最	最	*Adv.*	(indicates the superlative degree)	17
zuò	坐	坐	*V.*	to sit	11
zuò	做	做	*V.*	to make, to do	9, 14
zuǒbiān	左边	左邊	*N.*	on the left	15s
zuòfàn	做饭	做飯	*V.O.*	to cook	20

zuótiān	昨天	昨天	N.	yesterday	16
zuòyè	作业	作業	N.	homework, assignment	4s, 16
zúqiú	足球	足球	N.	soccer	16s
zūwū	租屋	租屋	V.O.	to rent a house	20s

英文索引 ENGLISH GLOSSARY

Each entry lists the English meaning, simplified character, traditional character, Pinyin, part of speech, and lesson number.

Note: The letter *s* indicates vocabulary supplementary to that lesson.

Measure Words (Classifiers) for

books, magazines	本	本	běn	*M.W.*	4
certain animals, or for one of a pair	只	隻	zhī	*M.W.*	6
clothes	件	件	jiàn	*M.W.*	13
companies, enterprises, stores, etc.	家	家	jiā	*M.W.*	21
people, characters, things in general	个	個	gè	*M.W.*	5
people (polite)	位	位	wèi	*M.W.*	9
piece of paper	张	張	zhāng	*M.W.*	13
rooms	间	間	jiān	*M.W.*	15s
school courses	门	門	mén	*M.W.*	10
skirts/pants	条	條	tiáo	*M.W.*	13
telephone calls	通	通	tōng	*M.W.*	9s
vehicles	辆	輛	liàng	*M.W.*	6

A

to ache	疼	疼	téng	*V.*	19
activity	活动	活動	huódòng	*N.*	22
address	地址	地址	dìzhǐ	*N.*	10
after, afterwards, later	以后	以後	yǐhòu	*Adv.*	8
afternoon	下午	下午	xiàwǔ	*N.*	10s
again	再	再	zài	*Adv.*	8
age, years	岁	歲	suì	*N.*	14
airplane	飞机	飛機	fēijī	*N.*	12
airport	机场	機場	jīchǎng	*N.*	12
all, both	都	都	dōu	*Adv.*	5
all, everybody	大家	大家	dàjiā	*N.*	6
already	已经	已經	yǐjīng	*Adv.*	22
also	也	也	yě	*Adv.*	1
altogether, in all	一共	一共	yígòng	*Adv.*	18
among (whom, which)	其中	其中	qízhōng		17
and	和	和	hé/hàn	*Conj.*	3

apartment	公寓	公寓	gōngyù	N.	7s
to apply	申请	申請	shēnqǐng	V.	21
to arrive	到	到	dào	V.	12
as early as, precisely	就	就	jiù	Adv.	10
to ask	问	問	wèn	V.	2
at, in	在	在	zài	Prep.	6
at the same time	一面	一面	yímiàn	Adv.	21
to attend class	上课	上課	shàngkè	V.O.	8
(attached to an adjective to transform the whole unit into an adverb when preceding a verb; describes manner of the verb)	地	地	de	Part.	19
automatic transmission (自排 in Taiwan)	自动排挡	自動排擋	zìdòngpáidǎng	Adj.	12s
autumn	秋	秋	qiū	N.	17

B

(a person with a) bachelor's degree	学士	學士	xuéshì	N.	21s
ball	球	球	qiú	N.	10
ball game, match	球赛	球賽	qiúsài	N.	16
baseball	棒球	棒球	bàngqiú	N.	16s
basketball	篮球	籃球	lánqiú	N.	16
bathroom, restroom	洗澡间	洗澡間	xǐzǎojiān	N.	15
bathroom, toilet	厕所	廁所	cèsuǒ	N.	15s
to be, (affirmative answer) yes	是	是	shì	V.	1
to be all right, to be okay	行	行	xíng	V.	8
to be at, to be in	在	在	zài	V.	6
to be away from	离	離	lí	V.	18
to be like, to seem	好像	好像	hǎoxiàng	V.	19
to be online	上网	上網	shàngwǎng	V.O.	9
bean curd	豆腐	豆腐	dòufu	N.	11s
beautiful	美丽	美麗	měilì	Adj.	22
because	因为	因為	yīnwèi	Conj.	22
bed	床	床	chuáng	N.	15s
bedroom	卧室	卧室	wòshì	N.	15
beef	牛肉	牛肉	niúròu	N.	11s
before, previously	以前	以前	yǐqián	N.	20
behind, at the back	后边	後邊	hòubiān	N.	15
beside, nearby	旁边	旁邊	pángbiān	N.	15

bicycle	自行车	自行車	zìxíngchē	N.	18
	单车	單車	dānchē	N.	18s
	(脚踏车)	(腳踏車)	(jiǎotàchē)		
big, large	大	大	dà	Adj.	7, 13s
birthday	生日	生日	shēngrì	N.	14
black	黑	黑	hēi	Adj.	13
to blow (wind)	刮风	刮風	guāfēng	V.O.	17
to blow	吹	吹	chuī	V.	14s
blue	蓝色	藍色	lánsè	Adj.	13s
body temperature	体温	體溫	tǐwēn	N.	19s
book	书	書	shū	N.	4
to borrow	借	借	jiè	V.	12
boss	老板	老闆	lǎobǎn	N.	22
bottle	瓶	瓶	píng	M.W.	11
bowl	碗	碗	wǎn	M.W.	11
boyfriend	男朋友	男朋友	nánpéngyou	N.	5s, 6
bread	面包	麵包	miànbāo	N.	11s
breakfast	早饭	早飯	zǎofàn	N.	8s
to bring over	带来	帶來	dàilái	V.C.	20
Britain	英国	英國	Yīngguó	N.	3
brown	棕色	棕色	zōngsè	Adj.	13s
	(咖啡色)	(咖啡色)	(kāfēisè)		
to burn the midnight oil	熬夜	熬夜	áoyè	V.O.	10s
bus	公共汽车	公共汽車	gōnggòngqìchē	N.	18
	公车	公車	gōngchē	N.	18s
	(巴士)	(巴士)	(bāshì)		
businessman	商人	商人	shāngrén	N.	6s
busy	忙	忙	máng	Adj.	4s, 9
busy season	旺季	旺季	wàngjì	N.	18s
but	但是	但是	dànshì	Conj.	20
but, however	不过	不過	búguò	Conj.	22
but, yet, however	可是	可是	kěshì	Conj.	4
to buy	买	買	mǎi	V.	13
by the way (a phrase used to start a new topic)	对了	對了	duìle	N.	3

C

cake	蛋糕	蛋糕	dàngāo	N.	11s, 14
calendar	日历	日曆	rìlì	N.	14s
California	加州	加州	Jiāzhōu	N.	21
to call, to be called	叫	叫	jiào	V.	2
to call, to make, to hit	打	打	dǎ	V.	9
calligraphy	书法	書法	shūfǎ	N.	22

can, may, be able to	能	能	néng	*Aux.*	12
can, be able to, know how to	会	會	huì	*Aux.*	3
can, may	可以	可以	kěyǐ	*Aux.*	12
Canada	加拿大	加拿大	Jiānádà	N.	3s
candle	蜡烛	蠟燭	làzhú	N.	14s
car	车	車	chē	N.	6
	汽车	汽車	qìchē	N.	18s
cat	猫	貓	māo	N.	6s
to catch a cold	感冒	感冒	gǎnmào	V.	19
to celebrate a birthday	庆生	慶生	qìngshēng	V.O.	14s
cell phone	手机	手機	shǒujī	N.	7
Celsius, Centigrade	摄氏	攝氏	shèshì	N.	17s
certainly, surely	一定	一定	yídìng	*Aux.*	14
chair	椅子	椅子	yǐzi	N.	15s
chef	厨师	廚師	chúshī	N.	6s
chicken	鸡肉	雞肉	jīròu	N.	11s
child	孩子	孩子	háizi	N.	6s
China	中国	中國	Zhōngguó	N.	3
Chinese (language)	中文	中文	Zhōngwén	N.	1s, 2
chopstick	筷子	筷子	kuàizi	N.	11
city	城市	城市	chéngshì	N.	22
class	班	班	bān	N.	21
class, lesson	课	課	kè	N.	8
classmate	同学	同學	tóngxué	N.	2
clean	干净	乾淨	gānjìng	*Adj.*	15s
clear, sunny	晴	晴	qíng	*Adj.*	17s
climate	气候	氣候	qìhòu	N.	17
to climb a mountain	爬山	爬山	páshān	V.O.	16s
clinic	诊所	診所	zhěnsuǒ	N.	19s
clothes	衣服	衣服	yīfu	N.	13s
cloudy, overcast	阴	陰	yīn	*Adj.*	17s
club	俱乐部	俱樂部	jùlèbù	N.	16s
coach, trainer	教练	教練	jiàoliàn	N.	16
coat	外套	外套	wàitào	N.	13s
coffee	咖啡	咖啡	kāfēi	N.	11s
cola	可乐	可樂	kělè	N.	11
cold	冷	冷	lěng	*Adj.*	17
cold, flu	感冒	感冒	gǎnmào	N.	19
colleague, co-worker	同事	同事	tóngshì	N.	22
college, university	大学	大學	dàxué	N.	10
college student(s)	大学生	大學生	dàxuéshēng	N.	4s, 21s
color	色	色	sè	N.	12
	颜色	顏色	yánsè	N.	13s
to come over	过来	過來	guòlái	V.C.	20

English	Simplified	Traditional	Pinyin	Type	Lesson
to come (also used before a verb to indicate that one is about to do something)	来	來	lái	V.	5
comfortable, well	舒服	舒服	shūfu	Adj.	19
company	公司	公司	gōngsī	N.	21
computer (used in Mainland China only)	计算机	計算機	jìsuànjī	N.	4s
computer (used in Taiwan, also used in Mainland China)	电脑	電腦	diànnǎo	N.	4s, 21
conscientious, serious	认真	認真	rènzhēn	Adj.	22
to cook	做饭	做飯	zuòfàn	V.O.	20
cooked rice, meal	饭	飯	fàn	N.	8
cool	凉	涼	liáng	Adj.	17s
correct, right	对	對	duì	Adj.	9
to cough	咳嗽	咳嗽	késòu	V.	19
country	国	國	guó	N.	3
cracker, cookie	饼干	餅乾	bǐnggān	N.	11s
cup	杯	杯	bēi	M.W.	11
currency of Hong Kong	港币	港幣	Gǎngbì	N.	13s
currency of Taiwan (New Taiwan dollars)	新台币	新台幣	Xīntáibì	N.	13s
currency of the People's Republic of China	人民币	人民幣	Rénmínbì	N.	13s

D

English	Simplified	Traditional	Pinyin	Type	Lesson
dance	舞	舞	wǔ	N.	14
to dance	跳舞	跳舞	tiàowǔ	V.O.	14s
dance party	舞会	舞會	wǔhuì	N.	14
day	日	日	rì	N.	10
	天	天	tiān	N.	10
to decide	决定	決定	juédìng	V.	21
degree	度	度	dù	N.	17
	学位	學位	xuéwèi	N.	21s
to deliver, to escort, to see off	送	送	sòng	V.	19
desk	书桌	書桌	shūzhuō	N.	15s
dessert	甜点	甜點	tiándiǎn	N.	11s
to dial a wrong number	打错了	打錯了	dǎcuòle	V.	9s
difficult	难	難	nán	Adj.	4
dining room	餐厅	餐廳	cāntīng	N.	15
dinner	晚饭	晚飯	wǎnfàn	N.	8s
dirty	脏	髒	zāng	Adj.	15s
disease, illness	病	病	bìng	N.	19
dish (type of food), cuisine	菜	菜	cài	N.	8

to do	做	做	zuò	V.	9
doctor	医生	醫生	yīshēng	N.	6s, 19
(a person with a) doctoral degree	博士	博士	bóshì	N.	21s
doctoral students	博士生	博士生	bóshìshēng	N.	21s
dog	狗	狗	gǒu	N.	6
dollar	块	塊	kuài	N.	13
door	门	門	mén	N.	15s
dorm	宿舍	宿舍	sùshè	N.	7
downstairs	楼下	樓下	lóuxià	N.	20s
drink	饮料	飲料	yǐnliào	N.	11s
to drink	喝	喝	hē	V.	11
to drive, to turn on, to open	开	開	kāi	V.	12
driver	司机	司機	sījī	N.	18s
dumpling (crescent-shaped)	饺子	餃子	jiǎozi	N.	11

E

early	早	早	zǎo	Adj.	10s
earring	耳环	耳環	ěrhuán	N.	13s
east	东	東	dōng	N.	18s
easy	容易	容易	róngyì	Adj.	4s
to eat	吃	吃	chī	V.	8
to eat, to have a meal	吃饭	吃飯	chīfàn	V.O.	8
eight	八/捌	八/捌	bā	Num.	7
elder brother	哥哥	哥哥	gēge	N.	6s
elder sister	姐姐	姐姐	jiějie	N.	6
electric, electricity	电	電	diàn	N.	7
email	电子邮件	電子郵件	diànzǐ yóujiàn	N.	10
to end class, class dismissed	下课	下課	xiàkè	V.O.	8
engineer	工程师	工程師	gōngchéngshī	N.	6
engineering	工程	工程	gōngchéng	N.	4
English (language)	英文	英文	Yīngwén	N.	2
to enter	进	進	jìn	V.	15
et cetera	等等	等等	děngděng	Part.	22
evening, night	晚上	晚上	wǎnshang	N.	9, 10s
every, each	每	每	měi	Pron.	10
every day	每天	每天	měitiān	Adj.	10
Every wish comes true.	心想事成	心想事成	xīnxiǎngshìchéng		22s
everywhere	到处	到處	dàochù	Adv.	22
exam	考试	考試	kǎoshì	N.	4s, 19
to exercise	锻炼	鍛煉	duànliàn	V.	16
	运动	運動	yùndòng	V.	16s
expensive	贵	貴	guì	Adj.	13s
extremely	极	極	jí	Adv.	17

F

face	面	面	miàn	N.	17
Fahrenheit	华氏	華氏	huáshì	N.	17
to fall ill, to get sick	生病	生病	shēngbìng	V.O.	19
far	远	遠	yuǎn	Adj.	18
fast	快	快	kuài	Adj.	16
father	爸爸	爸爸	bàba	N.	6
female	女	女	nǚ	N.	6s
few, little	少	少	shǎo	Adj.	4
first	先	先	xiān	Adv.	11, 18
first day	第一天	第一天	dìyītiān	N.	20
fish	鱼	魚	yú	N.	11s
five	五/伍	五/伍	wǔ	Num.	7
flu	流感 (流行性感冒)	流感 (流行性感冒)	liúgǎn (liúxíngxìng gǎnmào)	N.	19s
flu shot	流感疫苗	流感疫苗	liúgǎn yìmiáo	N.	19s
football	橄榄球	橄欖球	gǎnlǎnqiú	N.	16s
for (to do something for someone; used before the object of one's act of service)	为	為	wèi	Prep.	14
for a long time	久	久	jiǔ	Adj.	17
for example	比如	比如	bǐrú	Conj.	22
for public use, communal	公用	公用	gōngyòng	Adj.	15
for, to	给	給	gěi	Prep.	9
four	四/肆	四/肆	sì	Num.	6
four seasons	四季	四季	sìjì	N.	17s
France	法国	法國	Fǎguó	N.	3
French (language)	法文	法文	Fǎwén	N.	3
friend	朋友	朋友	péngyou	N.	5
from	从	從	cóng	Prep.	6
fruit	水果	水果	shuǐguǒ	N.	11s

G

Germany	德国	德國	Déguó	N.	3s
to get up	起床	起床	qǐchuáng	V.	10
gift	礼物	禮物	lǐwù	N.	14s
girlfriend	女朋友	女朋友	nǚpéngyou	N.	5s, 6s, 20
to give	给	給	gěi	V.	9
to give (as a present), to send	送	送	sòng	V.	14
to give or receive an injection	打针	打針	dǎzhēn	V.O.	19s
glasses	眼镜	眼鏡	yǎnjìng	N.	13s

to go	去	去	qù	*V.*	8
to go out	出去	出去	chūqù	*V.C.*	20
to go to bed, to sleep	睡觉	睡覺	shuìjiào	*V.O.*	9s, 10
gold	金黄色	金黄色	jīnhuángsè	*Adj.*	13s
good, well	好	好	hǎo	*Adj.*	1
good-looking	好看	好看	hǎokàn	*Adj.*	13
good luck	好运	好運	hǎoyùn		21
"Got it."	知道了	知道了	zhīdào le		9
to graduate	毕业	畢業	bìyè	*V.*	21
graduate school	研究生院	研究生院	yánjiūshēngyuàn	*N.*	21
graduate student	研究生	研究生	yánjiūshēng	*N.*	21s
green	绿	綠	lǜ	*Adj.*	11
gym (workout facility)	健身房	健身房	jiànshēnfáng	*N.*	16
gymnasium	体育馆	體育館	tǐyùguǎn	*N.*	16

H

half	半	半	bàn	*Adj.*	10
hand	手	手	shǒu	*N.*	7, 12
happy	愉快	愉快	yúkuài	*Adj.*	21
	高兴	高興	gāoxìng	*Adj.*	22
	开心	開心	kāixīn	*Adj.*	22
Happy birthday to you.	祝你生日快乐	祝你生日快樂	Zhù nǐ shēngrì kuàilè.		14s
hat	帽子	帽子	màozi	*N.*	13s
to have, there is/are	有	有	yǒu	*V.*	5
to have a fever	发烧	發燒	fāshāo	*V.O.*	19
to have a headache	头疼	頭疼	tóuténg	*V.*	19
have a pleasant journey	一路平安	一路平安	yílùpíng'ān		21
to have a taste	尝尝	嚐嚐	chángchang	*V.*	22
have as a surname	姓	姓	xìng	*V.*	2
to have free time	有空	有空	yǒukòng	*V.O.*	14
to have, to start (a vacation)	放	放	fàng	*V.*	17
to have a holiday or vacation	放假	放假	fàngjià	*V.O.*	17s
he, him	他	他	tā	*Pron.*	1
head	头	頭	tóu	*N.*	19
healthy	健康	健康	jiànkāng	*Adj.*	22s
to hear	听	聽	tīng	*V.*	18
(used in greeting or to attract attention) hello, hey	喂	喂	wèi (wéi)	*Int.*	9
to hear of, it is said that . . .	听说	聽說	tīngshuō	*V.*	18
to help	帮	幫	bāng	*V.*	13
a hike, hiking	远足	遠足	yuǎnzú	*N.*	16s
home, family	家	家	jiā	*N.*	6

homework	作业	作業	zuòyè	N.	16
homework, assignment	功课	功課	gōngkè	N.	4
	作业	作業	zuòyè	N.	4s
hospital	医院	醫院	yīyuàn	N.	19s
hot	热	熱	rè	Adj.	17
hour	钟头	鐘頭	zhōngtóu	N.	10s
	小时	小時	xiǎoshí	N.	10s
house, room	房子	房子	fángzi	N.	7s
housewife	家庭主妇	家庭主婦	jiātíng zhǔfù	N.	6s
how is it, how about it	怎么样	怎麼樣	zěnmeyàng	Pron.	8
how many	几	幾	jǐ		5
how many, how much	多少	多少	duōshǎo	Pron.	7
how old	多大	多大	duōdà		14
hundred	百	百	bǎi	Num.	17
hungry	饿	餓	è	Adj.	19

I

I, me	我	我	wǒ	Pron.	1
I'm sorry	对不起	對不起	duìbuqǐ		9
ice	冰	冰	bīng	N.	11
iced, ice-cold, with ice	冰	冰	bīng	Adj.	11
immediately	马上	馬上	mǎshàng	Adv.	20
immunization shot	预防针	預防針	yùfángzhēn	N.	19s
to improve	进步	進步	jìnbù	V.	12
in front of	前边	前邊	qiánbiān	N.	15
(to indicate an action in progress) in the process of, in the course of	正在	正在	zhèngzài	Adv.	9
(indicates assumption or suggestion)	吧	吧	ba	Part.	9
(indicates the superlative degree)	最	最	zuì	Adv.	17
inexpensive, cheap (pronounced as [piányí] in Taiwan)	便宜	便宜	piányi	Adj.	13s
inside	内	內	nèi	N.	7s
	里	裡	lǐ	N.	15
	里边	裡邊	lǐbiān	N.	15
interesting, enjoyable	有意思	有意思	yǒuyìsi	Adj.	21
Internet	网络 (网路)	網絡 (網路)	wǎngluò (wǎnglù)	N.	9s
internship	实习	實習	shíxí	N.	21
to introduce	介绍	介紹	jièshào	V.	5
introduction	介绍	介紹	jièshào	N.	5

(introduces the object of a verb)	把	把	bǎ	*Prep.*	20
to invite	请	請	qǐng	*V.*	14
it seems	看来	看來	kànlái		22

J

Japan	日本	日本	Rìběn	*N.*	3s, 8
jeans	牛仔裤	牛仔褲	niúzǎikù	*N.*	13s
job	工作	工作	gōngzuò	*N.*	6
juice	果汁	果汁	guǒzhī	*N.*	11s
to jump	跳	跳	tiào	*V.*	14s

K

kitchen	厨房	廚房	chúfáng	*N.*	15
to know, to be aware of, to realize	知道	知道	zhīdào	*V.*	9
to know, to recognize, to be acquainted with/ familiar with	认识	認識	rènshi	*V.*	5s, 8
Korea	韩国	韓國	Hánguó	*N.*	3s, 8

L

to lack, to be short of	差	差	chà	*V.*	10s
landlord	房东	房東	fángdōng	*N.*	20s
language	语言	語言	yǔyán	*N.*	3s
large	大	大	dà	*Adj.*	13s
late	晚	晚	wǎn	*Adj.*	10
lawyer	律师	律師	lǜshī	*N.*	6s
to learn, to master	学到	學到	xuédào	*V.C.*	22
to leave a message (used in Mainland China)	留言	留言	liúyán	*V.O.*	9
to leave a message (used both in Mainland China and Taiwan)	留话	留話	liúhuà	*V.O.*	9
to let, to allow	让	讓	ràng	*V.*	13
letter	信	信	xìn	*N.*	10
library	图书馆	圖書館	túshūguǎn	*N.*	10
life	生活	生活	shēnghuó	*N.*	10
to like	喜欢	喜歡	xǐhuān	*V.*	10
to listen	听	聽	tīng	*V.*	14s
literature	文学	文學	wénxué	*N.*	4

a little	一点儿	一點兒	yìdiǎr		3
	有点儿	有點兒	yǒudiǎr	Adv.	4s
little steamed buns with stuffing	小笼包	小籠包	xiǎolóngbāo	N.	22
to live	住	住	zhù	V.	7
living room	客厅	客廳	kètīng	N.	15
to look at, to see, to watch	看	看	kàn	V.	9
long	长	長	cháng	Adj.	17s
to love	爱	愛	ài	V.	6
lunch	午饭 (中饭)	午飯 (中飯)	wǔfàn (zhōngfàn)	N.	8s

M

machine	机	機	jī	N.	7
magazine	杂志	雜志	zázhì	N.	15s
major (used in Mainland China)	专业	專業	zhuānyè	N.	4s
major (used in Taiwan)	主修	主修	zhǔxiū	N.	4s
major, college department	系	系	xì	N.	4s
to make a phone call	打电话	打電話	dǎ diànhuà	V.O.	9
to make, to do	做	做	zuò	V.	14
male	男	男	nán	N.	6
manual transmission (手排 in Taiwan)	手排挡	手排擋	shǒupáidǎng	N.	12
many, much	多	多	duō	Adj.	4
map	地图	地圖	dìtú	N.	14
(a person with a) master's degree	硕士	碩士	shuòshì	N.	21s
maternal grandfather (mother's father)	外公	外公	wàigōng	N.	6s
maternal grandmother (mother's mother)	外婆	外婆	wàipó	N.	6s
mathematics	数学	數學	shùxué	N.	4s
matter, thing, business	事儿	事兒	shèr	N.	8
may I ask	请问	請問	qǐng wèn		2
meat, flesh	肉	肉	ròu	N.	11s
medical exam room	医务室 (医护室)	醫務室 (醫護室)	yīwùshì (yīhùshì)	N.	19s
medicine	药	藥	yào	N.	19
medium	中	中	zhōng	Adj.	13s
to meet each other	见面	見面	jiànmiàn	V.O.	17
menu	菜单	菜單	càidān	N.	11s
messy	乱	亂	luàn	Adj.	15s

Mexico	墨西哥	墨西哥	Mòxīgē	*N.*	3s
middle	中间	中間	zhōngjiān	*N.*	15
midnight snack	宵夜	宵夜	xiāoyè	*N.*	8s
minor	辅修	輔修	fǔxiū	*N.*	4s
minute	分	分	fēn	*N.*	10
	分钟	分鐘	fēnzhōng	*N.*	10s
	分钟	分鐘	fēnzhōng	*N.*	18
miss	小姐	小姐	xiǎojiě	*N.*	11
mister	先生	先生	xiānsheng	*N.*	11
money	钱	錢	qián	*N.*	13
month	月	月	yuè	*N.*	10
monthly calendar	月历	月曆	yuèlì	*N.*	14s
morning (around 7–9 A.M.)	早上	早上	zǎoshang	*N.*	10s
morning (roughly after 9 A.M.)	上午	上午	shàngwǔ	*N.*	10s
mother	妈妈	媽媽	māma	*N.*	6
to move	搬	搬	bān	*V.*	20
	搬家	搬家	bānjiā	*V.O.*	20s
movie	电影	電影	diànyǐng	*N.*	9s, 13
MRT (Mass Rapid Transportation) in Taiwan	捷运	捷運	jiéyùn	*N.*	18s
music	音乐	音樂	yīnyuè	*N.*	14s
must	必须	必須	bìxū	*Aux.*	20
must, have to	得	得	děi	*Aux.*	12

N

name	名字	名字	míngzi	*N.*	2
name card, business card	名片	名片	míngpiàn	*N.*	8s
near	近	近	jìn	*Adj.*	18
new	新	新	xīn	*Adj.*	22
New York	纽约	紐約	Niǔyuē	*N.*	6
next time	下次	下次	xiàcì		8
nine	九/玖	九/玖	jiǔ	*Num.*	7
no problem	没关系	沒關係	méiguānxi		20
noble, honored, expensive	贵	貴	guì	*Adj.*	2
noodle	面	麵	miàn	*N.*	11
noon	中午	中午	zhōngwǔ	*N.*	10s
north	北	北	běi	*N.*	18s
not bad, okay	还好	還好	hái hǎo		4s
not bad, pretty good	不错	不錯	búcuò	*Adv.*	13
(used to form a negative) not, no	不	不	bù	*Adv.*	1
to not have, to be without, there isn't/aren't	没有	沒有	méiyǒu	*V.*	5s, 6

not until, only then	才	才	cái	*Adv.*	10
notes	笔记	筆記	bǐjì	*N.*	19
now	现在	現在	xiànzài	*N.*	10s
				Adv.	16
number	号	號	hào	*N.*	7
	号码	號碼	hàomǎ	*N.*	7
nurse	护士	護士	hùshi	*N.*	6s, 19s

O

to occupy a (phone) line, the line is busy	占线	佔線	zhànxiàn	*V.O.*	9s
o'clock	点钟	點鐘	diǎnzhōng	*M.W.*	10s
o'clock (point on clock)	点	點	diǎn	*M.W.*	10
off campus	校外	校外	xiàowài	*N.*	7
off-season	淡季	淡季	dànjì	*N.*	18s
often, frequently	常	常	cháng	*Adv.*	5
on campus	校内	校內	xiàonèi	*N.*	7s
on the left	左边	左邊	zuǒbiān	*N.*	15s
on the right	右边	右邊	yòubiān	*N.*	15s
on top of, above, over	上边	上邊	shàngbiān	*N.*	15
one	一/壹	一/壹	yī	*Num.*	6
only	只要	只要	zhǐyào	*Adv.*	18
opportunity	机会	機會	jīhuì	*N.*	22
opposite	对面	對面	duìmiàn	*N.*	15
or	还是	還是	háishì	*Conj.*	11
or, either . . . or . . .	或者	或者	huòzhě	*Conj.*	13
orange	橙色 (橘色)	橙色 (橘色)	chéngsè (júsè)	*Adj.*	13s
to order	点	點	diǎn	*V.*	11
to order food	点菜	點菜	diǎncài	*V.O.*	11
organization	社团	社團	shètuán	*N.*	16s
outside	外	外	wài	*N.*	7
to be out	出	出	chū	*V.*	20
overseas, abroad	国外	國外	guówài	*N.*	21

P

pair	双	雙	shuāng	*M.W.*	11
pants	裤子	褲子	kùzi	*N.*	13
park	公园	公園	gōngyuán	*N.*	15
to park	停	停	tíng	*V.*	12
parking lot	停车场	停車場	tíngchēchǎng	*N.*	12
to participate, to join	参加	參加	cānjiā	*V.*	14
party (evening party)	晚会	晚會	wǎnhuì	*N.*	14s

to pass (time), to celebrate (birthday, holiday), to cross, to live	过	過	guò	V.	10s, 14, 17
paternal grandfather (father's father)	爷爷	爺爺	yéye	N.	6s
paternal grandmother (father's mother)	奶奶	奶奶	nǎinai	N.	6s
to pay	付	付	fù	V.	20
to pay the bill	买单	買單	mǎidān	V.O.	11s
peaceful, safe	平安	平安	píng'ān	Adj.	21
Peking Opera	京剧	京劇	jīngjù	N.	22
perhaps, maybe, possibly	可能	可能	kěnéng		21
person	人	人	rén	N.	3
pet	宠物	寵物	chǒngwù	N.	6s
phone	电话	電話	diànhuà	N.	7
to pick up	接	接	jiē	V.	12
place	地方	地方	dìfang	N.	22
plate	盘	盤	pán	M.W.	11
to play basketball/ badminton/tennis/ table tennis	打球	打球	dǎqiú	V.O.	10
to play, to have fun	玩	玩	wán	V.	12
(polite) please	请	請	qǐng		2
pork	猪肉	豬肉	zhūròu	N.	11s
to practice	练习	練習	liànxí	V.	12
to practice, to intern	实习	實習	shíxí	V.	21
(prefix indicating an ordinal number)	第	第	dì		20
to prepare	准备	準備	zhǔnbèi	V.	19
problem, question	问题	問題	wèntí	N.	12
professor	教授	教授	jiàoshòu	N.	1s
purple	紫色	紫色	zǐsè	Adj.	13s

Q

a quarter (of an hour)	刻	刻	kè	M.W.	10

R

rain	雨	雨	yǔ	N.	17
to rain	下雨	下雨	xiàyǔ	V.O.	17
really	真	真	zhēn	Adv.	15
to receive	收到	收到	shōudào	V.C.	22
red	红	紅	hóng	Adj.	11
relatively, comparatively	比较	比較	bǐjiào	Adv.	13

rent	房租	房租	fángzū	N.	20
to rent a house	租屋	租屋	zūwū	V.O.	20s
to rent, to hire, to lease	租	租	zū	V.	18
to research, to study/examine	研究	研究	yánjiū	N.	21
to rest	休息	休息	xiūxi	V.	8s, 19
restaurant	饭馆	飯館	fànguǎn	N.	11s
	餐厅	餐廳	cāntīng	N.	11s
resumé	简历	簡歷	jiǎnlì	N.	21s
	(履历表)	(履歷表)	(lǚlìbiǎo)		
(retroflex ending)	儿	兒	ér		3
to return	回	回	huí	V.	8
	回来	回來	huílai	V.	9
to review	复习	復習	fùxí	V.	19
to ride	骑	騎	qí	V.	18
to ride a bike	骑自行车	騎自行車	qí zìxíngchē	V.O.	16s
road	路	路	lù	N.	18
road, street	马路	馬路	mǎlù	N.	18s
room	房间	房間	fángjiān	N.	7
roommate	室友	室友	shìyǒu	N.	5
to run	跑	跑	pǎo	V.	16s
	跑步	跑步	pǎobù	V.O.	16s

S

salad	沙拉	沙拉	shālā	N.	11s
salesman, saleswoman	店员	店員	diànyuán	N.	13
same, similar	同	同	tóng		2
Saturday	星期六	星期六	xīngqīliù	N.	14
scenery	风景	風景	fēngjǐng	N.	18
scenery, view	景色	景色	jǐngsè	N.	18
school	校	校	xiào	N.	7
	学校	學校	xuéxiào	N.	18
scooter, motorcycle	摩托车	摩托車	mótuōchē	N.	18s
	(机车)	(機車)	(jīchē)		
seafood	海鲜	海鮮	hǎixiān	N.	11s
seashore	海滩	海灘	hǎitān	N.	18s
seaside	海边	海邊	hǎibiān	N.	18
season (of a sport)	球季	球季	qiújì	N.	16s
second	秒	秒	miǎo	M.W.	10s
to see	见	見	jiàn	V.	8
see you again, goodbye	再见	再見	zàijiàn		8
to seek, to look for	找	找	zhǎo	V.	21
to sell	卖	賣	mài	V.	13s
semester	学期	學期	xuéqī	N.	10

to send a short (cell phone) message	发短信 (送简讯)	發短信 (送簡訊)	fā duǎnxìn (sòng jiǎnxùn)	V.O. 9s
seven	七/柒	七/柒	qī	Num. 7
severe	严重	嚴重	yánzhòng	Adj. 19s
severely, very much	厉害	厲害	lìhài	Adj. 19s
she, her	她	她	tā	Pron. 1s, 2
ship	船	船	chuán	N. 18
shirt	衬衫	襯衫	chènshān	N. 13
shoes	鞋子	鞋子	xiézi	N. 13s
short	短	短	duǎn	Adj. 17
shorts	短裤	短褲	duǎnkù	N. 13s
should	应该	應該	yīnggāi	Aux. 12
siblings	兄弟姐妹	兄弟姐妹	xiōngdìjiěmèi	N. 6s
to sign a contract	签约	簽約	qiānyuē	V.O. 20s
silver	银灰色	銀灰色	yínhuīsè	Adj. 13s
to sing a song	唱歌	唱歌	chànggē	V.O. 14s
to sit	坐	坐	zuò	V. 11
six	六/陆	六/陸	liù	Num. 7
size	号	號	hào	N. 13s
to ski	滑雪	滑雪	huáxuě	V.O. 16s
skirt	裙子	裙子	qúnzi	N. 13
slow	慢	慢	màn	Adj. 16
small	小	小	xiǎo	Adj. 7, 13s
smooth	顺利	順利	shùnlì	Adj. 22s
snow	雪	雪	xuě	N. 17
to snow	下雪	下雪	xiàxuě	V.O. 17
soccer	足球	足球	zúqiú	N. 16s
socks	袜子	襪子	wàzi	N. 13s
some	一些	一些	yìxiē	Adj. 22
sometimes	有时候	有時候	yǒushíhou	Adv. 17
song	歌	歌	gē	N. 14s
soup	汤	湯	tāng	N. 11
the South	南部	南部	nánbù	N. 18
Spain	西班牙	西班牙	Xībānyá	N. 3s
to speak	说	說	shuō	V. 3
sports	运动	運動	yùndòng	N. 16s
spring	春天	春天	chūntiān	N. 17
spring break	春假	春假	chūnjià	N. 17
to start, to begin	开始	開始	kāishǐ	V. 22
to starve	饿	餓	è	V. 19
steamed rice	白饭	白飯	báifàn	N. 11s
step	步	步	bù	N. 16s
still, also	还	還	hái	11
to stir fry	炒	炒	chǎo	V. 11

stop, station	车站	車站	chēzhàn	N.	18s
store	店	店	diàn	N.	13
(a structural particle used to show possession)	的	的	de	*Part.*	2
student	学生	學生	xuésheng	N.	1
to study abroad	留学	留學	liúxué	*V.O.*	21
to study, to learn	学	學	xué	*V.*	1
	学习	學習	xuéxí	*V.*	15
subway	地铁	地鐵	dìtiě	N.	18s
(suffix used after a personal pronoun to show plural number)	们	們	men		4
summer	夏	夏	xià	N.	17
summer vacation	暑期	暑期	shǔqī	N.	21
	暑假	暑假	shǔjià	N.	17s, 21
surname, family name	姓	姓	xìng	N.	2
sweater	毛衣	毛衣	máoyī	N.	13s
to swim, swimming	游泳	游泳	yóuyǒng	*V.O.*	16
swimming pool	游泳池	游泳池	yóuyǒngchí	N.	16

T

table	桌子	桌子	zhuōzi	N.	15
take care	保重	保重	bǎozhòng		22s
to take medicine	吃药	吃藥	chīyào	*V.O.*	19
to take off (used with accessories)	摘	摘	zhāi	*V.*	13s
to take off (used with clothing in general)	脱	脱	tuō	*V.*	13s
tall building	大楼	大樓	dàlóu	N.	22
taxi	出租汽车 (计程车)	出租汽車 (計程車)	chūzūqìchē (jìchéngchē)	N.	18s
tea	茶	茶	chá	N.	11
to teach, to coach	教	教	jiāo	*V.*	16
teacher	老师	老師	lǎoshī	N.	1
T-shirt	T-恤衫	T-恤衫	tīxùshān	N.	13s
television	电视	電視	diànshì	N.	9
temperature	气温	氣溫	qìwēn	N.	17s
ten	十/拾	十/拾	shí	*Num.*	7s, 11
tenant	房客	房客	fángkè	N.	20s
tennis	网球	網球	wǎngqiú	N.	16s
to thank, to be grateful	感谢	感謝	gǎnxiè	*V.*	19
thanks	谢谢	謝謝	xièxie		9
that	那	那	nà/nèi	*Pron.*	4

then, after that, afterwards	然后	然後	ránhòu	*Adv.*	10
then (connects two clauses, the first being the premise of the second)	就	就	jiù	*Adv.*	12
therefore, consequently	所以	所以	suǒyǐ	*Conj.*	19
thing	东西	東西	dōngxi	*N.*	22
to think, to feel	觉得	覺得	juéde	*V.*	13
this	这	這	zhè/zhèi	*Pron.*	4
(on the phone) this is he/she speaking	我就是	我就是	wǒ jiù shì		9
this time	这次	這次	zhècì	*Pron.*	12
three	三/叁	三/叁	sān	*Num.*	7
thus, in this way, like this	这样	這樣	zhèyàng	*Pron.*	12
ticket	票	票	piào	*N.*	13
tidy	整齐	整齊	zhěngqí	*Adj.*	15s
time	时间	時間	shíjiān	*N.*	17
(the duration of) time, (a point in) time	时候	時候	shíhou	*N.*	9
tip	小费	小費	xiǎofèi	*N.*	11s
tired	累	累	lèi	*Adj.*	4s
today	今天	今天	jīntiān	*N.*	8
together	一起	一起	yìqǐ	*Adv.*	8
tomorrow	明天	明天	míngtiān	*N.*	12
too	太	太	tài	*Adv.*	4
train	火车	火車	huǒchē	*N.*	18, 18s
to travel	旅行	旅行	lǚxíng	*V.*	18
to try	试试	試試	shìshi	*V.*	13
tunnel	隧道	隧道	suìdào	*N.*	18s
two	两	兩	liǎng	*Num.*	5
	二/贰	二/貳	èr	*Num.*	7
two people (colloquial)	俩	倆	liǎ		16

U

under	下边	下邊	xiàbiān	*N.*	15s
underground walkway	地下道	地下道	dìxiàdào	*N.*	18s
United States	美国	美國	Měiguó	*N.*	3
upstairs	楼上	樓上	lóushàng	*N.*	20
U.S. dollar	美金	美金	Měijīn	*N.*	13s
to use	用	用	yòng	*V.*	12
(used after a verb to indicate a brief action)	一下	一下	yíxià		5
(used at the end of a sentence to indicate surprise)	啊	啊	a	*Int.*	20

(used at the end of a declarative sentence to transform it into a question)	吗	嗎	ma	*Part.*	1
(used at the end of an interrogative sentence)	呢	呢	ne	*Part.*	1
(used between a verb or an adjective and its complement to indicate a result, possibility, or degree)	得	得	de	*Part.*	16

V

vacation	假期	假期	jiàqī	*N.*	17s
vegetable	青菜	青菜	qīngcài	*N.*	11s
very	非常	非常	fēicháng	*Adv.*	16
very, quite	很	很	hěn	*Adv.*	3
to visit	参观	參觀	cānguān	*V.*	15

W

to wait	等	等	děng	*V.*	9
to wait for a moment, to hang on (on the phone)	等一下儿	等一下兒	děng yíxiàr	*V.*	9
waiter/waitress	服务员	服務員	fúwùyuán	*N.*	11
to walk	走	走	zǒu	*V.*	15
	走路	走路	zǒulù	*V.O.*	18
to want, to desire	要	要	yào	*V.*	9
to want, to think, to miss	想	想	xiǎng	*V.*	8
wardrobe	衣橱	衣櫥	yīchú	*N.*	15s
warm	暖和	暖和	nuǎnhuo	*Adj.*	17
warm-hearted	热心	熱心	rèxīn	*Adj.*	22
watch	手表	手錶	shǒubiǎo	*N.*	13s
water	水	水	shuǐ	*N.*	11
we, us	我们	我們	wǒmen	*Pron.*	4
to wear, to put on (used with accessories)	戴	戴	dài	*V.*	13s
to wear (used with clothing in general)	穿	穿	chuān	*V.*	13
weather	天气	天氣	tiānqì	*N.*	17s
Web site	网站	網站	wǎngzhàn	*N.*	9s
week	星期	星期	xīngqī	*N.*	14
to welcome	欢迎	歡迎	huānyíng	*V.*	15
the West	西部	西部	xībù	*N.*	18

wharf, dock, pier	码头	碼頭	mǎtóu	*N.*	18s
what	什么	什麼	shénme	*Pron.*	2
what happened, what's wrong	怎么了	怎麼了	zěnmele		19
when, at what time	什么时候	什麼時候	shénme shíhou		9
where	哪儿	哪兒	nǎr	*Pron.*	7
which	哪	哪	nǎ/něi	*Pron.*	3
what size	几号	幾號	jǐ hào	*Pron.*	13s
white	白	白	bái	*Adj.*	12
who, whom	谁	誰	shéi/shuí	*Pron.*	2
wind	风	風	fēng	*N.*	17
window	窗户	窗戶	chuānghu	*N.*	15s
winter	冬	冬	dōng	*N.*	17
winter vacation	寒假	寒假	hánjià	*N.*	17s
to wish	祝	祝	zhù	*V.*	10
with	跟	跟	gēn	*Prep.*	5
wonderful	棒	棒	bàng	*Adj.*	14
wonton	馄饨	餛飩	húntun	*N.*	11s
to work	工作	工作	gōngzuò	*V.*	6
to work for others, to be employed	打工	打工	dǎgōng	*V.O.*	21
to wrap	包	包	bāo	*V.*	16
to write	写	寫	xiě	*V.*	10
to write a letter (to the speaker)	来信	來信	láixìn	*V.O.*	22

Y

year	年	年	nián	*N.*	10
yellow	黄	黄	huáng	*Adj.*	13
yesterday	昨天	昨天	zuótiān	*N.*	16
you	你	你	nǐ	*Pron.*	1
(polite) you	您	您	nín	*Pron.*	2
(in reply to thank you) you're welcome, don't mention it	不客气	不客氣	búkèqi		9s, 14
(in reply to thank you) you're welcome	不谢	不謝	búxiè		9s
younger brother	弟弟	弟弟	dìdi	*N.*	6s
younger sister	妹妹	妹妹	mèimei	*N.*	6s, 12

Z

zero	零	零	líng	*Num.*	7s

写字簿的生字 CHARACTERS IN THE CHARACTER BOOK

The following list shows the 428 characters (Lessons 1–11: 205 characters & Lessons 12–22: 223 characters) that appear in the Character Book, grouped by the lesson in which they are first introduced. Students are required to memorize how to read and write these key characters to build up their literacy skills. The number of new characters introduced in each lesson is carefully controlled, and is provided in the list.

(1) 第一课　问候 (13 characters)
你 好 是 学 生 吗 我 呢 也 他 不 老 师

(2) 第二课　名字 (17 characters)
您 贵 姓 请 问 的 英 文 名 字 中 叫 什 么 她 谁 同

(3) 第三课　国籍和语言 (14 characters)
哪 国 人 很 对 了 法 美 说 会 一 点 儿 和

(4) 第四课　学习 (14 characters)
那 书 这 本 工 程 难 太 可 功 课 多 们 少

(5) 第五课　介绍 (14 characters)
朋 友 来 介 绍 下 室 有 几 两 个 都 常 跟

(6) 第六课　家 (16 characters)
家 大 从 在 四 爸 妈 姐 作 男 没 辆 车 只 狗 爱

(7) 第七课　地址 (21 characters)
住 宿 舍 号 房 间 电 话 小 码 二 三 五 六 七 八 九 手 机 校 外

(8) 第八课　见面、相约 (21 characters)
认 识 去 上 以 后 事 想 回 起 吃 饭 菜 今 天 次 怎 样 行 再 见

(9) 第九课　打电话 (22 characters)
打 喂 等 知 道 谢 吧 忙 正 看 视 做 网 就 位 留 言 时 候 晚 要 给

(10) 第十课　时间表 (29 characters)
活 期 门 每 床 睡 觉 半 才 刻 分 然 图 馆 午 喜 欢 球 写 信 子 邮 件 地 址 祝 年 月 日

(11) 第十一课　点菜 (24 characters)
红 茶 还 绿 服 务 员 坐 先 喝 杯 冰 水 瓶 乐 面 饺 盘 炒 十 碗 汤 双 筷

(12) 第十二课   请求 (24 characters)

借明用得场接妹飞玩到排挡开应该题白色停习练能进步

(13) 第十三课   衣服、逛街 (23 characters)

买衬衫店条裙或者裤黄错比较穿黑试帮让钱块张影票

(14) 第十四课   生日和庆祝 (15 characters)

岁空星过为舞参加定蛋糕送棒客气

(15) 第十五课   地点和位置 (18 characters)

前边迎观里厨公旁走厅面餐洗澡卧桌园真

(16) 第十六课   爱好和运动 (20 characters)

篮俩教游泳非快体育池健身锻炼现昨赛业包慢

(17) 第十七课   天气和四季 (22 characters)

春久放假夏秋冬其最暖短热华氏百度极刮风雨冷雪

(18) 第十八课   旅行和交通 (20 characters)

火旅离远只钟骑自共汽路近西部景船南听海租

(19) 第十九课   健康和医药 (23 characters)

感冒饿像舒头疼发烧咳嗽病考复所医药休息准备笔记

(20) 第二十课   看房和租房 (15 characters)

把带啊搬出关系但女必须第付楼马

(21) 第二十一课   未来计画 (18 characters)

暑毕决申研究院找司实脑班意思愉平安运

(22) 第二十二课   艺术和文化 (25 characters)

因已经丽城市处新些方动如京剧东笼尝始高兴收心板保重

图片供应者 PHOTO CREDITS